Creation, Cross and Everlasting Rest

A Guide to the Message of Three Great Oratorios

BY

Robert Bashford

The Latimer Trust

ISBN 978-1-906327-82-8 Published by the Latimer Trust April 2023.

Cover Image: Light and Clouds on Golgotha Hill – The Death and Resurrection of Jesus Christ and the Holy Cross by artplus (iStock)

The Latimer Trust (formerly Latimer House, Oxford) is a conservative Evangelical research organisation within the Church of England, whose main aim is to promote the history and theology of Anglicanism as understood by those in the Reformed tradition. Interested readers are welcome to consult its website for further details of its many activities.

The Latimer Trust

London N14 4PS UK

Registered Charity: 1084337

Company Number: 4104465

Web: www.latimertrust.org

E-mail: administrator@latimertrust.org

Acknowledgements

English Standard Version Anglicized (ESVUK), The Holy Bible, English Standard Version Copyright © 2001 by Crossway Bibles, a division of Good News Publishers.

Revised Standard Version Apocrypha
Copyright © 1957 by the Division of Christian Education of the National Council of the Churches of Christ in the USA.

English translation of Bach's *St Matthew Passion*
Copyright © Pamela Dellal, courtesy Emmanuel Music Inc., used by permission.

Eleanor Farjeon, "Morning has broken" in *Hymns for Today's Church* (London: Hodder and Stoughton, 1982)
Copyright © David Higham Associates Limited, used by permission.

Dr and Mrs Howard Taylor, *Biography of James Hudson Taylor* (London: Hodder and Stoughton, 1965)
Copyright © 1965 by OMF International (formerly Overseas Missionary Fellowship), used by permission.

C.S. Lewis, *Letters to an American Lady,* ed. C. Kilby (London: Hodder and Stoughton, 1969), Copyright © 1967 by Wm. B. Eerdmans Publishing Co., used by permission.

The following abbreviations are used:

AV = Authorised Version – otherwise known as the King James' Version
ESV = English Standard Version
GNB = Good News Bible
NEB = New English Bible
NIV = New International Version
RSV = Revised Standard Version
RV = Revised Version

Bible quotations are from the ESV, unless otherwise indicated.

Contents Page

Preface

All great oratorios have the power to inspire through both their music and their message. God is to be thanked for both. Music is one of his gifts to the whole human race - a gift that belongs to what is sometimes called God's 'common grace'. The message of great oratorios is God's word, the Bible, and that is by definition powerful. It is God personally speaking to men and women of every generation. The three great oratorios which are the focus of this study can only be called 'great' because they excel both as musical masterpieces and as clear expressions of biblical truth.

Undoubtedly, the greatest of all sacred oratorios is Handel's *Messiah*, which was the subject of an earlier study by this author and recently published by the Latimer Trust (*Focus on Jesus*, 2020). But the three oratorios which are examined in this work can be described as close runners-up in the list of great oratorios. They are certainly among my favourites and, I hope, they are (or may become) your favourites too.

The three selected oratorios can be enjoyed without the aid of this study. But if the following pages help to increase that enjoyment and, more importantly, to deepen understanding of their message, this work will have achieved its goal.

The three selected oratorios, individually, open a window on major doctrines of the Bible. Collectively, they present a panorama of a considerable expanse of the message of Holy Scripture.

Haydn's *The Creation* takes us to the beginning of all things in the physical domain. We are led through Genesis 1, with a glimpse of Genesis 2. We are invited to marvel at God's creative power displayed in the heavens and the earth, in vegetation and animal life in all its variety, and in the culmination of God's handiwork: the creation of humankind. Ominously, Haydn's oratorio ends with a strong hint of the tragic Fall of Genesis 3, which appropriately points towards our desperate need of a rescue – and that is the subject of the second oratorio.

From creation, we move on therefore to redemption, which is the theme of Bach's *St Matthew Passion.* Here, in one of the most moving musical compositions of all time, we come to the heart of God's great plan of salvation, conceived from all eternity, and put into operation at that specific time when God sent his Son to be born into this world, to die on the Cross of Calvary. Bach's work takes us through the Passion of the Lord Jesus Christ, as it unfolds in chapters 26 and 27 of Matthew's Gospel.

The third oratorio, Brahms' *Requiem,* directs our gaze again and again away from the sorrows and frustrations of this life towards the solid and lasting joys of heaven to come. The title used here for the third part of the study is 'Everlasting Rest', which is borrowed from the Puritan pastor and writer, Richard Baxter. As will be explained in the Introduction to that part of this study, he had heaven in mind when he used those words.

CREATION – CROSS – HEAVEN (or Everlasting Rest). These three topics may not cover the whole storyline of the Bible's narrative, but they do represent three of its main components. God created men and women; he has redeemed his people (all who put their trust in Christ crucified), and he purposes to bring his people to the heavenly inheritance that he has prepared for them.

Each of the three parts of the study follow the same approach. We begin with a brief introduction to the composer and to the oratorio. The major component in each part is a guide to the message of the work, scene by scene or movement by movement - followed each time by some comments on 'What to listen out for' in the music of that section. The aim has been to make the musical comments user-friendly, but readers may find it helpful to consult the Musical Glossary from time to time, which will be found as one of the Appendices. The whole study concludes with a reflection on our response to the message of these three oratorios. In the preparation of this book, I have found myself thrilled, humbled, and challenged by God's work of grace in the unfolding of his purposes in creation, the cross and all that is to come. My prayer is that others too may share that experience.

Part 1: Creation

Haydn's *The Creation*

Introduction

Introducing Joseph Haydn

Joseph Haydn was born at Rohrau in Austria in 1732, the son of a wheelwright. Both his parents were musical without being able to read music. As a boy, Haydn showed signs of musical talent, and at the age of 8 he was accepted as a chorister at St Stephen's Cathedral in Vienna, where he remained until the age of 16. His voice had, of course, broken by then, but the reason for his dismissal appears to have been a practical joke that he carried out on a fellow student. He now had to earn his living in various ways – for example taking on pupils – and he remained very poor for several years. During this time, however, he managed to train himself as a composer.

In 1759 he obtained an appointment with Count Morzin, which gave him a small but secure salary. Soon after this, Haydn entered into a marriage that proved to be a most unhappy one; it lasted until 1800, when his wife died. From 1761 to 1790, he was in the service of the enormously wealthy Esterhazy family. Prince Nicholas Esterhazy, who succeeded to the title in 1762, was one of the greatest benefactors of music during this period when, generally, musicians (and particularly composers) could only survive in the employment of a patron. Haydn had to wear the uniform of a servant, but he enjoyed good relations with his employer and a generous salary. He was given every encouragement to compose according to his own inclinations. He had control of an orchestra, a choir, solo singers and opera performances. Within a few years he became recognised as the greatest composer of the period.

Haydn spent 18 months in London in 1791-2, during which time he was awarded an honorary doctorate from Oxford University. He undertook a further visit to London in 1794-5. He enjoyed both visits and regarded his time in England as the happiest period of his life. Musically, they were very successful and remunerative visits. It was because of the second London visit that he was given the idea of writing *The Creation*, and more will be said about this a little later.

On his return to Vienna in 1795, Haydn again took up a position with the Esterhazys. By this time, he was a public figure in Vienna. In his later years, he suffered poor health and had to struggle to complete his final works. He died in 1809 at the age of 77.

His early style of composing was influenced by that of C.P.E. Bach (one of the sons of J.S. Bach), particularly in his use of what was then the new style of sonata and symphony. This led Haydn to produce over a hundred symphonies, about eighty string quartets and over fifty sonatas - as well as many other compositions. The most outstanding of Haydn's symphonies are those he wrote for London audiences, and they are known as the 'Salomon Symphonies': Salomon was the impresario who arranged the visits and commissioned the works.

Haydn befriended and mentored Mozart, his younger contemporary, and he also tutored Beethoven. Haydn's younger brother Michael was also a composer.

In his character, Haydn was known for his modesty and integrity. At the same time, perhaps because of his poverty in his early years, he became very astute in his business dealings. He was greatly respected by the Esterhazys. He had a sense of humour, which is apparent in some of his music. The best-known example of this is probably his *Surprise* Symphony (No.94 in G major), where – in the second movement – he follows a quiet passage with a sudden and unexpected loud chord, as if to wake up an audience who are in danger of falling asleep. He was a devout Catholic, and he normally began the manuscript of a new composition with the words 'In nomine Domini' ('In the name of the Lord') and ended it with 'Laus Deo' ('Praise be to God').

Introducing Haydn's *The Creation*

Composition of the work

During Haydn's time in London he attended various performances of Handel's oratorios and was greatly impressed by them - particularly *Messiah* and *Israel in Egypt*. On his return to Vienna, he felt inspired to try his hand at this musical form and composed two oratorios: *The Creation,* written between 1797 and 1798, and *The Seasons,* written in 1800. It is the first of these that has been recognised as a truly great musical masterpiece. *The Creation* (in German, *Die Schöpfung*), as the title suggests, depicts and celebrates the creation of the world and mankind, as related in the first two chapters of Genesis (mainly chapter 1). In addition to biblical texts, the oratorio uses John Milton's *Paradise Lost* as a source.[1] The poetic parts of the libretto imitate Milton's style and occasionally whole phrases are borrowed. As will be seen later on, one feature of the text in the opening scene owes more to Milton's storyline than it does to the Book of Genesis. In the Hoboken catalogue of Haydn's works, the oratorio is listed as Hob. XXI:2.[2]

Haydn clearly felt a great amount of enthusiasm about his composing of *The Creation.* An early biographer quoted Haydn as saying that he was "never so devout" as at the time he was working on *The Creation.* He is reported to have said, "Every day I fell to my knees and asked God to give me strength to enable me to pursue the work to a successful conclusion."[3]

The first performances of the work took place in 1798 under the auspices of the 'Gesellschaft der Associierten' (which means 'Society of the Associates'). This was a group of noblemen who loved music,

---

[1] J. Milton, *Paradise Lost* (Harmondsworth: Penguin Books Ltd, 2005), first published 1667.

[2] Anthony van Hoboken (1889 – 1983) was a Dutch musicologist, who compiled the official catalogue of Haydn's works. The category number XXI indicates that it is an oratorio. There are three works in this category: 1. *Il ritorno di Tobia,* 1775, 2. *The Creation,* 1797-8 and 3. *The Seasons,* 1800. It is the second of these that stands out as a masterpiece.

[3] G.A. Griesinger, *Biographische Notizen über Joseph Haydn* (Leipzig, 1810), 54f., quoted by B. Robins in 'Haydn: Late Oratorios - The Creation and The Seasons', *Early Music World* (www.earlymusicworld.com).

and Baron Gottfried van Swieten, a patron of music, organised them to sponsor concerts of serious music. The complete work was rehearsed before a full audience on 29 April of that year. The first performance, which was a private affair, took place the following day at the old Schwarzenberg Palace in Vienna, but a very large crowd turned up hoping to hear something of the music.

The first public performance was on 19 March 1799 at the old Burgtheater in Vienna. Forty more performances were held in Vienna during Haydn's lifetime. A number of these were put on for the benefit of the 'Tonkünstlersocietät', a charitable organisation for the support of widows and orphans of musicians.[4]

The Creation was published with the text in German and English in 1800.

The first London performance of *The Creation* was in 1800 at Covent Garden, where it was sung in English. Over the following years, the reputation of *The Creation* spread internationally, and it is still performed regularly today.

Looking at the content and structure of the work

The Creation is structured in three parts. The first deals with the creation of light, heaven and earth, the sun and moon, the land and water, and plants. The second is taken up with the creation of the animals, and of man and woman. The final part describes Adam and Eve during their blissful time in the Garden of Eden, in perfect harmony with God, with each other and with the newly formed world. The oratorio centres on the Bible account of what happened before the Fall. The entry of sin into the world, related by Genesis 3, is not part of the work's agenda, although the final scene of the oratorio gives a strong hint of what will happen.

By the end of the eighteenth century, the intellectual climate of Western Europe had been dominated for decades by the Enlightenment, which asserted the supremacy of human reason. Scientific and philosophical debates had undermined the very concept

---

[4] 'Tonkünstlersocietät' means 'Society of Composers'.

of creationism. So, an oratorio that focused on the role of God the Creator in bringing the universe, the world and mankind into being must be regarded as a significant challenge to the society of Haydn's time. In the twenty-first century too, where secularism holds sway, people need to hear the Bible's message that God is the one 'who made the world and everything in it' and that he is 'Lord of heaven and earth' (Acts 17:24).

In terms of the singers who are to perform the oratorio, *The Creation* is scored for three soloists (soprano, tenor and bass - plus a contralto solo part in the finale) and for a four-part chorus (soprano, contralto, tenor and bass). In Parts I and II, the three soloists represent angels who narrate and comment on the six days of creation: Gabriel (soprano), Uriel (tenor) and Raphael (bass).[5] In Part III, Adam is sung by a bass and Eve by a soprano. In most performances, these two parts are sung by the same soloists who took the parts of Raphael and Gabriel respectively in Parts I and II, but some conductors prefer to use different soloists in Part III. Uriel (unlike Raphael and Gabriel) has a role in Part III both at the beginning and the end. The word 'chorus' (used above) has two meanings. It refers to the choral singers or choir, and to the four-part items for them to sing. Throughout the oratorio, several of the choruses celebrate the end of each day of creation.

To elaborate a little further on the shape of the oratorio: the account of each day of creation in Parts I and II consists of biblical recitative (verses from Genesis 1), poetic description in the style of Milton, and choruses with words which include paraphrases of psalms.

Haydn intended the orchestra to be a large one, consisting of strings; woodwind (2 flutes, 2 oboes, 2 clarinets, 2 bassoons and a contrabassoon); brass (2 horns, 2 trumpets, 3 trombones); timpani, and

---

[5] Of these three names, only Gabriel is mentioned in the Bible (in both Daniel and Luke). The inclusion of these three angels in *The Creation* derives from John Milton's *Paradise Lost,* but listeners to this oratorio do not need to know anything about the part they play in that literary work. Uriel is mentioned in the apocryphal book, Esdras 2, and in the Book of Enoch (an ancient Hebrew apocalyptic religious text). Raphael is mentioned in the apocryphal book, Tobit, and in the Book of Enoch. More will be said about the Apocrypha in the Introduction to Brahms' *Requiem.*

continuo. Haydn clearly wanted a big sound: at the first public première there were about 120 instrumentalists and 60 singers.

Musically, there are three features about *The Creation* which mark it out as one of the most outstanding of Haydn's works. The first is the majestic impact of the choruses, which clearly owe so much to the example of Handel's oratorios. The second is the descriptive quality of Haydn's composition: the phrase 'tone painting' is sometimes used in this connection, meaning Haydn's superb ability to conjure up a picture of the scene that a particular musical item is intended to suggest. Handel had used this technique in his oratorios, so we can again detect Haydn's indebtedness to his illustrious predecessor. The third outstanding feature of *The Creation* is Haydn's consummate skill in his orchestration, which reaches the same level of excellence as in his 'Salomon' symphonies.

A performance of *The Creation* lasts about one hour and 45 minutes.

Looking at the English libretto

As was mentioned above, Haydn wrote *The Creation* using both German and English words. But the story of the English text of *The Creation* is a complex one and leaves at least two questions unanswered.

The first of these questions is: *Who was responsible for the English libretto?* The London impresario Salomon gave Haydn an English libretto on the subject of the Creation, together with the suggestion that Haydn might set it to music. This original libretto is lost, and it is not at all clear who had written it. Various suggestions have been made, but we can only speculate. Haydn is reported as saying that the idea came from an Englishman with the name Lidley - but he did not say that Lidley wrote the words. Possibly Haydn misheard, or misunderstood, the name 'Lidley'. It is more probable that he meant Thomas Linley, who was a keen promoter of oratorio in London. While the identity of the individual who compiled the original libretto remains a mystery, it is known that the text was originally put together for Handel, but Handel never made use of it.

The second question is: *Why is the English libretto (in the earliest form available to us) so inconsistent in its quality?* As mentioned above, the original English libretto (which was given to Haydn in 1795) is now lost. The earliest version of the English libretto which we have is the one published in 1800. Some parts of it are very well written, but other parts are very laboured and disappointing. It must be remembered, of course, that poetry, which is deliberately borrowed from, or modelled on, Milton will sound rather archaic and quaint. After all, as noted above, *Paradise Lost* was published in 1667. But this comment about some parts of the English libretto being 'laboured and disappointing' applies to wording and sentence-structure which have no connection with Milton.

While we cannot be sure - which is why we must describe this question as another 'unanswered' one - the explanation would appear to be something like the following. It is undisputed that, on his return to Vienna, Haydn gave the libretto to Baron van Swieten, who, as we have seen, later became involved in arranging for performances of *The Creation*. Van Swieten shortened the text and translated it into German. He also made suggestions about the setting of individual items within the work. For the quotations from the Bible, van Swieten chose to stick very closely to the English Authorised Version of the Bible (1611). Haydn and van Swieten would have realised that English audiences would not welcome changes to the words of Scripture. So far, we are on sure ground.

But it is in the 'poetic' material that we find the mixture of good and less good. Most probably, van Swieten not only shortened the text in places but also added other passages, working them out first in German and then translating them back into his own version of English. Van Swieten was not a fully fluent speaker of English, and the task which he undertook may well have exceeded his capabilities. We might, therefore, guess that the parts where the text is impressive are those from the original libretto which van Swieten left untouched. Similarly, we might guess that the less successful parts are those which he attempted to rework.

Mercifully, most English audiences are shielded from the worst examples of van Swieten's less successful efforts by the alterations to the English libretto introduced by Vincent Novello (1781 - 1861). He was an English musician, best known for promoting the popularity of many works now considered part of the standard musical repertoire. Also, together with his son, he created a major publishing house. Novello published his first English edition of the vocal score of *The Creation* in 1860, and we are indebted to him for some considerable improvements to the earlier van Swieten version of the text. (An appendix in this study shows the alterations that Novello made.) Novello's version of the libretto became the standard text in performances of the oratorio in English. Today, despite the introduction of other competently revised versions of the English libretto, the Novello version is still widely used.

Comments on the study in the following pages

In the pages that follow, it is the text of the Novello edition that is used, since this is probably the one with which readers are most familiar. The verses from the Book of Genesis are, therefore, essentially the text of the Authorised Version (1611), but with a few minor changes (e.g., the change of an occasional word), which will not be commented on. We shall also find that, while Parts I and II of *The Creation* work their way through Genesis 1, not every single verse is included. No doubt, Haydn or van Swieten, or perhaps both, decided that a more compressed version of the Bible text would work better. Comments will be included in the following study about Bible material that has been excluded. As noted earlier, verses selected from the Book of Psalms are paraphrased in the libretto.

At the beginning of each scene, the relevant parts of the libretto will be provided. Bible material (both the verses from Genesis 1 and the paraphrases of verses from Psalms) is set out in italics. Poetic material appears in ordinary print (without italics). But references within the discussion from both the biblical and the poetic material will appear in italics. In the discussions of the biblical material, quotations (other than those directly from the libretto) will be made from the English Standard Version (ESV).

The programme notes for many performances and recordings set out the libretto of *The Creation* as a series of 'scenes', which makes good sense, particularly in Parts I and II, which describe the six days of creation. It is that scheme that is followed in this study. Part III is similarly presented as consisting of a few scenes. The titles given to the scenes of Part III are my own. In addition, the individual items within the work are also numbered, to make it easier for them to be identified. These items will be designated here as 'movements', by analogy with the word used for the sections which make up a symphony or a concerto. The numbers for the movements used in this study are those to be found in the Novello edition.

A comment on the use of the names Adam and Eve may be helpful. In the Bible, the name 'Adam' is used not only as a proper name but also to mean 'mankind'. The word is derived from the Hebrew word for 'ground' because it was from the dust of the ground that man was created (Genesis 2:7). The first clear use of the word 'Adam' as a name is in Genesis 2:20.[6] The name 'Eve' is first used in Genesis 3:20 (after the Fall), and it is Adam who calls her by this name, because - we are told in that verse - 'she was the mother of all living'. The Hebrew words for 'Eve' and 'life' are connected. In this study, the names Adam and Eve will be used only in the discussion of Part III of the oratorio, because Parts I and II are concerned mainly with the account of creation in Genesis 1, where those proper names are not found. Instead, the pair will be referred to as 'the man' and 'the woman'. Part III of the oratorio is focused on the happy state of the first human couple in the Garden before the Fall, so even here the use of the name 'Eve' is premature, but as the oratorio refers to them in Part III as 'Adam' and 'Eve', it makes sense to do the same in this study.

The comments on the more poetic parts of the libretto will be mainly concerned with their contribution to the message of this oratorio, rather than examining their literary quality. Footnotes will draw attention to obvious borrowings of words or phrases from *Paradise Lost,* and will explain some words which are not familiar in modern English. Very little Bible material is used in Part III of the oratorio, so the discussion of that part of *The Creation* will be shorter.

---

[6] The Authorised Version introduces the name 'Adam' in the previous verse (Genesis 2:19). The Revised Version and the Revised Standard Version retain 'man' or 'the man' in Genesis 2:20 and do not introduce the name 'Adam' until Genesis 3:17.

The discussion of Part I Scene 1 will be the longest, partly because the opening verses of Genesis 1, which are central to the opening section of the oratorio, are the most important in setting out the Bible's teaching on creation, and partly because the influence of Milton's *Paradise Lost* on the opening scene of the oratorio needs to be discussed. There will also be a substantial comment on Part II Scene 2, which is concerned with the events of the sixth day (the creation of living creatures on earth and of the first man and woman), and with the completion of the six days of creation.

It will be evident from the text of the libretto that apostrophes are frequently used. This is to indicate for the soloists and chorus that there is no separately enunciated syllable at that point. So, for example, in Scene 2 of Part I, 'marvellous' is printed as 'marv'llous'.

It will be beyond the scope of this book to examine the relationship between Christianity and science, except to make a couple of comments now at the end of this Introduction. First, there can be no conflict between Christianity and science, because they look at God's creation from two different perspectives and each asks a different question. Science aims to look at *how* things happen, while Christianity looks at *why* things happen. Secondly, throughout the past centuries many influential scientists have been Christian believers, and that is still true today. In fact, it is the Christian faith that has inspired the western world to engage in scientific enquiry. Johannes Kepler, the German astronomer (1571 – 1630), said that in his scientific investigation he was "thinking God's thoughts after him."[7] It is highly appropriate, therefore, that the words of Psalm 111:2 are to be found on the door of both the old and the new Cavendish Laboratories in Cambridge. On the doors of the old Laboratory they were in the Latin Vulgate version.[8] On the doors of the new Laboratory the words of the Authorised Version are used: 'The works of the Lord are great, sought out of all them that have pleasure therein.'

---

[7] Quoted by R.J. Berry in 'The Research Scientist's Psalm' in *Science and Christian Belief,* Vol.20, No.2, 161.

[8] 'Magna opera Domini exquirenda in cunctis voluntatibus suis.'

The Message of Haydn's *The Creation* and what to listen out for in the music

Part One

1. Overture – The Representation of Chaos

Scene 1: The First Day

2. Recitative and chorus

RAPHAEL

In the beginning God created the heaven and the earth; and the earth was without form, and void; and darkness was upon the face of the deep. (Genesis 1:1-2a)

CHORUS

And the Spirit of God moved upon the face of the waters. And God said, Let there be light: and there was light. (Genesis 1:2b-3)

Recitative

URIEL

And God saw the light, that it was good: and God divided the light from the darkness. (Genesis 1:4)

3. Aria and chorus

URIEL

Now vanish before the holy beams
the gloomy shades of ancient night.
The first of days appears.
Now chaos ends, and order fair prevails.
Affrighted fly hell's spirits black in throngs:
down they sink in the deep abyss
to endless night.

CHORUS
Despairing cursing rage attends their rapid fall.
A new-created world springs up at God's command.

A surprise element in this oratorio's account of creation

There is something about the opening of Haydn's *The Creation* which may take us by surprise. Readers may possibly have noticed something in the text of Scene 1, given above, which has prompted a question. There *is* something here that we do not normally associate with the Bible's teaching on creation - something that needs to be checked out. Whether or not you have already spotted that 'something', it is going to be left to one side for the moment, but more will be revealed very shortly. First, we shall focus on the content of Genesis 1:1-4, which make up the content of the first half of Scene 1.

Setting the scene

It would be difficult to over-emphasise the extreme importance of the opening words of the Bible in Genesis 1:1-5. Verses 1-4 are the first sung words of the oratorio (Movement 2). Here we have an introduction to the whole of God's work of creation (verses 1-2), followed by the account of the first day of creation (in verses 3-4). Strictly speaking, the account of the first day should also include verse 5, which is omitted from the libretto: 'God called the light Day, and the darkness he called Night. And there was evening and there was morning, the first day.' A comment about the first part of verse 5 will be included a little later. For now, we should notice that the second part of verse 5 presents the pattern which is adopted at the end of each day of creation, namely: "And there was evening and there was morning, the *nth* day" - and each time, throughout the scenes of Parts I and II, this formula is omitted.[9] To make up for the exclusion of this pattern from the libretto, in each scene of Parts I and II one of the soloists or the chorus informs us which day of creation it is that is being, or has been, presented to us.

In order to underline the importance of the Bible's opening words, it will be helpful to work our way through all of them, focusing on single words or short phrases:

---

[9] The six verses, or half-verses, of Genesis 1 that provide the pattern of enumerating the days of creation are: 5b, 8b, 13, 19, 23 and 31b.

The whole of God's work of creation

- *In the beginning ...*

This is more than an expression of time. Here we are glimpsing back before time into eternity, just as we are invited to do in other parts of the Bible. Psalm 90:2 tells us: 'Before the mountains were brought forth, or ever you had formed the earth and the world, from everlasting to everlasting you are God.' In Isaiah 40:28 we read: 'The LORD is the everlasting God, the Creator of the ends of the earth.' The New Testament too gives us the same perspective on eternity, particularly John's Gospel, which opens with the words: 'In the beginning was the Word ...' (John 1:1). Jesus' prayer before his arrest includes these words: 'And now, Father, glorify me in your own presence with the glory that I had with you before the world existed.' (John 17:5)

- *... God ...*

It is no accident that God is the subject of the first sentence of the Bible, for this Book is primarily about him. God is eternal - he is before and beyond creation. We sometimes use the word 'transcendent' in this connection. God is separate from his creation - he is not part of it. He is unique, saying of himself, '"... for I am God, and there is no other; I am God, and there is none like me."' (Isaiah 46:9) It is he - and he alone - who is the author of creation.

- *... created ...*

The word used here (*bārā'* in Hebrew) is used in Genesis 1 to mark three great beginnings: 'the heavens and the earth' (v 1); living creatures (v 21); and mankind (v 27). Another verb, normally translated as 'made' ('*āśâ* in Hebrew), is used throughout this chapter and in chapter 2 verses 3 and 4 it is used in parallel with 'created' to cover everything that God has made. It is very rare among the religions of the world to find a Creator God. Normally, the gods appear long after creation. The Christian understanding of creation is that it is - to use the technical expression - *creatio ex nihilo,* which means '"creation out of nothing'. There was no pre-existent matter that God made use of in his work of creation. The writer of the Letter to the Hebrews tells us: 'By faith we understand that the universe was created by the word of God, so that what is seen was not made out of things that are visible' (Hebrews 11:3).

- *... the heaven and the earth ...*

Normally, 'heaven' means God's own place. But here *the heaven* (or 'the heavens') has a physical sense, meaning everything above us. This phrase, *the heaven and the earth,* embraces the whole of the created order, just as the Nicene Creed tells us that God is the 'maker of heaven and earth, of all that is, seen and unseen'.[10] Similarly, the apostle John writes of the role of the Divine Word in creation and says: 'All things were made through him, and without him was not any thing made that was made.' (John 1:3)

- *... and the earth was without form, and void ...*

The first part of verse 2 provides an expansion of the statement made in verse 1. From here on, we are to view the unfolding work of creation from the perspective of earth. *Without form, and void* is the translation of a pair of rhyming Hebrew words (*tōhû* and *bōhû*). The English phrase 'topsy-turvy' captures something of the sense and the feel of the two words. Augustine refers to this description as 'formless matter entirely without feature.'[11] John Calvin uses the phrase 'confused emptiness' to describe this and the following expression.[12] So, it describes the condition of what God initially brought into being, and now - we are told - he is about to change formlessness into form by his creative word.

- *...and darkness was upon the face of the deep.*

The formless waste of verse 2 is also described as a *darkness ... upon the face of the deep*. The *deep* is, of course, the sea, and the whole of this phrase might be construed as suggesting terror or even an alien power. But we are told here clearly that the *deep*, even in its *darkness*, is part of God's creation. Just as with *the earth ... without form,* God will bring order and pattern and beauty.

- *And the Spirit of God moved upon the face of the waters.*

The ESV uses the words 'was hovering' to translate *moved*. The word has connotations of gentleness and love – and of being ready for action.

---

[10] *Common Worship* (London: Church House Publishing, 2000), 173.

[11] *Augustine, Confessions* (Harmondsworth: Penguin Books Ltd, 1961), Book XII.3, 282.

[12] J. Calvin, *A Commentary on Genesis* (Edinburgh: The Banner of Truth Trust, 1965), 73. First published in Latin in 1554.

The word is used in one other place in the Bible, namely in Deuteronomy 32:11, where it is translated as 'flutters'. The context is God's loving guidance and care for his people in bringing them out of slavery in Egypt to the borders of the Promised Land: 'Like an eagle that stirs up its nest, that flutters over its young, spreading out its wings, catching them, bearing them on its pinions ...' This verse pictures for us a father or mother eagle, eager that their baby eagle should learn to fly. In order for this to happen, they have to push it out of the nest. However, so that the young bird will not fall to the ground, they hover to catch it and care for it and protect it. So, the use of this word in Genesis 1:2 spells out the gentleness and care of the Spirit of God hovering over the face of the waters. While verse 1 has told us about the 'transcendence' of God, verse 2 shows that at the same time God is intimately involved in creation. The word used in this connection is God's 'immanence'. The Creator God is both transcendent and immanent: separate from his creation, and yet intimately involved in caring for it and sustaining it.

A hint of the Trinity

The Bible nowhere uses the word 'Trinity' in relation to God, but it nevertheless points clearly to the correctness of affirming that he is one God in three persons. The first three verses of Genesis may be regarded as providing evidence of this.

'God' in the New Testament is often a shorthand way of referring to God the Father, who is the planner and initiator of things, and this is the role of 'God' in Genesis 1:1.

God the Son, the Lord Jesus Christ, is given the title 'the Word' (John 1:1), and we have seen already that it is by his word that God created light on the first day (Genesis 1:3) – just as happens with God's further acts of creation on the succeeding days. The apostle John clearly had that identification in mind when he wrote of the Word: 'All things were made through him' (John 1:3). Similarly, the apostle Paul tells us of the role of Christ in creation: 'For by him (i.e., the Son) all things were created, in heaven and on earth, visible and invisible, whether thrones or dominions or rulers or authorities – all things were created through him and for him.' (Colossians 1:16)

God the Holy Spirit, as has just been noted, is clearly in view in Genesis 1:2. Thus, all three persons of the Trinity are in evidence in the Bible's account of creation. Augustine wrote these words (but identifying the Son with God's 'Wisdom', which might be said to be embodied in the incarnate Word of God):

When I read that your Spirit moved over the waters, I catch a faint glimpse of the Trinity which you are, my God. For it was you, the Father, who created heaven and earth in the Beginning of our Wisdom – which is your Wisdom, born of you, equal to you, and co-eternal with you – that is in your Son ... Here, then, is the Trinity, my God, Father, Son and Holy Ghost, the Creator of all creation.[13]

The first day

After the introductory first two verses of the chapter, we come to what constitutes the work of the first day of creation:

- *... and God said, Let there be light: and there was light. And God saw the light, that it was good: and God divided the light from the darkness.*

These are verses 3 and 4 of the chapter, and we need to add in also the first part of verse 5 (omitted from the libretto): 'And God called the light Day, and the darkness he called Night.' God's act of creation on the first day, therefore, consisted of four things.

First, God *said*. Here we meet the important teaching of the Bible about revelation. The Lord God is not only a *creating* God (as v 1 tells us) and a *caring* God (as shown by v 2), but he is also a *communicating* God (v 3). The phrase *God said* occurs ten times in this chapter (v 3, 6, 9, 11, 14, 20, 24, 26, 28 and 29): God speaks – and creation takes place. Psalm 33 comments on this: 'By the word of the LORD the heavens were made, and by the breath of his mouth all their host. ... For he spoke, and it came to be; he commanded, and it stood firm.' (Psalm 33:6, 9) Because God speaks, he makes it possible for men and women to enter into a relationship with him – but that is to anticipate the creation of human beings, which belongs to the work of the sixth day. What we find in verse 3 is that God's word is all-powerful. God speaks

[13] Augustine, *Confessions,* Book XIII.5, p.314.

the word of command, and creation takes place. The first thing to be created is *light.* This is highly appropriate, since light speaks of God's character, particularly his purity and holiness.

Second, God *saw.* He examines his work, and his assessment is that *it was good.* This phrase recurs in chapter 1, on each day of creation. Sin had not yet entered into God's perfect creation, as it would do in chapter 3.

Third, God *divided.* This is another recurring phrase in the chapter, as God makes certain distinctions. Separations that are set in place on the first, second and third days have a bearing on developments on the fourth, fifth and sixth days respectively. So, on the first day God divides between light and darkness (v 4) – just as on the fourth day God makes the sun and moon to 'rule' the day and night respectively (v 14-18). On the second day, God separates between the waters under the expanse and the waters above the expanse (v 6, 7) – just as on the fifth day he makes the birds to fly across the heavens and the sea monsters and fish to swim in the seas (v 20, 21). On the third day, God separates between the dry earth and the seas (v 9, 10 – just as on the sixth day he makes animals to inhabit the earth and human beings to have dominion over them (v 24-27). Also, God separates between male and female (v 27 and 2:18-25). Most importantly, God separates between good and evil (as the unfolding of the narrative from chapter 3 onwards will make clear). It is important to recognise the principle, inherent in creation, that God has made several of distinctions.

Fourth, God *called.* God's right to 'call' (or name) what he has created expresses his lordship over them. Remarkably, one aspect of the authority that God will confer on the first man is his right to name every living creature (2:19, 20).

Errors to avoid

The truths about God and his creation, spelt out by the opening verses of Genesis 1, rule out certain wrong understandings which have appeared in human history and are still in circulation today.

There is no place for 'pantheism' – that is the idea that God and his creation are essentially all one. This is found in many eastern religions, such as Hinduism, and also in New Age thinking. When people personify nature and speak of it as if it was spelt with a capital letter, with the implication that 'Nature' itself directs events on this planet, they are falling into this error. The Bible's opening words, 'In the beginning God created the heaven and the earth', establish the truth that God is separate from his creation.

There is no place for 'materialism' – that is the idea that this world and the universe are all that there is, and that the ultimate meaning for everything is to be found in those things. The Bible's opening words rule out this way of thinking. The writer of the Book of Ecclesiastes deliberately explores the implications of examining everything 'under the sun' – which is his way of describing materialism – and his conclusion is that this leads to meaninglessness: "Vanity of vanities ... All is vanity" (Ecclesiastes 1:2, 3). The closing verses of this Bible book affirm that life only makes sense with an acknowledgement of God's sovereign control and our accountability to him (Ecclesiastes 12:13, 14).

There is no place for 'mysticism' – by which is meant the idea that there is a division between what is 'material' (which is bad) and what is 'spiritual' (which is good). This approach has entered many religions and has even crept into some forms of Christianity. It is found, for example, in Buddhism, where the ideal is to become a disembodied brain. Asceticism, the idea of deliberately renouncing things as evil, has affected the monastic movement. However, we come back once more to the Bible's statement that *in the beginning God created the heaven and the earth* – also its repeated assertion in connection with creation that *God saw ... that it was good.* The apostle Paul tells us that 'God ... richly provides us with everything to enjoy' (1 Timothy 6:17).

There is no place for 'polytheism' – which is, of course, the idea that there are many gods. This is found in the religions of ancient Greece and Rome, and in Hinduism. The Bible's teaching on creation points us to what we call 'monotheism': there is only one God. He says of himself, "I am the first and I am the last; besides me there is no god" (Isaiah 44:6).

There is no place for 'dualism' – that is the idea that there are two equal forces, a good force and an evil force. This understanding, which has an ancient history, belongs today to New Age thinking. In Christian thinking, the idea has occasionally surfaced that, when something terrible has occurred, Satan has won a victory. But the Bible tells us that, although Satan is real, his power is in no way comparable to that of the Lord God. The Bible's monotheism has no room for dualism, just as it has no room for polytheism. One of the most important Bible verses for Jewish people, and affirmed by Jesus, is: "Hear, O Israel: the LORD our God, the LORD is one." (Deuteronomy 6:4; Mark 12:29).

A return to the surprise element in this oratorio's account of creation

Now, at last, the mystery of the surprising 'something', mentioned at the beginning of the discussion of this scene, will be explained. In so doing, this study will sound a note of criticism about the oratorio's beginning. This oratorio rightly deserves its reputation as a masterpiece, both musically and theologically. In terms of the music, *The Creation* shows Haydn at his best. In terms of the subject matter, we should be grateful that this oratorio puts the spotlight on such an important biblical topic. Nevertheless, we must face up to a problem about the way the oratorio begins.

Creation is not the only focus in the oratorio's opening. There is also a focus on *Chaos*. But the word 'chaos' seems to be used in two different ways. Before each of them is explored in more detail, it can be stated now that one of the uses of the concept of 'chaos' is *physical,* while the other one is *spiritual.* They are referring to two totally different things. But the fact that both these understandings of 'chaos' are presented to the listener within the first few minutes of the oratorio is extremely confusing. A high degree of sophistication is expected of an audience to work out that the word is to be understood differently each time. In addition, the word 'chaos' is not a biblical word at all, and that is part of the problem. The fact that the word is used at all - let alone that it appears twice - is totally unnecessary.

We need to look more closely now at the two different ways the word 'chaos' is used in the oratorio.

First, there is the Overture (Movement 1), which is given the title 'The Representation of Chaos'. This is the word 'chaos' being used in a *physical* sense. What we have here needs to be understood as a musical interpretation of Genesis 1:2a: *And the earth was without form, and void; and darkness was upon the face of the deep.* The musical comment on this scene which follows shortly will explain the reason for this interpretation of Movement 1. Someone listening to this oratorio might well gain the impression that this 'chaos' was 'formless primordial matter' (one definition of 'chaos'), which already existed *before* God began his work of creation. After all, we must wait for Movement 2 before we have the announcement in Genesis 1:1 that *God created the heaven and the earth.* But, as we have seen in the earlier discussion, this does not accurately reflect what the beginning of Genesis 1 is telling us. God created 'the heaven and the earth' out of *nothing*. The matter which was *without form, and void* was the first stage of God's creation in verse 1, before he brought form and order out of that which was formless.

However, in Haydn's defence, we do need to notice that throughout the oratorio Haydn provides the sung verbal explanation *after* the orchestral portrayal. But this only becomes clear, though, as we make our way through the whole work: at the beginning of the work there is no indication that this is the procedure he will adopt. Also, no doubt, Haydn wanted to begin his oratorio with a quiet introduction, in order to heighten the dramatic effect of the creation of light at the end of Movement 2, and this may be a further reason for his giving us his musical interpretation of verse 2a before that of verse 1. Haydn's understanding, therefore, of the opening verses of Genesis 1, was almost certainly the correct one. For him, 'chaos' meant the earth being *without form, and void* following God's initial act of creation. But the placing of the orchestral representation of verse 2a before the soloist's announcement of verse 1 has blurred the clarity of the Bible account.
Second, there is another 'chaos' which we hear about in Uriel's aria (Movement 3), where he sings:

> *Now vanish before the holy beams*
> *the gloomy, dismal shades of ancient night.*
> *The first of days appears!*
> *Now chaos ends and order fair prevails.*
> *Affrighted fly hell's spirits, black in throngs;*
> *down they sink in the deepest abyss*
> *to endless night.*

And the chorus respond with:

> *Despairing, cursing rage attends their rapid fall.*
> *A new-created world springs up at God's command.*

Here are the words *ancient night* and *chaos.* This 'chaos' has more to do with 'utter confusion' (another dictionary definition) than with 'formless primordial matter'. This is no physical 'chaos' - rather, it concerns the *spiritual* domain, because we are told of *hell's spirits* fleeing in fear and sinking into *the deepest abyss* and *endless night.* We are informed of *their rapid fall.* That, of course, raises the question: Where in the Bible's account of creation is there any mention of hell and the spiritual forces of evil?

The straightforward answer to that question is that what we have here is *not* drawn from the Book of Genesis. Rather, it has to do with the influence of John Milton's *Paradise Lost.* This long poetic work is an imaginative and powerful reworking of the first three chapters of the Bible. But Milton goes beyond the Bible's account of creation of the world and of man and woman, and its account of the Fall (Adam and Eve's disobedience of God and their ejection from the Garden of Eden). Milton fills in what might be described as the gaps, particularly with his description of the person and role of Satan. *Paradise Lost* tells us of events that took place before Genesis 1. God had already created angels, one of whom (Satan) rebelled against God and carried many other angels with him. This leads to war in heaven and to the defeat of Satan and his forces. These things have already happened at the point where the poem begins. Milton tells us in his 'Argument' (or summary) of Book I that:

> Satan, with his Angels, now fallen into Hell – described here not in the Centre (for heaven and earth may be supposed as yet not made, certainly not yet accursed), but in a place of utter darkness, fitliest called Chaos.[14]

[14] Milton, *Paradise Lost,* 5.

This sentence from John Milton explains very clearly where those references in the opening scene of *The Creation* to *hell, darkness* and *chaos* come from, and it explains that *hell's spirits* are Satan's fallen angels. It may well be the case that modern audiences at performances of *The Creation* are not as familiar with *Paradise Lost* as was once the case. Those who listened to the oratorio in the early 1800s are more likely to have been acquainted with this background information.

The line *Now chaos ends and order fair prevails* may cause some readers to think of a well-known hymn by John Marriott (1780-1825), which begins: 'Thou, whose almighty word / *Chaos* and darkness heard / And *took their flight*" (my emphasis). This hymn provides a robust statement of the involvement of all three Persons of the Trinity in the work of creation. The first three verses of the hymn focus in turn on the role of the Father, the Son and the Holy Spirit in creation, and the fourth verse combines all three. It would be interesting to know whether Marriott was influenced by the opening scene of *The Creation*, since it was only a few years after the oratorio's appearance that he wrote the hymn, and included this statement about chaos taking its flight. It would also be interesting to know whether Marriott had in mind only the 'confused emptiness' of Genesis 1:2a (to repeat Calvin's phrase), or whether he was also thinking of Milton's poetic work.[15]

The other major thing that it is useful to know from *Paradise Lost* is that, following God's overthrow of Satan's rebellion, God chooses to put into effect his plan to create the world and mankind. That, in turn, leads to Satan's decision to spoil God's creation by tempting the first human pair into sin. And so, the poem moves into territory which we know well from the first three chapters of Genesis.

It would be wrong for us to dismiss Milton's work out of hand and to regard it as wild imagining of things about which the Bible is silent. There are, in fact, verses and passages in the Bible that relate to the fall of Satan. We turn now to four of them.

---

[15] J. Marriott, 'Thou, whose almighty word,' written in 1813 and first published in Dr Raffle's *Collection* in 1816.

What the Bible has to say about war in heaven

First, *Luke 10:18,* here Jesus says: "I saw Satan fall like lightning from heaven." In the previous verse, seventy-two disciples have returned with joy from a mission on which he has sent them, and they have said, "Lord, even the demons are subject to us in your name!"

What is Jesus referring to in his reply of verse 18 concerning the fall of Satan? There are three possibilities. One is that he has in mind an event in pre-history (which would link in with the storyline of *Paradise Lost*). A second possibility is that his words are to be understood as what we might describe as a prophetic past tense (but referring to the future defeat of Satan, to be brought about by his work on the Cross - or it could be the future final defeat of Satan at the end of time). A third possibility is that Jesus was describing what he saw at that point of time (a graphic description of what his disciples' successful mission had accomplished).

Any one of those three explanations could be the correct one, but the first or the second probably makes best sense. At the very least, Luke 10:18 in its immediate context does tell us certain things for certain. It tells us that:

- Satan's home had been in heaven with God
- Satan fell from that blissful position
- there is a spiritual war going on
- God's people have power over the Enemy
- the names of God's people are written in the same heaven from which Satan fell (Luke 10:20)

Second, *Revelation 12*. The main purpose of the Book of Revelation, including this chapter, is to give pastoral encouragement to Christians facing persecution, but it does shed light on the origin of Satan. Verses 7-9 of Revelation 12 describe the following:

> Now war arose in heaven, Michael and his angels fighting against the dragon. And the dragon and his angels fought back, but he was defeated, and there was no longer any place for them in heaven. And the great dragon was thrown down, that ancient serpent, who is

> called the devil and Satan, the deceiver of the whole world - he was thrown down to the earth, and his angels were thrown down with him.

Among other things, we learn here that:

- Satan had been an inhabitant of heaven, an angelic being who rebelled
- Satan was cast out of heaven along with 'his' angels
- earth is now the sphere of his operations, and he attacks the church

Third, *Ezekiel 28*. The chapter is written in poetic language, which means that we need to exercise caution, so that we do not read into it more than we should. However, certain things are made very clear. The first ten verses of the chapter speak of the prince of Tyre, while the nine following verses consist of a lamentation over the king of Tyre. While the language used of the prince of Tyre is appropriate to a man (and he is referred to as a 'man'), the language used of the king of Tyre really could not be used of any human being. However, the same spirit dominates both prince and king. Both have tremendous beauty, wisdom and power, and both defy the living God. It might reasonably be understood that the prince is the understudy of the king: he is dominated by the spirit of the ultimate ruler of Tyre, who is Satan himself.

The words spoken about the prince of Tyre (Ezekiel 28:1-10) will be left to one side, but here is part of the following section of words spoken about the king of Tyre:

> Thus says the Lord GOD:
> "You were the signet of perfection, full of wisdom and perfect in beauty.
> You were in Eden, the garden of God;
> every precious stone was your covering,
> sardius, topaz, and diamond, beryl, onyx, and jasper, sapphire, emerald, and carbuncle;
> and crafted in gold were your settings and your engravings.

> On the day that you were created they were prepared.
> You were an anointed guardian cherub.
> I placed you; you were on the holy mountain of God;
> in the midst of the stones of fire you walked.
> You were blameless in your ways from the day you were created,
> till unrighteousness was found in you.
> In the abundance of your trade you were filled with violence in your midst,
> and you sinned;
> so I cast you as a profane thing from the mountain of God,
> and I destroyed you, O guardian cherub, from the midst of the stones of fire.
> Your heart was proud because of your beauty;
> you corrupted your wisdom for the sake of your splendour.
> I cast you to the ground..."
> (Ezekiel 28:12b-17a)

It must be said that these words do appear to apply to a fallen angelic spirit.

Fourth, *Isaiah 14*. Ostensibly, the opening part of this chapter, from verse 3 onwards, consists of a taunt against the king of Babylon. But as with the passage from Ezekiel 28, the words used seem better fitted to addressing a more sinister figure, who stands behind the Babylonian king. Here is part of that chapter:

> "How you are fallen from heaven, O Day Star, son of Dawn!
> How you are cut down to the ground, you who laid the nations low!
> You said in your heart, 'I will ascend to heaven;
> above the stars of God I will set my throne on high;

I will sit on the mount of assembly in the far
reaches of the north;
I will ascend above the heights of the clouds;
I will make myself like the Most High.'"
(Isaiah 14:12-14)

These words too seem to describe the fall of an angelic being.

Conclusion

Dare we say that *The Creation* creates confusion with the word 'chaos'? At the very least, there is the danger that it may do so. And the confusion, as we have seen, is twofold, because of the two different uses of the word 'chaos', one carrying a *physical* sense, the other a *spiritual* one.

First, Movement 1, 'The Representation of Chaos', can wrongly give the impression that God used pre-existent 'chaotic' matter in his work of creation.

Second, the reference to the 'chaos' of Milton's *Paradise Lost* in Movement 3 may not be understood by modern audiences. Neither is this theme developed in any part of the rest of the oratorio. It is true that the Bible passages that have just been examined point to the origin and character of Satan. Also, it is true that Milton's poetic creation has more of a biblical foundation than might at first appear to be the case.[16] However, the inclusion of the pre-creation 'chaos' theme in the opening scene of the oratorio, alongside the 'creation' theme of the work as a whole, should probably be regarded as an error of judgement. If the oratorio were to have included an account of the Fall as well as an account of Creation, the Miltonian reference to war in heaven would have made better sense, because further information about the Tempter in the Garden would have been helpful. As it is, the oratorio

[16] Other Bible verses which refer to the fall of Satan and of other angels are Jude 6 ('And the angels who did not stay within their own position of authority, but left their proper dwelling, he has kept in eternal chains under gloomy darkness until the judgement of the great day') and 1 Timothy 3:6 ('... or he may become puffed up with conceit and fall into the condemnation of the devil.') This last phrase should be understood to mean that the devil is the one who is condemned, not that he is the one who condemns.

focuses on Genesis 1 and, briefly, Genesis 2 (the creation of the heavens and the earth and of the first human pair), and the only hint of a reference to Genesis 3 (the Fall) is a comment in the final scene of the oratorio in a recitative from Uriel.

What to Listen Out For in the Music of Part I Scene 1

Movement 1: Overture – The Representation of Chaos

Listen out for features in this movement which mark it out as a good example of 'tone painting', referred to earlier. An alternative phrase might be 'musical onomatopoeia'. The music seeks to paint a picture for us by its sounds. Haydn was influenced by Handel's use of this technique in his oratorios.

Listen out for:

(a) the slow tempo of the movement – and its seemingly formless shape (although, in fact, it is in the classical sonata form). This slow introduction suggests that Haydn was *not* influenced in this movement by the Miltonian idea of 'chaos' representing a pre-creation war in heaven. Otherwise, the music would surely have been fast and furious. Rather, Haydn must have had in mind the formless state of the earth, described in Genesis 1:2 as being at first *without form, and void.* There is an atmosphere of mysteriousness about the movement.

(b) the minor key of the movement. Given that the minor key normally suggests mournfulness, or – to express that slightly differently – the lack of something fully positive, Haydn is telling us musically that the *good* (and the *very good*) of later in the chapter has not yet been reached. The key here is C minor, which is significant because, when the anticipated major key later appears in Movement 2 (in connection with the creation of light), it is the key of C major that is used. It is not being suggested here that there is particular significance attached to the use of the key of C. The point is that it is the same key that is being used, but switched from the minor to the major. Also, significantly, the key of C major is used in Movement 14, at the end of Part I of the oratorio, where the soloists and chorus celebrate how the heavens tell the glory of God.

Listen out for prominent contributions from woodwind and brass. For example, there is a two-octave ascending run from the clarinet about halfway through. Do touches like this give hints of the creation to come?

Movement 2: Recitative and chorus
Listen out for the continuation of the key of C minor in the bass soloist's recitative about the earth being *without form, and void* (already represented in the Overture).

Listen out for the chorus's rendition of Genesis 1:2b-3: for the most part quiet, and still at a slow tempo. Then comes a dramatic moment. The chorus sing God's words, *Let there be light,* which is immediately followed by a quiet pizzicato chord from the strings. Then the chorus sing quietly, unaccompanied and in unison, *and there was* – and that is immediately followed by the word *light,* sung suddenly and very loud (taking by surprise those who do not know what is coming!). Most significantly, the chorus sing the word as a chord of C *major,* which makes a dramatic contrast with the tonality of C minor which has dominated this far. The chorus hold the chord for a full bar, with loud chords of C major from the orchestra. In the first performance of *The Creation* that moment caused a great sensation of amazement, and still today it can make a powerful impact on the audience.

Movement 3: Aria and chorus
Listen out for the totally different mood of this movement, which refers to the defeat of Satan's forces, as depicted in *Paradise Lost.* The key is A major.

Listen out for more instances of 'tone painting' – for example, the (appropriately) descending musical figure from both tenor soloist and orchestra on the words *Down they sink in deepest abyss,* and the chorus's singing of the spirits' *despairing, cursing rage.* This is a short fugal passage (i.e. the same musical phrase being sung by the different voices one after the other), which intensifies the sense of confusion among the defeated enemies.

Then comes the chorus's repeated phrase, *A new-created world,* a delightful moment which brings this scene to an end.

SCENE 2: The Second Day
(PART I of the oratorio)

4. Recitative

RAPHAEL
And God made the firmament, and divided the waters which were under the firmament from the waters, which were above the firmament: and it was so. (Genesis 1:7)

Now furious storms tempestuous rage,
like chaff, by the winds impelled are the clouds,
by sudden fire the sky is inflamed,
and awful thunders are rolling on high.
Now from the floods in steam ascend reviving showers of rain,
the dreary wasteful hail, the light and flaky snow.

5. Aria and chorus

GABRIEL
The marv'llous work behold amaz'd
the glorious hierarchy of heaven;
and to th' ethereal vaults resound
the praise of God, and of the second day.[17]

CHORUS
And to th' ethereal vaults resound
the praise of God, and of the second day.

CHORUS
And to th' ethereal vaults resound
the praise of God, and of the second day.

---

[17] *ethereal* (here) = belonging to the sky (cf. the word 'ether') rather than the modern meaning of delicate or dainty.
Cf. Milton, *Paradise Lost,* VII.274-5: 'So even / And morning chorus sung the second day.'

Looking at the biblical account of the second day

Three verses of the Bible's first chapter give the account of the second day, Genesis 1: 6-8:

> 6: And God said, "Let there be an expanse in the midst of the waters, and let it separate the waters from the waters."
> 7: And God made the expanse and separated the waters that were under the expanse from the waters that were above the expanse. And it was so.
> 8: And God called the expanse Heaven. And there was evening and there was morning, the second day.

This scene gives us only verse 7 (in Movement 4), which takes us to the heart of the action of the second day. It is a pity that verse 6 is omitted, since it reinforces the theme of the creative power of the word of God.

The word *firmament* (or 'expanse', ESV) refers to the sky. The word means something firm: it is pictorial language, like our expression 'the vault of heaven'. So, what we are being told is that God separates between the waters under the expanse (i.e. the oceans and seas) and the waters above the expanse (i.e. the water vapour in the atmosphere). The word "Heaven" (v 8) is the physical heaven, in other words the sky (as in the ESV footnote).

Poetic celebration of the second day of creation

The poetic section for this scene (Movement 5) draws attention to some of the phenomena we associate with the sky: storms, wind and clouds, lightning, thunder, rain, hail and snow. The observation that *from the floods in steam* ascend *reviving showers of rain* shows awareness of the rain-cycle (rain-bearing clouds being produced by rising water vapour).

What to Listen out for in the Music of Part I Scene 2

Movement 4: Recitative

Listen out for the second part of the bass soloist's recitative (following the verses from Genesis 1). We return to the key of C major. This movement gives us further instances of 'tone painting' applied to different types of meteorological phenomena - the orchestral representation of each precedes the soloist's naming of it. Listen out for the inventive depictions of storms, wind, fire (i.e., lightning), thunders (with timpani used here), rain, hail and snow.

Movement 5: Aria and chorus

Listen out for the use again of the key of C major in this joyful movement.

Listen out for the way Haydn combines the parts sung by the soprano soloist and by the chorus. The aria consists of a four-line poem, and the chorus reinforce the third and fourth lines of it a few times.

SCENE 3: The Third Day
(PART I of the oratorio)

6. Recitative

RAPHAEL

And God said, Let the waters under the heavens be gathered together to one place, and let the dry land appear: and it was so. And God called the dry land earth, and the gathering of waters called he seas: and God saw that it was good. (Genesis 1:9-10)

7. Aria

RAPHAEL

Rolling in foaming billows,
Uplifted, roars the boisterous sea.
Mountains and rocks now emerge,
their tops among the clouds ascend.[18]
Through th' open plains, outstretching wide,
in serpent error rivers flow.[19]
Softly purling, glides on[20]
through silent vales the limpid brook.[21]

8. Recitative

GABRIEL

And God said, Let the earth bring forth grass, the herb yielding seed, and the fruit-tree yielding fruit after his kind, whose seed is in itself, upon the earth: and it was so. (Genesis 1:11)

---

[18] Cf. Milton, *Paradise Lost*, VII.285-7: 'Immediately the mountains huge appear / Emergent, and their broad bare backs upheave / Into the clouds; their tops ascend the sky.'

[19] Cf. Milton, *Paradise Lost*, VII.302: 'With serpent error wandering...'
serpent = serpentine, winding (like a snake).
error = wandering (the Latin sense of the word).

[20] *purling* = swirling.

[21] *limpid* = clear.

9. Aria

GABRIEL

With verdure clad the fields appear,[22]
delightful to the ravish'd sense;[23]
by flowers sweet and gay
enhanced is the charming sight.
Here fragrant herbs their odours shed;
here shoots the healing plant.
With copious fruit the expanded boughs are hung;[24]
in leafy arches twine the shady groves;
o'er lofty hills majestic forests wave.

10. Recitative

URIEL

And the heavenly host proclaimed the third day, praising God and saying,

11. Chorus

CHORUS

Awake the harp, the lyre awake,
and let your joyful song resound.
Rejoice in the Lord, the mighty God;
For he both heaven and earth
has clothed in stately dress.

Looking at the biblical account of the third day

The Bible verses that relate what happened on the third day are Genesis 1:9-13. The complete version of those verses is:

> 9: And God said, "Let the waters under the heavens be gathered together into one place, and let the dry land appear." And it was so.

---

[22] *verdure* = growing vegetation.
Cf. Milton, *Paradise Lost*, VII.313-6: 'Earth ... / Brought forth the tender grass, whose verdure clad / Her universal face with pleasant green.'

[23] *ravish'd* = delighted.

[24] Cf. Milton, *Paradise Lost*, VII.325: 'Their branches, hung with copious fruit...'

> 10: God called the dry land Earth, and the waters that were gathered together he called Seas. And God saw that it was good.
> 11: And God said, "Let the earth sprout vegetation, plants yielding seed, and fruit trees bearing fruit in which is their seed, each according to its kind, on the earth." And it was so.
> 12: The earth brought forth vegetation, plants yielding seed according to their own kinds, and trees bearing fruit in which is their seed, each according to its kind. And God saw that it was good.
> 13: And there was evening and there was morning, the third day.

The oratorio gives us verses 9-11 (Movements 6 and 8). The first part of verse 12 is essentially a repetition of verse 11: what is stated in verse 11 as a command becomes a reality in verse 12. The second part of verse 12 affirms again, as on the first day in verse 4 (and as already on the third day in verse 10), the goodness of God's creation, and it is important for us to be reminded of the sheer excellence of all that God created.

In these verses, the separation of dry land from the sea takes place, and we begin to meet the theme of fullness and fruitfulness, which will be given even greater emphasis later in the chapter. On the third day, vegetation and plants and trees appear.

Poetic celebration of the third day of creation

Raphael's aria (Movement 7) focuses on the different forms that water on earth assumes – in particular seas, rivers, brooks. Gabriel's aria (Movement 9) picks up the sense of verses 11 and 12, moving from fields, flowers and herbs to the trees of orchards, groves and forests.

What to Listen out for in the Music of Part I Scene 3

Movement 6: Recitative

A brief recitative for the bass soloist.

Movement 7: Aria

Listen out for more 'tone painting' in the bass soloist's aria about the different forms of water upon earth. An orchestral introduction depicts the *foaming billows* of the *sea*. The description of the way the tops of mountains and rocks *ascend* from the waters is accompanied by ascending scales in the accompaniment. The *serpent error* of the rivers is expressed by a series of descending scales from the soloist.

Listen out for the change of key from D minor to D major in the second half of the aria, which focuses on *the limpid brook*. Although this is the theme of only two lines of the soloist's words, the repeated treatment of them occupies the full second half of the movement. Not only has the key changed from minor to major (giving a more positive tone to the piece), but also the mood of this second half is calmer. Triplets in the orchestral accompaniment suggest the gentle flowing of the water.

Movement 8: Recitative

A brief recitative for the soprano soloist.

Movement 9: Aria

Listen out for the A-B-A shape of this lovely aria for the soprano soloist. The A section is made up of the first 6 lines (from *With verdure clad* to *the healing plant*), and the B section consists of lines 7 to 9 (from *With copious fruits* to *forests wave*). There is a change of key between the A and B sections: the A section is in the key of B flat major, and the B section is in the closely related key of E flat major.

Listen out for the 'siciliana' rhythm of the movement (which means that the time signature is a slow 6/8 or 12/8 with a lilting rhythm). This piece is in 6/8 (i.e., two beats in the bar, each consisting of a dotted crotchet). The Christmas carol 'Silent Night' is a well-known example of a piece making use of the 'siciliana' rhythm.

Listen out for the embellished phrasing on the word *enhanced* and on the phrase *the healing plant.*

Movement 10: Recitative

A brief recitative for the tenor soloist.

Movement 11: Chorus

Listen out, in this triumphant chorus of praise, for another example of the A-B-A structure. The words of the A sections give the commands to praise God, while the central B section gives the reason why people should praise.

Listen out, in the central section, for the four-part fugue on the words *For he both heaven and earth has clothed in stately dress.* This central section (the reason for people to praise) is both preceded and followed by what we might describe as 'block chord' treatment of the words. The technical term for this is 'homophonic'.

SCENE 4: The Fourth Day
(PART I of the oratorio)

12. Recitative

URIEL

And God said, Let there be lights in the firmament of heaven, to divide the day from the night, and to give light upon the earth; and let them be for signs, and for seasons, and for days, and for years. He made the stars also. (Genesis 1:14, 15b and 16c)

13. Recitative

URIEL

In splendour bright is rising now the sun,
and darts his rays; a joyful happy spouse,
a giant proud and glad
to run his measur'd course.
With softer beams, and milder light,
steps on the silver moon through silent night.
The space immense of th' azure sky,
a countless host of radiant orbs adorns.
And the sons of God announced the fourth day,
in song divine, proclaiming thus his power:

14. Trio and chorus

CHORUS

The heavens are telling the glory of God;
the wonder of his work displays the firmament. (Psalm 19:1)

GABRIEL, URIEL and RAPHAEL

To day that is coming speaks it the day;
the night that is gone to following night. (Psalm 19:2)

CHORUS

The heavens are telling ...

GABRIEL, URIEL and RAPHAEL

In all the lands resounds the word,
never unperceived, ever understood.

CHORUS
The heavens are telling ...

Looking at the biblical account of the fourth day

On the fourth day, God created the sun, the moon and the stars. Again, the biblical material in the soloist's recitative has been edited. The account of the fourth day occupies Genesis 1:14-19:

> 14: And God said, "Let there be lights in the expanse of the heavens to separate the day from the night. And let them be for signs and for seasons, and for days and years,
> 15: and let them be lights in the expanse of the heavens to give light upon the earth." And it was so.
> 16: And God made the two great lights—the greater light to rule the day and the lesser light to rule the night—and the stars.
> 17: And God set them in the expanse of the heavens to give light on the earth,
> 18: to rule over the day and over the night, and to separate the light from the darkness. And God saw that it was good.
> 19: And there was evening and there was morning, the fourth day.

Uriel's recitative (Movement 12) makes use of parts of verses 14 and 15, and the last few words of verse 16. The libretto omits what is presumably regarded as repetitions and omits another of the statements about God seeing the goodness of his creation. However, it brings out the roles of the sun and the moon, both to provide light on the earth and 'for signs and for seasons, and for days and years' – in other words, to mark the calendar, which would be important for the people of Israel, in the time to come, for observing regular festivals for worshipping God (Leviticus 23:4).

Attention should be drawn to the closing words of verse 16: *He made the stars also.* These words should surely be regarded as one of the greatest throw-away lines that have ever been written. We, with our radio-telescopes, can now begin to understand something of the truly amazing size of the universe and of the unimaginable number of stars that exist in the universe. All this is compressed into this short phrase, which in Hebrew consists of just two words (one of which may be regarded simply as a linking word). The Bible tells us that God is well able to identify each individual star. We read: 'He determines the number of the stars; he gives to all of them their names.' (Psalm 147:4) The Book of Isaiah makes a similar comment about the stars:

> Lift up your eyes on high and see: who created these?
> He who brings out their host by number, calling them all by name,
> by the presence of his might, and because he is strong in power not one is missing.
> (Isaiah 40:26).

An important inference to draw from this comment about the stars (and the same applies to the sun and the moon in these verses) is that they are all part of God's creation. Therefore, there is no place for anything to do with astrology or any idea that the stars can be our masters and determine our destiny. It is significant also that the Hebrew word for *lights* is used in these verses, instead of the specific words for 'sun' and 'moon', in case they could be wrongly understood to be deities. Readers of horoscopes today need to dismiss their superstitious ideas.

Poetic celebration of the fourth day of creation

Uriel's next recitative (Movement 13) provides a poetic description of the sun, moon and stars. The words about the sun are a reference to Psalm 19:4c-5, where the sun is imaginatively compared to two individuals, both of whom display vitality and eagerness. First, there is a *spouse* (or, more exactly in the psalm, 'a bridegroom') splendidly clothed, eagerly setting out from his home to claim his bride. Secondly, there is the *giant* (or, again to be more precise, in the terms of the psalm, 'a strong man') – perhaps we should imagine a runner – who joyfully runs his race.

'The heavens are telling the glory of God'

The following trio and chorus (Movement 14) make the fullest use of the first part of that same psalm, Psalm 19, as a paraphrase of some of its verses. This movement is probably the best-known part of the whole oratorio and is often sung as a single item. Psalm 19 is in two parts: the first part focuses on the theme of God's revelation through 'the heavens' (i.e., the sky – particularly the stars of the night sky and the sun), and the second part on the theme of God's revelation through 'the law of the LORD'. Here are the verses of the first part of the psalm:

> 1: The heavens declare the glory of God, and the sky above proclaims his handiwork.
> 2: Day to day pours out speech, and night to night reveals knowledge.
> 3: There is no speech, nor are there words, whose voice is not heard.
> 4: Their voice goes out through all the earth, and their words to the end of the world. In them he has set a tent for the sun,
> 5: which comes out like a bridegroom leaving his chamber, and, like a strong man, runs its course with joy.
> 6: Its rising is from the end of the heavens, and its circuit to the end of them, and there is nothing hidden from its heat.

The words of trio and chorus (Movement 14) are based on verses 1, 2 and 4 (the first part of the verse), and the last part of verse 4 and verse 5, as mentioned above, have been referenced in Movement 13.

Psalm 19:1-6 gives Christian believers a strong encouragement to express joy and wonder at God's creation. The opportunity to enjoy and marvel at the breath-taking beauty of the night sky is not readily available to most of us. Streetlights, cloudy skies, and the cold nights of winter are major factors in preventing us from stargazing with godly awe, as David had clearly done. But David has in mind the sky by day as well as by night when he includes the sun in these verses. He writes here of what might be described as the silent eloquence of the heavens:

they speak so powerfully of God's glory and praise him for his 'marvellous craftsmanship' (in the words of the New Living Translation), even though they do not utter a word. In fact, they are almost like missionaries, taking the message of the power and majesty of God 'though all the earth' and 'to the end of the world' (v 4). Interestingly, the apostle Paul picks up on this point when he quotes Psalm 19:4 in Romans 10:18. He does so in a paragraph in which he urges his readers to take seriously the need to take the message of the Gospel to people of all nations – and, of course, to preach it, for there is to be nothing silent about Christian witness!

It is possible that Paul also had Psalm 19:1-6 in mind when he wrote, in Romans 1, about the clear evidence of God's power and Lordship in everything that he has made:

> For the wrath of God is revealed from heaven against all ungodliness and unrighteousness of men, who by their unrighteousness suppress the truth. For what can be known about God is plain to them, because God has shown it to them. For his invisible attributes, namely, his eternal power and divine nature, have been clearly perceived, ever since the creation of the world, in the things that have been made. So they are without excuse.
> (Romans 1:18-20)

God has revealed enough of himself through his creation to bring people to an awareness of his reality and their accountability to him. While they still need the Gospel to point them to Christ, the witness of creation clearly confronts every human being. To ignore that witness leaves those who do so 'without excuse'.

What to Listen out for in the Music of Part I Scene 4

Movement 12: Recitative
A brief recitative for the tenor soloist.

Movement 13: Recitative
Listen out for the 'tone painting' at the very beginning of this movement, representing sunrise. A sense of anticipation is created by the slow orchestral introduction. There is a crescendo from *pianissimo* to *fortissimo* with a gradually ascending series of notes, then a purposefully downward series of notes from the lower instruments, and then a series of triumphant chords before the soloist makes his entry. Further majestic phrases from the orchestra intersperse the soloist's description of the sun as *a happy spouse* and as *a giant proud and glad.*

Listen out for the contrasting depiction of the moon. The music is slower and quieter – more languid, but again with a rising scale passage.

Listen out for the third short section of this piece, depicting the stars, with the return of a more triumphant tone.

Movement 14: Trio and chorus
Listen out for the use of C major, as at the end of the earlier Movement 2. It is appropriate that that key, which was clearly linked with the beginning of creation and the triumph of light over darkness, should re-appear at the end of Part I in this magnificent and much-loved chorus, praising God for the wonder of the heavens.

Listen out for the alternation between the majestic sections sung by the chorus, celebrating God's work, and the more meditative sections sung by the three vocal soloists as a trio.

Listen out for the chorus's third contribution of their words. This time, it takes the form of a fugue on the words *and the wonder of his work displays the firmament,* which is followed by a final homophonic ('block chord') section.

Listen out for the extended ending of the movement, with Haydn piling up coda upon coda almost every time we expect the item to finish.

Part Two

SCENE 1: The Fifth Day

15. Recitative

GABRIEL

And God said, Let the waters bring forth abundantly the moving creature that hath life, and fowl that may fly above the earth in the open firmament of heaven. (Genesis 1:20)

16. Aria

GABRIEL

On mighty pens uplifted soars[25]
the eagle aloft, and cleaves the air,
in swiftest flight, to the blazing sun.
His welcome bids to morn the merry lark,
and cooing calls the tender dove his mate.
From ev'ry bush and grove resound
the nightingale's delightful notes;
no grief affected yet her breast,
nor to a mournful tale were tun'd
her soft enchanting lays.[26]

17. Recitative

RAPHAEL

And God created great whales, and every living creature that moveth; and God blessed them, saying, Be fruitful, all, and multiply. (Genesis 1:21a and 22a)

Ye winged tribes, be multiplied,
and sing on every tree; multiply,
Ye finny tribes, and fill each wat'ry deep;
be fruitful, grow, and multiply,

---

[25] *pens* = wings.

[26] *lays* = songs. These few lines refer to the conceit (i.e. the fanciful idea) that, just after the Creation, the nightingale's song was not melancholy.

and in your God and Lord rejoice.

18. Recitative

RAPHAEL

And the angels struck their immortal harps,
and the wonders of the fifth day sung.

19. Trio

GABRIEL

Most beautiful appear, with verdure young adorn'd,[27]
the gently sloping hills; their narrow sinuous veins
distil, in crystal drops, the fountain fresh and bright.

URIEL

In lofty circles play, and hover in the air,
the cheerful host of birds; and as they flying whirl
their glitt'ring plumes are dy'd as rainbows by the sun.

RAPHAEL

See flashing through the deep in thronging swarms
the fish a thousand ways around.
Upheaved from the deep, th' immense Leviathan[28]
sports on the foaming wave.

GABRIEL, URIEL and RAPHAEL

How many are thy works, O God!
Who may their number tell?

20. Trio and chorus

TRIO and CHORUS

The Lord is great, and great his might,
his glory lasts for ever and for evermore.

---

[27] *verdure* = growing vegetation.

[28] *Leviathan* = the whale. This is certainly the meaning here, as also in Milton, *Paradise Lost*, I.201 and VII.412. In the Bible, the identification of Leviathan is less certain. In Job.41:1-34 it seems to be the crocodile. Elsewhere, it seems to indicate an aquatic monster and is also used figuratively of the Egyptian Pharaoh, Assyria and Babylonia.

Looking at the biblical account of the fifth day

Genesis 1:20-23 provides the account of the fifth day of creation, which saw the appearance of sea-creatures and birds. The verses in full are:

> 20: And God said, "Let the waters swarm with swarms of living creatures, and let birds fly above the earth across the expanse of the heavens."
> 21: So God created the great sea creatures and every living creature that moves, with which the waters swarm, according to their kinds, and every winged bird according to its kind. And God saw that it was good.
> 22: And God blessed them, saying, "Be fruitful and multiply and fill the waters in the seas, and let birds multiply on the earth."
> 23: And there was evening and there was morning, the fifth day.

As with previous scenes, the libretto gives a compressed account of the Genesis account.

As indicated in the discussion of the first day, the word *created* in verse 21 translates the Hebrew word bārā, which is used to mark three great beginnings. This is the second of them, because here we have the creation of living creatures in the sea and in fresh water, and in the air.

The moving creature that hath life (v 20) and *living creature* (v 21) is the same expression in the Hebrew. The translation both times in the ESV is 'living creatures'. The word *nepeš* is used, which can also be translated as 'soul', but here it is the equivalent of 'life'.

A significant new feature, at this point in the account of creation, is God's command to these creatures to *be fruitful ... and multiply*; we shall meet this again in verse 28 with the creation of man.

The *whales* of verse 21, as the AV translates the word, are 'great sea creatures'. No doubt, whales and suchlike are what is meant. In the world of the early Old Testament people, great sea creatures were regarded as a threat and they represented the powers of chaos. But in the Bible, they are magnificent creatures.

Poetic celebration of the fifth day of creation

Gabriel's aria (Movement 16) focuses on the creation of birds, and singles out eagles, larks, doves and nightingales. Gabriel's recitative (Movement 17) deals with sea creatures in a more general way. The trio (Movement 19), in its three successive stanzas from the three soloists, celebrates the creation – respectively – of hills and springs (somewhat surprisingly in this scene), birds, and sea-life. The common feature of each of these three is the abundant fruitfulness of God's creation.

What to Listen out for in the Music of Part II Scene I

Movement 15: Recitative

A brief recitative for the soprano soloist.

Movement 16: Aria

Listen out for the orchestral introduction to this aria with a prominent contribution from the flute. As this aria concerns the creation of birds, the flute might be regarded as well suited to represent them. Prokofiev uses the flute to represent the bird in his 'symphonic fairy tale for children', *Peter and the Wolf*.

Listen out for the expressive nature of the soprano soloist's aria, as she sings, firstly, about the creation of the eagle, lark and dove. Each of these three birds is depicted in turn. The eagle, who *soars ... aloft,* is represented by a few stately ascending scales and upward leaps in the vocal line and accompaniment, the lark's song is suggested by a couple of phrases from the clarinet, and the dove's call is imitated by the soloist's embellished phrases, particularly on the word *cooing*.

Listen out for the second half of the aria, which concerns the nightingale. The flute provides accompaniment for part of this.

Movement 17: Recitative

Listen out for the way this movement, despite being labelled a recitative, consists of a short recitative (the words taken from Genesis 1:21 and 22), followed by a short aria.

Listen out for the way the bass voice is well suited to convey the words of God in the recitative, giving his command to the creatures to *be fruitful ... and multiply* – which is developed in the short aria.

Listen out for the orchestral accompaniment in this movement. The violins do not play, and instead we hear only the lower strings, with both violas and cellos being divided into two parts. This feature intensifies the 'bass' texture of the movement, which may be considered appropriate for a piece that concerns, among other things, such deep-sea creatures as *great whales*.

Movement 18: Recitative

A brief recitative for the bass soloist.

Movement 19: Trio

Listen out for the three stanzas which form the main content of this movement – each stanza sung by a different soloist. First, we hear the soprano soloist singing about hills and springs. Next, we hear the tenor soloist singing about the birds, The musical content is an exact repeat of the first stanza. Then we hear the bass soloist singing about sea-life. As his lines include *th' immense Leviathan* (which is to be identified as the whale), the bass voice is appropriate, and – also appropriately for a stanza about *the deep* – the bass's vocal line includes two downward leaps of an octave (another touch of 'tone painting', of course).

Listen out for the three voices coming together for the last two lines of praise – partly singing as a fugue, and partly converging with each other.

Movement 20: Trio and chorus

Listen out for the way this movement follows on directly from the previous one as a further expression of praise to God.

Listen out for the three soloists singing as a trio, and then the chorus joining in with a repeat of what the soloists have sung - while the soloists continue with their own vocal lines, sometimes merging with what one or other voice in the chorus is singing, at other times singing quite separately from them. But Haydn combines it all into a gloriously harmonious whole, which is sustained for several pages.

Listen out for fast, embellished passages in all this from the soprano and tenor soloists.

Listen out, in the final section, for a twice-repeated ascending series of steps of one semi-tone at a time in the choral bass vocal line on the words *his glory lasts, his glory lasts.* Technically, this is called a ‘chromatic’ sequence, and it produces a striking effect on the harmonic progression at that point.

SCENE 2: The Sixth Day
(*PART II of the oratorio*)

21. Recitative

RAPHAEL

And God said, Let the earth bring forth the living creature after his kind, cattle, and creeping thing, and beast of the earth after his kind. (Genesis 1:24a)

22. Recitative

RAPHAEL

Straight opening her fertile womb,
the earth obey'd the word,
and teem'd creatures numberless,
in perfect forms and fully grown.[29]
Cheerful, roaring, stands the tawny lion.[30]
With sudden leap the flexible tiger appears.
The nimble stag bears up his branching head.[31]
With flying mane, and fiery look,
impatient neighs the noble steed.
The cattle, in herds, already seek their food
on fields and meadows green.[32]
And o'er the ground, as plants, are spread
the fleecy, meek and bleating flocks.
Unnumber'd as the sands, in swarms
arose the hosts of insects.
In long dimension creeps,

---

[29] Cf. Milton, *Paradise Lost,* VII.453-6: 'The Earth obeyed, and, straight / Opening her fertile womb, teemed at a birth / Innumerous living creatures, perfect forms, / Limbed and full grown.' *straight* = straightaway.

[30] Cf. Milton, *Paradise Lost,* VII.463-4: '... now half appeared / The tawny lion ...'

[31] Cf. Milton *Paradise Lost,* VII.469-70: '... the swift stag from underground / Bore up his branching head ...'

[32] Cf. Milton, *Paradise Lost,* VII.460: 'The cattle in the fields and meadows green; ...'

with sinuous trace, the worm.[33]

23. Aria

RAPHAEL

Now heaven in fullest glory shone;
earth smil'd in all her rich attire;[34]
the room of air with fowl is filled;[35]
the water swell'd by shoals of fish;
by heavy beasts the ground is trod.
But all the work was not complete;
there wanted yet that wondrous being,[36]
that, grateful, should God's power admire,[37]
with heart and voice his goodness praise.

24. Recitative

URIEL

And God created Man in his own image, in the image of God created he him. Male and female created he them. He breathed into his nostrils the breath of life, and Man became a living soul. (Genesis 1:27 and 2:7b)

25. Aria

URIEL

In native worth and honour clad,[38]
with beauty, courage, strength, adorn'd,

---

[33] Cf. Milton, *Paradise Lost*, VII.481: 'with sinuous trace' – referring to insects.
sinuous = winding.
worm can refer to a snake or serpent.

[34] Cf. Milton, *Paradise Lost*, VII.501-2: 'Earth, in her rich attire / Consummate lovely smiled; ...'

[35] *room* = empty space.

[36] Cf. Milton, *Paradise Lost*, VII.505: 'There wanted yet the master-work ...'
wanted = was lacking.

[37] Cf. Milton, *Paradise Lost*, VII.512-3: 'But grateful to acknowledge whence his good / Descends; ...'

[38] Cf. Milton, *Paradise Lost*, IV.289: '... with native honour clad ...'

erect, with front serene, he stands[39]
a man, the lord and king of nature all.[40]
His large and arched brow sublime[41]
of wisdom deep declares the seat!
And in his eyes with brightness shines
the soul, the breath and image of his God.[42]
With fondness leans upon his breast
the partner for him form'd,
a woman, fair and graceful spouse.
her softly-smiling virgin looks,
of flow'ry spring the mirror,
bespeak him love, and joy, and bliss.

26. Recitative

RAPHAEL

And God saw every thing that he had made, and, behold, it was very good. (Genesis 1:31a)
And the heavenly choir, in song divine, thus closed the sixth day:

27. Chorus

CHORUS

Achieved is the glorious work;
the Lord beholds it, and is pleas'd.
In lofty strains let us rejoice,
our song let be the praise of God.

27A. Trio

GABRIEL, URIEL

On thee each living soul awaits;
from thee, O Lord, all seek their food;
thou openest thy hand,

---

[39] Cf. Milton, *Paradise Lost,* VII.508-9: '... might erect / His stature, and upright with front serene ...'
front = brow.
[40] Cf. Milton, *Paradise Lost,* IV.290: '... seemed lords of all ...'
[41] Cf. Milton, *Paradise Lost,* IV.300: 'His fair large front and eye sublime ...'
[42] Cf. Milton, *Paradise Lost,* IV.291-2: '... for in their looks divine / The image of their glorious Maker shone.'

and fillest all with good. (Psalm 104:27-28)

RAPHAEL
But when thy face, O Lord, is hid,
with sudden terror they are struck;
thou tak'st their breath away,
They vanish into dust. (Psalm 104:29)

GABRIEL, URIEL and RAPHAEL
Thou sendest forth thy breath again.
and life with vigour fresh returns;
revived earth unfolds new strength
and new delights. (Psalm 104:30)

27B. Second chorus
CHORUS
Achieved is the glorious work;
our song let be the praise of God.

Glory to his name for ever.
He sole on high exalted reigns.
Hallelujah! (Psalm 148:13)

Looking at the biblical account of the sixth day

The remarkable thing about the oratorio's treatment of the Genesis account of the sixth day is how much it omits. Here is Genesis 1:24-31, the full narrative of the final day of creation – the parts included in the libretto are printed in bold:

> 24: **And God said, "Let the earth bring forth living creatures according to their kinds—livestock and creeping things and beasts of the earth according to their kinds."** And it was so.
> 25: And God made the beasts of the earth according to their kinds and the livestock according to their kinds, and everything that creeps on the ground according to its kind. And God saw that it was good.

26: Then God said, "Let us make man in our image, after our likeness. And let them have dominion over the fish of the sea and over the birds of the heavens and over the livestock and over all the earth and over every creeping thing that creeps on the earth."
27: **So God created man in his own image, in the image of God he created him; male and female he created them.**
28: And God blessed them. And God said to them, "Be fruitful and multiply and fill the earth and subdue it, and have dominion over the fish of the sea and over the birds of the heavens and over every living thing that moves on the earth."
29: And God said, "Behold, I have given you every plant yielding seed that is on the face of all the earth, and every tree with seed in its fruit. You shall have them for food.
30: And to every beast of the earth and to every bird of the heavens and to everything that creeps on the earth, everything that has the breath of life, I have given every green plant for food." And it was so.
31: **And God saw everything that he had made, and behold, it was very good.** And there was evening and there was morning, the sixth day.

It will be seen that the libretto includes part of Genesis 2:7 as an extension of Genesis 1:27, in connection with the creation of man. It is true that a large part of the omitted material consists of what might be regarded as repetitions. But some of the omissions are regrettable. The following comments will seek to cover the important things that the Bible text tells us.

The first creative act of the sixth day brings into existence "living creatures" (v 24). It is the same expression that we met in verse 20, and which we shall meet in a moment in Genesis 2:7. The phrase *creeping thing* refers not only to reptiles but also to other creatures whose movement might be described as crawling. So, the three kinds of animal in verse 24 are what we might call domesticated animals, small creatures, and game.

Next, we come to God's creation of human beings in verses 26-29. God's words "Let us make ..." (v 26) have provoked much discussion. Who is God speaking to? While some people think that it suggests some sort of heavenly council, we need to remember the words of Isaiah 40:14 in connection with God's activity in creation: 'Whom did he consult, and who made him understand?' The better suggestion is that we have here a pointer to the nature of the Lord God as the Trinity (or a 'triunity'), reinforcing earlier comments in this study about this topic, in connection with Genesis 1:2. It is significant that the Hebrew word for 'God' is a plural: *'ĕlōhîm*.

God's purpose is expressed in the words: "Let us make man in our image, after our likeness" (v 26). There is no 'and' between the two parts of this phrase, so that "in our image" and "after our likeness" should be understood as standing in parallel with each other, both expressing a very special relationship with God, not shared by any part of his creation. Mankind is both *like* and *unlike* the rest of living beings within the created order. Mankind shares the following with the rest of the world of living creatures: created like them on the sixth day; being made of dust as they are (Genesis 2:7 and 19); feeding just as they feed (Genesis 1:29 and 30), and reproducing with a blessing similar to the one given to them (Genesis 1:22 and 28a). But mankind is distinct from all other living creatures. Whereas God said of the animal kingdom, "Let the earth bring forth living creatures ..." (v 24), he said of mankind, "Let *us* make man in our image, after our likeness ..." (v 26, my italics). Mankind is set apart to be "over" all other forms of life (v 26), to "subdue" the earth and to "have dominion" over all other living things (v 28). But mankind's most distinctive aspect is to enjoy a special relationship with God. This will be expressed by the fact that God and the first human pair speak to each other and enjoy fellowship together (Genesis 2:16-17; 3:8 [hinting at the fellowship normally enjoyed] and 3:9-19). The Fall, in Genesis 3, does not destroy the fact of mankind being in God's image. This is restated in God's words to Noah after the

Flood: "… for God made man in his image." (Genesis 9:6) In the New Testament, James writes that people 'are made in the likeness of God' (James 3:9). But the Fall has seriously damaged that 'image' and 'likeness', so that – in response to Christ's reconciling death for us – men and women need 'to put on the new self, created after the likeness of God …' (Ephesians 4:24 and Colossians 3:10 use similar terms).

The AV wording of Genesis 2:7, included in the libretto, about God breathing into the man *the breath of life,* and man becoming *a living soul,* might appear to indicate an additional aspect of what it means to be a human being. Already, the distinctiveness of mankind has been marked by being in the *image* and *likeness* of God (Genesis 1:26), but this is the first time that the AV has used the word *soul.* However, as noted above, *a living soul* is the AV's translation of the same Hebrew phrase that we have met in Genesis 1:22 and 24, where it has been translated as 'living creatures'.

Genesis 1:27 also tells us that God created mankind *male and female.* When Pharisees asked Jesus a question about divorce, he quoted this verse, together with Genesis 2:24: "Therefore a man shall leave his father and his mother and hold fast to his wife, and they shall become one flesh." (Mark 10:6-9; Matthew 19:4-6) Jesus clearly regarded these two verses from Genesis as foundational to the Bible's teaching on marriage. Man and woman together complement each other, and they share a spiritual equality, as is also affirmed by the New Testament. The apostle Paul teaches that in Christ 'there is no male and female, for you are all one in Christ Jesus' (Galatians 3:28), meaning that there can be no talk of superiority or inferiority between men and women. And the apostle Peter instructs husbands that their wives are 'heirs with you of the grace of life' (1 Peter 3:7) - 'heirs together' in the AV. There will be a further comment about God's purposes for men and women in the discussion of Part III of *The Creation.*

The completion of God's work of creation

The libretto includes the words of Genesis 1:31a: *And God saw every thing that he had made, and, behold, it was very good.* This verse concludes the series of repetitions of this formula (*God saw … it was good),* which has appeared on each day of creation except the second (and twice on both the third and the sixth day).[43] The libretto of the oratorio has included only two of the earlier instances (in verses 4 and 10), plus this one in verse 31. This, the last occurrence, is distinctive because this time God's assessment of his craftsmanship is that it was *very good* (my emphasis); the word *behold* reinforces this. God has now created man (male and female), and this is the climax of his work.

There should be no chapter-division between 1:31 and 2:1, because Genesis 1:31 prepares us for the great statement of Genesis 2:1-4:

> 1: Thus the heavens and the earth were finished, and all the host of them.
> 2: And on the seventh day God finished his work that he had done, and he rested on the seventh day from all his work that he had done.
> 3: So God blessed the seventh day and made it holy, because on it God rested from all his work that he had done in creation.
> 4: These are the generations of the heavens and the earth when they were created, in the day that the LORD God made the earth and the heavens.

The word 'rested' in verses 2 and 3 is literally 'ceased' and relates to the word for 'sabbath'. It is the rest of achievement, not of inactivity. God continues to sustain what he has created. Paul tells us that in Jesus, who is the image of the invisible God, 'all things hold together' (Colossians 1:15-17): without his continuing control of his creation, everything would fall apart. Words spoken by the Lord Jesus Christ, in the context of a dispute with the Jewish leaders about a miracle of healing performed on the Sabbath, are very important: "My Father is working until now, and I am working." (John 5:17)

Significantly, there is no rounding-off formula this time, to tell us that there was evening and there was morning. The strong suggestion that this carries is that the seventh day continues into the future. The Letter

[43] The references are: Genesis 1:4, 10, 12, 18, 21, 25 and 31.

to the Hebrews picks up on the reference to God's 'rest' in Psalm 95:11, in order to direct our attention to the future 'rest' of heaven, which is the promised inheritance of all Christian believers.[44]

Poetic celebration of the sixth day of creation

It will be evident, from the number of footnote-references attached to Raphael's recitative (Movement 22) and aria (Movement 23), that the libretto for these two items borrows significantly from Milton's *Paradise Lost.*

Movement 22 enumerates eight of the animals that God created: the lion, the tiger, the stag, the horse (i.e., four animals that might be described as noble or impressive); cattle, sheep (i.e. two domesticated species); insects, and the worm (or snake – the reference to *long dimension* indicates that it is the latter that is meant) (i.e. representatives of the *creeping thing*). All of these, except the horse, are found in the account of the sixth day of creation in Milton. The libretto borrows phrases from Milton, but without reproducing Milton's dynamic descriptions of fully grown animals breaking their way free from the ground out of which they have been formed.

In passing, it may be of interest to readers to point out that a modern-English version of Milton's poetic description of the creation of animals out of the ground can be found in the writing of C. S. Lewis. This comes in *The Magician's Nephew,* when Lewis describes the creation of animals in the fictional world of Narnia. He too – like Milton – gives a special mention of the creation of the stag: 'The stags were the queerest to watch, for of course the antlers came up a long time before the rest of them, so at first Digory thought they were trees.'[45]

---

[44] The passage in Hebrews which picks up on this theme of God's 'rest' is 3:7 – 4:11. The theme of 'rest' will be explored more fully in the third section of this study, concerning the message of Brahms' *Requiem.*

[45] C.S. Lewis, *The Magician's Nephew* (Harmondsworth: Penguin Books Ltd, 1963), 106.

Raphael's aria (Movement 23) comments on the wonder of earth full of all kinds of animal life, but still incomplete because God's crowning work of creation – mankind – is yet to appear.

Uriel's aria (Movement 25) focuses on the creation of the first man and then the first woman. The man's physical, moral, and mental qualities are extolled, and important phrases from Genesis 1 and 2 are referred to: *the lord and king of nature all* (reflecting the 'dominion' that man is to exercise under God over the creatures of the world, according to Genesis 1:28); *the soul, the breath and image of his God* (Genesis 2:7 and 1:27). In the description of the woman, it is her love for her husband that is singled out. The word *partner* points to her equal status, which was commented on above.

Some commentators are of the opinion that the words of this aria reflect the values of the Enlightenment, particularly the way that certain qualities are attributed to the man and not to the woman. Debate will no doubt continue on this point, but provided the words of the aria are interpreted with reference to the biblical framework, there should be no problem.

It appears that this aria was the last item from *The Creation* that Haydn heard a few days before his death in 1809. A French military officer in Vienna, a member of Napoleon's invading army, sang it to him as a token of respect.

Praise to God who completes his creation and provides for its physical and spiritual needs

The concluding chorus of Part II (Movement 27 – and repeated in the first part of Movement 27B) praises God for the triumphant completion of his work of creation in Genesis 1:31. Then come paraphrases of extracts from two psalms.

The first of these two psalms is Psalm 104, and we hear a version of verses 27-30. Readers may find it worthwhile to look at the whole of Psalm 104, which can be described as the Bible's own commentary on Genesis 1. Each fresh stage of creation is used as a starting point for praise throughout the psalm.

Gabriel and Uriel sing a setting of Psalm 104:27-28 (Movement 27A). The ESV wording of these two verses is:

> These all look to you,
> to give them their food in due season.
> When you give it to them, they gather it up;
> when you open your hand, they are filled with good things.

Almost the same words appear in Psalm 145:15-16. A comment was made above about God continuing to sustain what he has created. That is exactly the point that is reinforced here. These two verses paint a lovely picture of the intended harmonious relationship between living beings (mankind is chiefly in view, but other creatures are surely included in the 'all' – or 'every living thing' in Psalm 145:16) – and their Creator. Those created by God look to him in dependence for their every need, as we are taught to do in the Lord's Prayer: 'Give us this day our daily bread' (Matthew 6:11). God gives generously – open-handedly – and 'every living thing' is fully satisfied.

With sadness, we must recognise that the Fall has spoilt God's perfect creation, so that the ideal harmonious relationship does not work out as it should. The world that God has created provides for every man's need, but not for every man's greed. The Fall has given rise to a sinful humanity, but it has also brought about a disorder in the fabric of the world, so that - as the apostle Paul puts it - 'the whole creation has been groaning together in the pains of childbirth until now.', We look forward to Christ's Return, when 'the creation itself will be set free from its bondage to corruption and obtain the freedom of the glory of the children of God.' (Romans 8:22 and 21)

The three soloists continue in this same movement with a paraphrase of the next two verses from the same psalm: Psalm 104:29-30

> When you hide your face, they are dismayed;
> when you take away their breath,
> they die and return to their dust.
> When you send forth your Spirit, they are created,
> and you renew the face of the ground.

Here we are brought face to face with the fact of death, which is referred to nowhere else in this oratorio. Death is a result of the Fall, the penalty for sin which entered into the world when the first human couple disobeyed God. God's clear command to them was: "You may surely eat of every tree of the garden, but of the tree of the knowledge of good and evil you shall not eat, for in the day that you eat of it you shall surely die." (Genesis 2:16-17) So, when they did eat the forbidden fruit, death came in. Physically, the process of dying began at that very point of time, even though the day of their death lay many years ahead. Spiritually, they died immediately in terms of their close intimate relationship with the living God, and they were expelled from the Garden. The whole human race, who are 'in Adam', similarly find themselves under a sentence of death (both physically and spiritually). But mercifully, the Big Picture of the Bible tells us of God's plan of salvation through the Lord Jesus Christ, who has taken upon himself the judgement that was due to those who put their trust in him, so that they may be rescued from the prospect of eternal separation from God. 'For the wages of sin is death, but the free gift of God is eternal life in Christ Jesus our Lord.' (Romans 6:23)

Despite the fact that death is the consequence of sin, as indicated by Genesis (and as Paul expounds – e.g., Romans 5:12ff and Romans 6:23), Psalm 104 is silent about the link between sin and death. It focuses on the fact of death, not its origins. Death comes to all living creatures; as verse 29 of this psalm puts it, God takes away their breath, they die and return to their dust. Significantly, however, the thrust of these two verses (29 and 30) is positive. We move not from life to death, but from death to life. The fact of death is answered by God sending forth his Spirit, so that new life is created. This is not the full answer to death that we find in the Gospel, namely that there is new life in Christ for all who will repent and believe. But God has not given up on his creation. He continues to provide for the human race, as one generation is succeeded by the next. And with the fuller revelation that Jesus has given by his coming into the world, we can see in verse 30 at least a hint of the new creation that God has prepared for those who love him. Men and women who 'look to'" the Lord God (v 27) and 'die and return to their dust' (v 29) will live by the *Spirit* and God will *renew* them in that new creation (to pick up on two words in verse 30 which I have italicized).

The second chorus (Movement 27B) repeats words already sung, and fittingly brings Part II of *The Creation* to an end on a note of praise, as it continues with a paraphrase of Psalm 148:13. In the ESV, that verse reads: 'Let them praise the name of the LORD, for his name alone is exalted; his majesty is above earth and heaven.' The whole of this psalm (only 14 verses long) is worth reading. It calls on the whole of God's creation to praise him; the word 'praise' is used 13 times in this psalm. Those called upon to praise God are God's angels and hosts (i.e. his armies); sun, moon and stars; highest heavens and waters above the heavens; great sea creatures and the deeps; fire, hail, snow, mist, stormy wind; mountains and hills; fruit trees and cedars; beasts and all livestock; creeping things and flying birds; kings of the earth and all people; princes and rulers of the earth; young men and maidens, and old men and children. The list reads like a rollcall of God's creation in Genesis 1.

Verse 13 of this psalm, the one used in the libretto, matches verse 5. The two verses share a similarity, but there is a difference. That earlier verse of the psalm is addressed to the celestial bodies of verses 3 and 4 (sun, moon and stars), together with the highest heavens and waters, and they are commanded, 'Let them praise the name of the LORD! For he commanded and they were created.' Inanimate creations as they are, they are commanded to praise God for their existence. Verse 13, however, is addressed to people (the whole human race, verses 11 and 12). While they too are commanded, 'Let them praise the name of the LORD,' the reason for them to praise the LORD is different. Here are men and women, created in the image and likeness of God, created to be able to have a relationship with God. They are to praise God because they are conscious beings who have received the revelation that 'his name alone is exalted; his majesty is above earth and heaven.'

The following verse of the psalm (verse 14) is linked to verse 13 by 'and' in the Hebrew. The two verses must therefore be regarded as a single unit. This final verse of the psalm points us beyond God's creation to God's redemptive love: 'He has raised up a horn for his people, praise for all his saints, for the people of Israel who are near to him.' (v14) God's raising up 'a horn for his people' means that he has raised up a strong deliverer for his people – and brought his people 'near to him'. Here too, just as with Psalm 104:29-30, we are given a strong anticipatory hint of the Gospel of Christ. Zechariah, the father of John the Baptist, recognised that in Jesus God was raising up 'a horn of salvation' for his people (Luke 1:69). After the Fall, mankind found themselves far removed from fellowship with God, but now that Jesus has opened for us 'the new and living way' into God's presence, we are invited to 'draw near' (Hebrews 10:19-22).

The above comment about an anticipatory hint of the Gospel of Christ should not be taken to imply that this biblical connection was necessarily in the mind of the librettist. Neither is it being claimed that the biblical connection between a verse that is not sung in the oratorio and a verse in Luke 1 would naturally occur to hearers of this work. Rather, this comment is included in order to draw attention to the Bible's Big Picture which includes salvation as well as creation. When we recognise that verses 13 and 14 of Psalm 148 belong together, it becomes clear that we should 'praise the name of the LORD' for all that he has done, including the 'horn for his people', referring to their salvation.

What to Listen out for in the Music of Part II Scene 2

Movement 21: Recitative

A brief recitative for the bass soloist.

Movement 22: Recitative

Although this item is called a 'recitative', it is not of the same kind that we have met so often, presenting Bible verses - like the previous movement. It is really an aria, but is termed a 'recitative' nevertheless, no doubt because of the deliberate changes of tempo, key, and rhythm throughout the piece.

Listen out for further examples of 'tone painting' in this movement in the portrayal of the newly created animals. We can imagine Haydn making full use of his sense of humour in his composition of this piece. The musical portrayal of each animal is given before that animal is mentioned in the bass's recitative. So, we have the lion, following a trombone and contrabassoon note representing its roar; the tiger, following a series of fast ascending runs which suggest its *sudden leap;* the stag, following its introductory phrase which suggests a mixture of stately trotting and running, and the horse, portrayed by what might be described as a cantering movement in the accompaniment. After these four noble animals, the music changes key and tempo and takes on a gentle, lilting rhythm, as we meet cattle and flocks. Insects are preceded by rapid, but quiet series of pizzicato chords, representing their humming. Finally, the tempo slows again, as the bass soloist sings notes near the lower end of his register to tell us of the *worm.* The bass soloist, if he is able to do so, will often sing his final note, D, on that word an octave lower than Haydn has written it. What is this creature? It is not only the refence to *long dimension* which tells us that this creature is to be understood as the snake; there is a dark, mysterious, sinister tone here. We should note a subtle hint of the serpent of Genesis 3.

Movement 23: Aria

Listen out for the triumphant tone of this piece, which reflects the words of the text, expressing wonder and admiration at all that has been accomplished so far.

Listen out for the touch of 'tone painting' in connection with the words *by heavy beasts the ground is trod,* which are sung twice. The bass soloist's phrase is pitched on suitably low notes, and the chromatic progression in part of this adds to the effect. In addition, the bassoons and contrabassoon intensify the hint of laboriousness conveyed by the soloist's last note.

Listen out for pauses in the bass soloist's vocal line at three points: within the phrase *there wanted yet that wondrous being,* then in the phrase *that, grateful, should God's pow'r admire,* and on the words *with heart and voice.* These pauses help to heighten the sense of anticipation of the final work of creation, still to come.

Movement 24: Recitative

A recitative for the tenor soloist, brief but by no means unimportant since it announces the creation of man.

Movement 25: Aria

Listen out for the joyful and unaffected quality of this delightful aria,

Listen out for the tenor soloist's expressive final phrase, *joy and bliss* - particularly the long note on the word *joy* (a full two and a half bars, plus a pause).

Movement 26: Recitative

A brief recitative for the bass soloist.

Movement 27: Chorus
Movement 27A: Trio
Movement 27B: Second chorus

Musically, these three items belong together. They can be regarded as one single movement in ternary form (i.e., with an A-B-A shape). While the first and third items (Movements 27 and 27B) are not identical (the second chorus is greatly extended and includes extra words - as well as omitting some of those that were used the first time), they both begin with the same words and both are in the key of B flat major. The central item (Movement 27A) is in the key of E flat major and, as will become apparent in a moment, itself has a ternary shape.

Listen out for the majestic tone of the opening chorus, which will become even more majestic in the second chorus (Movement 27B). This is very fitting for the final musical section of Part II of the oratorio, with its praise of God for his finished work of creation.

Listen out for the short fugal section, in the first chorus, on the words *In lofty strains let us rejoice.*

Listen out for the change of mood in the central section (Movement 27A), as the three soloists sing their paraphrase of verses from Psalm 104. This section is slower and more meditative. First, it is just the soprano and tenor who sing as a duet of God's generous provision for all living beings - this is the first part of the central item's ternary structure. The woodwind, particularly the clarinet and flute, are prominent in the accompaniment.

Listen out for the further change of mood, as the bass soloist sings his paraphrase of the next part of the psalm on the theme of death. Appropriately, the music switches to the minor key. The strings play quiet pizzicato chords in repeated triplets on the first half of each beat during much of this section, producing an impression of life stuttering as earthly creatures *vanish into dust*, in the soloist's words. All this is the second part of the central item.

Listen out for yet another change of mood in Movement 27A, as the three soloists sing as a trio of God sending his breath again. We return to the major key. Here we have the third part of the central item. But this third part is more developed musically than the first, and there are some striking upward scales, which begin in the bass soloist's vocal line and run seamlessly into the tenor's and soprano's vocal lines.

The chorus returns, in Movement 27B. As mentioned above, this second chorus is a developed version of Movement 27. It is a thrilling item, incorporating sections of fugue. It is also a classic example of Haydn's skill in sustaining a complex and substantial piece of choral composition.

Part Three

SCENE 1: The New World

28. Orchestral introduction (morning) and recitative

URIEL
In rosy mantle appears,
by music sweet awak'd,
the morning, young and fair.[46]
From heaven's angelic choir
pure harmony descends
on ravish'd earth.[47]
Behold the blissful pair,
where hand in hand they go:[48]
their glowing looks
express the thanks that swell their grateful hearts.
A louder praise of God
their lips shall utter soon;
then let our voices ring,
united with their song.

'Morning has broken'

The well-known hymn, which begins with the words of this heading, may be taken as a commentary to place alongside the words of Uriel's recitative (Movement 28), describing the newly created world, where everything was 'very good' (Genesis 1:31) - pure and fresh and vibrant. Here are the words of the hymn in full:

Morning has broken like the first morning;
blackbird has spoken like the first bird:
praise for the singing, praise for the morning,
praise for them springing fresh from the word!

---

[46] Cf. Milton, *Paradise Lost,* V.1-2: 'Now Morn, her rosy steps in the eastern clime / Advancing ...'

[47] *ravish'd* = delighted.

[48] Cf. Milton, *Paradise Lost,* IV.321: 'So hand in hand they passed ...'

Sweet the rain's new fall, sunlit from heaven,
like the first dew fall on the first grass:
praise for the sweetness of the wet garden,
sprung in completeness where his feet pass.

Mine is the sunlight, mine is the morning
born of the one light Eden saw play:
praise with elation, praise every morning,
God's re-creation of the new day![49]

That hymn is more than an evocation of the Garden of Eden before the Fall because it speaks of 'God's *re-creation* of the new day' (my italics), which refers to all that God has brought into being through the Lord Jesus Christ. Because Jesus has died and has risen, there is now a 'new creation' (Galatians 6:15 – and this verse, so near the end of Galatians, is meant to be understood in the light of the theme of the whole Letter, namely salvation by faith in Christ alone). Whenever an individual Christian is 'in Christ' (i.e., brought into a relationship with him through being born again), that is 'new creation' (2 Corinthians 5:17). God says, "Behold, I am making all things new." (Revelation 21:5) So, the experience of Christian believers here and now is the 'new creation' – and there is far more to look forward to in the life that is to come.

The above paragraph serves to remind us of that hymn's Christ-centred meaning. But if the hymn is *more* than an evocation of pre-Fall Eden, it is surely *no less* than that. The words of the hymn beautifully express the sense of wonder that Adam and Eve would have experienced, in the early days of their time in the newly created paradise that God had prepared for them. It is not just poetic imagination that conjures up such a picture – this is thoroughly biblical. Among the early verses of Genesis 2, we find such descriptive phrases as: 'a mist was going up from the land and was watering the whole face of the ground. ... And

---

49 Eleanor Farjeon, 'Morning has broken' in *Hymns for Today's Church* (London: Hodder and Stoughton, 1982), Hymn 265. Copyright David Higham Associates Limited.

out of the ground the LORD God made to spring up every tree that is pleasant to the sight and good for food.' (Genesis 2:6 and 9)

All this is expressed in the libretto of the oratorio at this point. We may ask: What is meant by *A louder praise of God their lips shall utter soon?* Louder than what? The German version of the words, translated into English, says, 'Soon their mouth shall sing the Creator's praise in a loud tone.'[50] There is no comparative in the German text. An extra syllable was required to make the line scan in English! So, it may be a mistake to make too much of this detail in the English text.

---

[50] The German text at this point is: 'Bald singt in lautem Ton / ihr Mund des Schöpfers Lob.'

What to Listen out for in the Music of Part III Scene I

Movement 28: Orchestral introduction (morning) and recitative
Listen out for the slow and gentle orchestral introduction before the tenor soloist sings. This is intended to be a representation of morning. Haydn provides us with a beautiful piece in his attempt to do justice to the beauty of the dawn of the very first morning of human existence in God's creation.

Listen out for the very first chord of the movement. It should sound very different from everything that has been played or sung so far. It is a long chord of E major, which is the key of this piece. There is no particular significance in the choice of this key, except for its remoteness from, and therefore difference from, the keys of previous moments. This may be a deliberate attempt to suggest the difference between heaven and earth.

Listen out for contributions in the orchestra from the flute and the horn.

SCENE 2: The Wonders of God's Creation
(PART III of the oratorio)

29. Duet and chorus

ADAM, EVE
By thee with bliss, O bounteous Lord,
both heaven and earth are stor'd.
This world so great, so wonderful,
thy mighty hand has fram'd.

CHORUS
For ever blessed be his power,
his Name be ever magnified.

ADAM
Of stars the fairest, pledge of day,
that crown'st the smiling morn;
and thou, bright sun, that cheer'st the world,
thou eye and soul of all!

CHORUS
Proclaim in your extended course
th' almighty power and praise of God.

EVE
And thou that rul'st the silent night
and all ye starry hosts,
ev'rywhere spread wide his praise
in choral songs about.

ADAM
Ye mighty elements, by his power
your ceaseless changes make;
ye dusky mists, and dewy streams,
that rise and fall thro' th' air.

ADAM, EVE, CHORUS
Resound the praise of God our Lord.

Great his name, and great his might.
EVE
Ye purling fountains, tune his praise;[51]
and wave your tops, ye pines.
Ye plants, exhale, ye flowers, breathe
to him your balmy scent.

ADAM
Ye that on mountains stately tread,
and ye that lowly creep;
ye birds that sing at heaven's gate,
and ye that swim the stream;

ADAM, EVE, CHORUS
Ye creatures all, extol the Lord;
him celebrate, him magnify.

ADAM, EVE
Ye valleys, hills, and shady woods,
made vocal by our song,
from morn till eve you shall repeat
our grateful hymns of praise.

CHORUS
Hail! bounteous Lord! Almighty, hail!
Thy word call'd forth this wondrous frame,
The heavens and earth thy power adore;
We praise thee now and evermore.

'This world so great, so wonderful'

The theme of this scene is Adam and Eve's praise to God for the wonders of his creation, interspersed with praises to God from the chorus and further urgings from them to the created order, to join in with their adoration. So, with that theme of praise connecting everything together, the duet and chorus range over the greatness of heaven and earth: the stars, the sun and the moon; the water that gives

[51] *purling* = swirling.

rise to mists and streams; springs, trees, plants and flowers; mountains, birds and fish, and valleys, hills and woods.

As listeners to the oratorio, we are reminded of the earlier scenes – and we too are encouraged to respond with praise.

What to Listen out for in the Music of Part III Scene 2

Movement 29: Duet and chorus

This movement is the longest of the whole oratorio (its duration is over 10 minutes), and it consists of three sections.

Listen out for the gently flowing tone of the *first* section. The triplet rhythm from the orchestra contribute to this effect.

Listen out for the prominent oboe in the first part of the introduction.

Listen out for the way the two soloists (Adam and Eve), although singing a harmonious duet made up of the same words, sing their words independently of each other – particularly in the early part of this section. This may well be an attempt to simulate normal conversation and does much to eliminate any sense of artificiality.

Listen out for the way the chorus (possibly representing onlooking angels who offer praise to God) join in with their separate words, while the two soloists repeat their own words of adoration.

Listen out for the contrast between, on the one hand, the style of the soloists and the orchestra, who maintain the triplet rhythm throughout this first section, and, on the other hand, the style of the chorus's contributions, which make no use of the triplet rhythm at all. It is as if there were two languages: that of earth (Adam and Eve) and that of heaven (the angels, if the chorus do indeed represent an angelic choir). And yet the two languages blend into a harmonious whole.

Listen out for the beginning of the *second* section, which follows a definite break in the music. This section is marked by a change of key and a slightly faster speed.

Listen out for the sequence of component parts in this section, as the couple praise God for different aspects of his creation, either individually or as a duet. After Adam's first entry in this section, the chorus respond with further words of praise in a short fugue. The chorus make two further contributions in this section, echoing and reinforcing the couple's words of praise.

Listen out for a prominent entry by the flute, accompanying Adam's second contribution in this section.

Listen out for the beginning of the *third* section, which begins with the words 'Hail, bounteous Lord!' This time, there is no definite gap between the sections – the chorus simply break in at the end of the couple's duet. This third section is sung by the chorus alone. It is another example of majestic choral singing. The central part of this section consists of a short fugue, but the beginning and end parts are homophonic (i.e., made up of 'block chords'). Alternations between loud and soft towards the end heighten the dramatic effect.

SCENE 3: A Celebration of Marriage
(PART III of the oratorio)

30. Recitative

ADAM
Our duty we have now perform'd,
in offering up to God our thanks.
Now follow me, dear partner of my life,
thy guide I'll be; and every step
pours new delights into our breasts,
shows wonders everywhere.
Then mayst thou feel and know
the high degree of bliss
the Lord allotted us,
and with devoted heart
His bounties celebrate.
Come, follow me, thy guide I'll be.

EVE
O thou for whom I am,
my help, my shield,
my all, thy will is law to me;
so God our Lord ordains;
and from obedience grows
my pride and happiness.[52]

31. Duet

ADAM
Graceful consort, at thy side
softly fly the golden hours;
ev'ry moment brings new rapture,
ev'ry care is lull'd to rest.

EVE
Spouse adored, at thy side
purest joys o'erflow the heart;

---

[52] Cf. Milton, *Paradise Lost*, IV.635-8: 'My author and disposer, what thou bidd'st / Unargued I obey; so God ordains: / God is thy law, thou mine: to know no more / Is woman's happiest knowledge, and her praise.'

life and all I have is thine;
my reward thy love shall be.

ADAM, EVE
The dew-dropping morn, O how she quickens all![53]
The coolness of even, O how she all restores!
How grateful is of fruits the savour sweet!
How pleasing is of fragrant bloom the smell!
But, without thee, what is to me
the morning dew, the breath of even,
the sav'ry fruit, the fragrant bloom?
With thee is every joy enhanced,
with thee delight is ever new,
with thee is life incessant bliss,
thine, thine it all shall be.

Husbands and wives

The main theme of this scene in the oratorio is the ideal marriage relationship of Adam and Eve. Here are expressions of mutual love and commitment.

Rightly, the recitative of Adam (Movement 30) begins with acknowledgement to God of their *duty* of thanksgiving to him, which they have been singing in the previous scene. *'Duty'* may seem a cold word to use in connection with thanksgiving. But mankind is indebted to God for the creation of the world it occupies, and when that thanks is given willingly, duty becomes a delight.

Adam declares his determination to be a godly leader in the marriage relationship: *'Come, follow me, thy guide I'll be.'* Eve responds with willingness that she will give her obedience, which will be her *'pride and happiness'*. In case such wording may seem quaint in modern ears, we should note that the libretto at this point is encapsulating the Bible's own instructions to husbands and wives. The most obvious passage to refer to is **Ephesians 5: 22-33**. Without working our way through the whole of that passage, we highlight the main points of the apostle Paul's instructions.

---

[53] *quickens* = gives life to.

Wives are told: '... submit to your own husbands, as to the Lord.' (Ephesians 5:22), and husbands receive the command: '... love your wives, as Christ loved the church and gave himself up for her.' (Ephesians 5:29) So, on the one hand, there is an instruction to wives to submit (or obey). On the other hand, there is an instruction to husbands to love their wives to the extent that they would be prepared to die for them. It must be asked: Is one of these two commands more challenging than the other? Surely, the answer is that they are both equally demanding! The Bible in no way endorses the suggestion that the husband should be tyrannical or that the wife should be limp or lifeless. Rather, each should seek the good of the other. The Ephesians passage ends with these words: 'However, let each one of you love his wife as himself, and let the wife see that she respects her husband.' (Ephesians 5:33)

It should be noted that the Bible envisages the marriage relationship expressing itself as teamwork. The mutuality of marriage has already been touched on from the Ephesians passage. But, in addition, God made Eve for Adam so that she might be '"a helper fit for him."' (Genesis 2:18, 20). Literally, the phrase is 'a help as opposite him' – hence the footnote in the ESV, 'corresponding to'. Eve is given to Adam as a partner and for fellowship.

What to Listen out for in the Music of Part III Scene 3

Movement 30: Recitative

A straightforward recitative from a musical point of view, with first Adam and then Eve singing.

Movement 31: Duet

This piece is made up of two sections.

Listen out for the lovely first section, with the couple singing of their love for each other. First, Adam sings a stanza. Then Eve sings a second stanza to the same tune. This immediately leads into the two vocal lines becoming intertwined, but with each of the pair repeating their separate words.

Listen out for the second section, marked by a faster tempo. Initially, the couple share the words between them, and then they sing together, before the whole piece is repeated.

Listen out for some charming bits of accompaniment from woodwind instruments, and a prominent horn entry at the halfway point of this section of the movement.

SCENE 4: Whispers of the Fall and of Salvation
(PART III of the oratorio)

32. Recitative

URIEL
O happy pair! And happy still might be
if not misled by false conceit.
Ye strive at more than granted is;
and more desire to know, than know ye should.

33. Quartet and chorus

Sing the Lord, ye voices all,
magnify his name thro' all creation,
celebrate his power and glory,
let his name resound on high.
Praise the Lord. Utter thanks.
Jehovah's praise for ever shall endure. Amen.

The anticipation of Paradise Lost

It has already been mentioned that the final scene of *The Creation* gives the only direct, explicit mention of the tragic Fall of the first human pair: their act of disobedience to God's clear command. Adam and Eve were indeed *'happy'* in their relationship with God, with each other and with the created order around them – the word appears twice in the first line of Uriel's recitative (Movement 32). Everything was in perfect harmony. And that state of bliss might have continued, had it not been for the Fall.

The earlier discussion of the beginning of the oratorio required some examination of the person and role of Satan, because of the inclusion of the theme of a pre-creation 'chaos' – a war in heaven – which was drawn from John Milton's *Paradise Lost*. This theme is a legitimate one and, as was shown, is referred to in various places in Scripture, even though the Bible nowhere relates it to God's work of creation. However, here, at the end of the oratorio, where the libretto makes a reference to the tragic event of **Genesis 3**, nothing is said at all about the part played by Satan in tempting Eve to eat the forbidden fruit. The blame is laid fully at the door of Adam and Eve. Their fault was, as Uriel's recitative

(Movement 32) puts it, to *'strive at more than granted is; and more desire to know, than know [they] should.'* At the end of Genesis 3, of course, all three of them – Adam, Eve and Satan – have God's judgement pronounced upon them.

Within the perfect paradise of the Garden, God provided everything that the human couple needed, and that provision was generous and comprehensive. But it was a provision to be enjoyed in a relationship of trust in, and dependence on, their Creator God. God had laid one prohibition on the human couple, as was noted in the discussion of Part II Scene 2. 'And the LORD God commanded the man, saying, "'You may surely eat of every tree of the garden, but of the tree of the knowledge of good and evil you shall not eat, for in the day that you eat of it, you shall surely die."' (Genesis 2:16-17). To transgress against that one single prohibition would be to step out of that trusting dependence on God for all things, because it would be an assertion of their own right to determine what is '"good and evil"' rather than trust the loving wisdom of God to be the one to direct them.

The serpent of Genesis 3 can be identified as Satan, even though that name is not used here. When the great red dragon appears in Revelation 12, he is described as 'that ancient serpent, who is called the devil and Satan, the deceiver of the whole world' (Revelation 12:9). That verse leaves us in no doubt about the identity of the one who is at work in Genesis 3. The temptations of the Lord Jesus by the devil (Matthew 4:1-11, Luke 4:1-13) are to be understood as a contrast with the Fall in Genesis 3: while Eve, together with Adam, yielded to Satan's temptation, Jesus stood firm.

It was that one single prohibition, regarding the tree of the knowledge of good and evil, that Satan used as the means to deceive Eve in Genesis 3. He questioned God's clear statement of his command: '"Did God actually say, 'You shall not eat of any tree in the garden?'"' (v 1). There are two things to note here. First, the suggestion that we may sit in judgement on God's word is flattering to human pride. Secondly, Satan deliberately misquoted God's words and suppressed his gracious and generous provision ('"You may surely eat of every tree of the garden ..."'), suggesting that God was keeping good things away from her. In so doing, he provoked Eve into wrongly remembering God's actual words, so that she fell into the trap of making God's command sound more restrictive than it was. She replied to the serpent, '"... but God said, 'You shall not eat of the fruit of the tree that is in the midst of the garden, *neither shall you touch it,* lest you die.'"' (v 3, my italics) God had said nothing about touching the fruit. Next, the serpent contradicted God's word: '"You will not surely die."' (v 4) The next step in the seduction was to appeal to Eve's desire for the knowledge (representing, as explained above, a unilateral declaration of independence against God) that was forbidden to her: '"For God knows that when you eat of it your eyes will be opened, and you will be like God, knowing good and evil."' (v 5) This was the heart of the temptation: in Uriel's words, to 'strive at more than granted is; and more desire to know, than know you should.' Sin has always been, in essence, the desire to be 'like God'" – to be our own 'god' – and set the boundaries where we wish, rather than to follow the clear word of God. Eve desired the apparent good that the tree represented, and which God apparently was withholding from her, and turned her back on God's word: '... the woman saw that the tree was good for food, and that it was a delight to the eyes, and that the tree was to be desired to make one wise ...' (v 6). She ate the fruit, and so too did Adam (v 6).

Thus, the downward steps in the path of disobedience were:

- to assume the right to sit in judgement on God's word;
- to question the clarity of God's word;
- to exaggerate the restrictive nature of God's word (as if God were holding back something good);
- to contradict God's word – or to agree with those who do so, and
- to give in to the desire to be '"like God"' and to seek self-gratification at all costs.

This path was not the way of wisdom, nor did it lead to wisdom. It was the way of folly. And it led, literally, to Paradise Lost.

The anticipation of Paradise Regained

Mercifully, this is not the end of the Bible's account of God's purposes for mankind. Otherwise, the prospects for all of us would be exceedingly bleak. Genesis 3 includes an announcement of the Saviour who would come and defeat the devil and his works, and bring rescue and restoration to the men and women who would look to him. In his words of judgement on the serpent, God says:

> I will put enmity between you and the woman,
> and between your offspring and her offspring;
> he shall bruise your head,
> and you shall bruise his heel. (Genesis 3:15)

In this verse we are given the Bible's first prophecy of the coming of the Messiah, or the Christ, the one whom God would send to crush the head of Satan, even at the cost of injury to himself (spoken of here as his heel being bruised). With the fuller revelation of the whole Bible, we know that the anticipation of the coming of the Messiah grew throughout the Old Testament and was gloriously fulfilled in Jesus Christ: his birth, life, death, resurrection, and ascension.

It is beyond the scope of this study to develop this theme further. *The Creation* takes us through Genesis 1, with a glimpse into chapter 2, and it ends with a hint of the tragedy of Genesis 3. We need to look elsewhere for the Bible's account of God's rescue-plan, achieved by the death of Jesus Christ in the place of sinners. That will be the focus of the next part of our study, as we examine the message of Bach's *St Matthew Passion.*

But one further comment about the good news of salvation needs to be made at this point. With the fuller revelation of the whole Bible, we also know that God was not taken by surprise by the Fall. The opening verses of Paul's letter to the Ephesians tell us this plainly: God '... chose us in him (i.e. in Christ) before the foundation of the world ... he predestined us for adoption as sons through Jesus Christ ...' (Ephesians 1:4-5). The breath-taking opening of Ephesians 1 includes the statement that God's eternal plan has always been that in Christ God's people should have "redemption through his blood, the forgiveness of our trespasses' (Ephesians 1:7). Amazingly, from before the very beginning of time – from eternity itself – God planned not only the creation of the world, but also the death of his Son as the Saviour of the world, and chose who his people would be.

A final note of praise

The concluding quartet and chorus (Movement 33) is a song of praise to God. The command to praise him is addressed to *'ye voices all'* – which must include us too. In view of the last part of the above discussion, we should be praising God not only for his creation but also for his new creation through his Son, the Lord Jesus Christ.

What to Listen out for in the Music of Part III Scene 4

Movement 32: Recitative

A brief recitative for the tenor soloist.

Movement 33: Quartet and chorus

Listen out for the slow, jubilant introduction to this movement sung by the chorus in 'block chords'.

Listen out for the fugal section from the chorus that follows, with a quartet of soloists interspersing with the choral sections. The quartet consists of the three soloists (soprano, tenor and bass) who have already sung, plus a contralto voice (often drafted in from the chorus).

In the final section of this movement the chorus has a homophonic section, bringing the whole oratorio to a grand conclusion.

Part 2: Cross

Bach's *St Matthew Passion*

Introduction

Introducing Johann Sebastian Bach

Johann Sebastian Bach was born in 1685 in Eisenach, in central Germany. There was a long tradition of musicianship in Bach's family, so it was taken for granted that this would be the career for the young Bach, and therefore he received musical training from an early age. When he was 10, his father died and he went to live with his older brother Johann Christoph at Ohrdruf. His musical education continued there and subsequently at Lüneburg, where Bach became a pupil at the Michaelisschule for three years.

After a short period in the service of Duke Johann Ernst III, the younger brother of the reigning Duke of Weimar, Bach obtained his first independent appointment as the organist at the New Church at Arnstadt. While there, in 1705, he undertook the longest journey of his life, to Lübeck, in order to hear the celebrated organist, Buxtehude. The distance was nearly 300 miles each way, and apparently Bach made the journey on foot. In 1707, he moved to become the organist at St Blasius's Church in Mühlhausen.

The following year he began his first important post, that of organist at the Ducal Court of Weimar. His duties required him to provide works which he then performed on the organ in the castle chapel. Many of his organ preludes, fugues and toccatas were written during this time. He was promoted to be 'Konzertmeister' (i.e. musical director) in 1714, which obliged him to write a new church cantata each month. In 1717, Bach fell out of favour in Weimar and for the next six years he became 'Kapellmeister'(another term meaning 'musical director') in the service of Prince Leopold of Anhalt-Köthen. He was responsible for the court music, which – despite the reference to the German word for 'chapel' in Bach's official title – was of a secular nature. Bach's orchestral suites, the concertos, and the sonatas and suites for the violin belong to this period.

In 1723, Bach was appointed to be the Cantor at St Thomas's Church in Leipzig, and he remained in Leipzig for the rest of his life. His duties were demanding. One of them was to provide some 59 cantatas each year. Over 200 of them are still in existence today. He was granted the title of court composer in 1736 by his sovereign, Augustus (Elector of Saxony and King of Poland). It was while he was at Leipzig that Bach wrote his *St Matthew Passion* and *St John Passion* and other great choral works, such as the *Mass in B minor*. In the last decades of his life he reworked and extended many of his earlier compositions. He died of complications after eye surgery in 1750 at the age of 65.

It will be evident from the above summary of Bach's life that his different types of composition were dictated by the demands of whichever appointment he held at the time. The three major categories of his music are works for the organ (many written in his earlier years in Weimar), pieces for other instruments and the orchestra of his day (much of this output dating from his time in Anhalt-Köthen), and choral works for church (from his later time in Weimar and from the years in Leipzig). But, within these constraints, Bach enjoyed the liberty to compose as his inclinations led him.

Bach played many instruments, and he was acknowledged as a brilliant performer on the clavichord, the harpsichord, and the organ. While his compositions were regarded, during his lifetime, as competent, he was largely forgotten after his death. The revival of interest in Bach's works came about as the result of a monograph written in 1802 by Johann Forkel (1749 – 1818), an organist and director of music at the university in Göttingen, and then through the efforts of a number of individuals, not least the composer Felix Mendelssohn (1809 – 1847). In England, the Bach Society was founded in London in 1849 by William Sterndale Bennett and others, with the intention of introducing Bach's works to the English public.[54] Gradually, recognition and appreciation of Bach's genius has grown to such an extent that he is now held in high esteem as one of the greatest composers of all time.

Bach was a devout Lutheran, and his sacred music expresses his own personal identification with the Christian truths conveyed by his compositions. His library at the time of his death consisted largely of theological works.

Bach married twice (his first wife died in 1720) and he was the father of 20 children, not all of whom survived infancy. Some of his sons achieved a measure of fame 8as musicians. Two to mention by name are Carl Philipp Emmanuel Bach (1714 – 1788) and Johann Christian Bach (1735 – 1782). The former held a position at the court of Frederick the Great and was a notable composer, being remembered particularly as the chief founder of the sonata-symphony style, later developed by Haydn, Mozart, and Beethoven. The latter moved to England and became an opera and concert director and music master in the family of George III and is known as 'the English Bach'.

---

54 William Sterndale Bennett (1816 – 1875): English composer, pianist, conductor, and music educator.

Introducing Bach's *St Matthew Passion*

Composition of the work

The *St Matthew Passion*, as stated above, was written during the time when Bach was Cantor at St Thomas's Church in Leipzig. The original Latin title is *Passio Domini nostri J.C. secundum Evangelistam Matthaeum* (which translates as 'The Passion of our Lord J[esus] C[hrist] according to the Evangelist Matthew'). The *St Matthew Passion* is the second of two Passion settings by Bach that have survived in their entirety, the first being the *St John Passion*, first performed in 1724. The *St Matthew Passion* was written in 1727 and probably first performed on 11 April (Good Friday) of that year in St Thomas's Church. It used to be thought that the first performance was as late as Good Friday in 1729, but the earlier date is now generally preferred. Certainly, it was performed on that later date, and also on Good Friday in 1736 (with some revisions) and again in 1742. Bach revised it again between 1743 and 1746. The *St Matthew Passion* is listed officially as BWV 244.[55]

When the Bach revival occurred in the nineteenth century, Mendelssohn arranged a centenary performance of the *St Matthew Passion* in 1829. The first English performance of the *St Matthew Passion* took place on 6 April 1854 under the direction of Bennett and the Bach Society.

Content of the work

The text of the *St Matthew Passion* is a mixture of three kinds of writing. First, there is the Bible text, consisting of chapters 26 and 27 of Matthew's Gospel in the Luther Bible. Part One of the oratorio sets words from Matthew 26:1–56, and Part Two, words from Matthew 26:57–75 and 27:1–66. The Bible text is presented mainly by means of recitatives. An Old Testament verse, Song of Solomon 6:1, is also used

---

[55] BWV stands for *Bach-Werke-Verzeichnis,* which means 'list of Bach's works'. This is a catalogue of compositions by Bach, first published in 1950, edited by Wolfgang Schmieder (1901 – 1990), a German music librarian and musicologist. The catalogue's second edition appeared in 1990.

in the opening aria of Part Two (and sung by the chorus). Second, there are items of free verse which are used in recitatives and arias, and also in the large-scale choral movements that open and close the Passion. Much of this material was written by a Leipzig poet, Christian Friedrich Henrici, who used Picander as his pen name.[56] Other sections of free verse come from publications by Salomo Franck[57] and Barthold Heinrich Brockes.[58] Third, the oratorio includes a number of chorales. The texts for these, together with their melodies, would have been well known to those attending those first Good Friday services at Leipzig, when the work was performed. One of them dates back to 1525, and nine of the eighteen chorale stanzas included come from three hymns by Paul Gerhardt.[59] The arias and chorales, interspersed between sections of Gospel text, provide personal reflection and prayer as application of those Bible verses.

The music of the work

The *St Matthew Passion* is set for two choirs and two orchestras. We will focus first on the vocal features of the work and then turn our attention to the instrumental accompaniment.

Bach was used to working with a double-choir format in his compositions for Sunday services. St Thomas's Church in Leipzig had two organ lofts. There was a large organ loft that was used throughout the year for musicians performing in Sunday services. Also, there was a small organ loft, situated opposite the large one, that was used additionally for the grander services associated with Christmas and Easter. Bach's intention with the *St Matthew Passion* was for it to be performed from both organ lofts at the same time – Chorus and Orchestra I occupying the large organ loft, and Chorus and Orchestra II performing from the small organ loft. Clearly, in the initial

[56] Christian Friedrich Henrici (1700 – 1764) (pen name: Picander): German poet and librettist.

[57] Salomo (or Salomon) Franck (1659 – 1725): a German lawyer, scientist and poet, who worked in Weimar at the same time as Bach.

[58] Barthold Heinrich Brockes (1680 – 1747): a German poet.

[59] Paul Gerhardt (1607 – 1676): German theologian, Lutheran minister and hymnodist.

performances, the number of performers would have been limited by the space available.

The number of soloists in a performance of the *St Matthew Passion* is a decision for the conductor or musical director. There are solo items for a soprano, a contralto (or countertenor), a tenor and a bass. Many of the solo items are recitatives and arias of a reflective or meditative nature. A tenor soloist (who may be the same individual just mentioned or a separate soloist) takes on the role of 'Evangelist' (i.e., the Gospel writer Matthew) and provides the narrative parts of the Gospel texts. He does so in *secco* recitative (which means that he is accompanied only by continuo). A bass soloist (again, this may – or may not – be the same soloist referred to above) sings the words of Jesus, and these words are treated distinctively. There are special *accompagnato* recitatives for these (which means that the words are accompanied not only by continuo but also by the entire string section of the orchestra, playing long sustained notes and highlighting certain words). This effect is sometimes referred to as Jesus' 'halo'. Only the words of Jesus' cry of dereliction (the Aramaic words *Eli, Eli, lema sabachthani?*)[60] are sung without this 'halo'.

There are also named parts for Judas (bass), Peter (bass), two high priests (bass), Pontius Pilate (bass), Pilate's wife (soprano), two witnesses (contralto and tenor) and two maids (soprano). These parts may be sung by individuals within the chorus. Two duets are sung by a pair of soloists, who represent two individuals speaking simultaneously. A number of passages for several speakers are sung by one of the two choirs or both.

We turn now to a few comments about the use of orchestral instruments. In Bach's setting, separate parts were included for the following instruments in each of the two orchestras (the same for both):

> 2 violins (i.e., 2 violin parts – there would be several of each)
> viola

---

[60] 'My God, my God, why have you forsaken me?' (Matthew 27:46).

viola da gamba (but in modern performances, the cello is normally used)
double bass
2 flutes (and 2 recorders)
2 oboes (or, instead of them, in certain movements, oboes d'amore or oboes da caccia – but in modern performances, the cor anglais is used)
bassoon

There was also a continuo organ and harpsichord.

In many arias, a solo instrument (or more than one) will create a specific mood. Prominent use of a particular instrument throughout a movement is referred to as *obbligato* – the instrument becomes an equal partner with the vocal soloist.

A performance of the *St Matthew Passion* lasts a little under three hours.

Comments on the study in the following pages

Bach did not number the individual movements, but musicologists have done this since early in the twentieth. It is a help in identifying specific items within the whole composition. The *Bach-Werke-Verzeichnis* (BWV, mentioned earlier) divides the work into 78 numbers, while the *Neue Bach-Ausgabe* (NBA) divides the oratorio into 68 movements.[61] Movement numbers in this study follow the BWV numbering system, which is adopted by the widely used Novello edition of the *St Matthew Passion*.

The shape of the *St Matthew Passion* is determined by the biblical text. The only division that Bach indicated within the work is that between Part One and Part Two, which comes about halfway through: Part One takes us up to the arrest of Jesus, and Part Two focuses on the trials, scourging, crucifixion, and burial. Within that structure, it is possible to recognise – within Bach's oratorio – what might be described as separate 'scenes', which correspond to the major stages of action of the

---

[61] *Neue Bach-Ausgabe* means New Bach Edition. It was published by Bärenreiter between 1954 and 2007.

Bible text. Bach did not himself indicate separate scenes. The choice of the number of scenes in this study is determined by major changes of location or focus. Each scene begins with part of the Gospel text sung by the Evangelist, except the first scene of each of the two parts of the work. Chorales and arias follow, providing a meditation on that part of the Passion account. (At one point in the study, the decision has been made to switch to a new scene in the middle of a movement consisting of recitative (Movement 73)). For each scene, in this study, the text and the comments on the message of the oratorio will be followed by the musical comments.

Audiences at performances of the work will hear the text sung in either the original German or an English translation. If it is sung in German, programme-notes will probably provide an English translation. If the work is sung in an English translation, it is most often the words of the translation found in the Novello edition that are used. That translation generally follows the Authorised Version of the Bible (1611) for the biblical material, but it has to handle the free verse and chorales somewhat loosely in order to fit the syllables to the music. In this study, the translation is by Pamela Dellal, and is used with her kind permission. It has the benefit of being a faithful rendering of the German text, both in the passages of Matthew 26 and 27 from the Luther Bible and in the content of the arias, recitatives, and chorales.[62] Since this translation is not designed to be a sung version of the text, the rendering of the poetic sections is free from the constraints of having to fit into the structure and metre of the original German.

The relevant section of text, in the following study, is printed out at the beginning of each scene. An attempt has been made to indicate clearly which movements are renderings of the Bible text, which are sections of free verse (most of it by Picander), and which movements are chorales. Bible verses are in italics, with the verse references being given each time at the end of that section of scriptural material. At times, two or more successive movements continue the narrative or the dialogue from Matthew 26 and 27 – so readers will need to look on to

[62] Luther's New Testament was published in 1522, and the whole Bible in 1534.

the conclusion of the sequence to find the reference for those verses. Free verse is set out in ordinary print (without italics). Chorales are printed in bold.

In the discussion of each scene, Bible verses will normally be quoted from the English Standard Version (ESV). Quotations from the translation by Pamela Dellal will be in italics.

The discussion of the Bible material for each scene will be followed by an 'Application' section, where attention will be given to the choruses, chorales and arias for that scene – also the recitatives (other than those which take us through Matthew 26 and 27). They form a major part of the work, and their value lies in the way they urge us as listeners to this *Passion* to reflect on the Bible's account of Jesus' way of the cross and to apply its message to ourselves. These comments will be related to individual movements and will be concise.

It was mentioned earlier that Bach composed the oratorio for two choirs. Scores of the work indicate which choir should sing which chorus or choral. But this will not be referred to in the following discussion, except where it plays a significant role – for example in Movement 1, where both choirs sing but do so antiphonally (i.e., one choir asks a question, which is answered by the other choir).

The Message of Bach's *St Matthew Passion* and What to Listen out for in the Music

Part One

SCENE 1: Devotion and Plotting

1. CHORUS and CHORALE
Come, daughters, help me lament.
Behold! – Whom? – The Bridegroom!
Behold him! – How? – As a Lamb.
Behold! – What? – Behold the patience.
Look! – Where? – At our guilt.
See him, out of love and graciousness
bear the wood for the Cross himself.

> **O innocent Lamb of God,**
> **slaughtered on the trunk of the Cross,**
> **patient at all times,**
> **however you were scorned.**
> **You have borne all sins,**
> **otherwise we would have to despair.**
> **Have mercy on us, O Jesus.**

2. RECITATIVE
(Evangelist) *When Jesus had finished this speech, he said to his disciples,* (Jesus) *You know that after two days it will be Passover, and the Son of Man will be handed over to be crucified.* (Matthew 26:1-2)

3. CHORALE
Heart's beloved Jesus, how have you transgressed,

that such a harsh sentence has been pronounced?
What is the crime, of what kind of misdeed
are you accused?

4. RECITATIVE
(Evangelist) *Then the high priests and the scribes and the elders of the people gathered in the palace of the high priest, who was named Caiaphas, and took council how with deception they could seize Jesus and kill him. They said however:*

5. CHORUS
Not, indeed, during the festival, so that there will not be an uproar among the people.

6. RECITATIVE
(Evangelist) *Now when Jesus was in Bethany, in the house of Simon the leper, a woman came to him with a cup filled with valuable water; and she poured it upon his head, as he sat at the table. When his disciples saw this, they were against it and said:*

7. CHORUS
What purpose does this foolishness serve? This water could have been sold for a high price and given to the poor.

8. RECITATIVE
(Evangelist) *When Jesus heard this, he said to them:*
(Jesus) *Why do you trouble this woman? She has done a good deed for me. You will have the poor with you always, but you will not always have me. She has poured this water on my body, because I will be buried. Truly I say to you: wherever this Gospel will be preached in the whole world, they will tell, in her memory, what she has done.* (Matthew 26:3-13)

9. RECITATIVE (Contralto)
O you, dear Saviour,
when your disciples foolishly protest
that this virtuous woman prepares your body
with ointment for the grave,
in the meantime let me,
with the flowing tears from my eyes,

pour a water upon your head!

10. ARIA (Contralto)
Repentance and regret, repentance and regret
rips the sinful heart in two.
Thus the drops of my tears,
desirable spices,
are brought to you, loving Jesus.

11. RECITATIVE
(Evangelist) *Then one of the twelve, named Judas Iscariot, went to the high priests and said:*
(Judas) *What will you give me? I will betray him to you.*
(Evangelist) *And they offered him for thirty silver pieces. And from then on, he sought opportunity to betray him.* (Matthew 26:14-16)

12. ARIA (Soprano)
Bleed out, you loving heart!
Alas! A child that you raised,
that nursed at your breast,
threatens to murder its caretaker,
since it has become a serpent.[63]

Matthew 26:1-16

The first two verses of Matthew 26 mark a point of transition. Matthew begins his account of the Passion with the same (or very similar) formula of wording which he has used for the end of each of the major blocks of Jesus' teaching in this Gospel: 'When Jesus had finished all these sayings, ...'[64] 'These sayings' refer to all that Jesus has spoken since his Triumphal Entry into Jerusalem at the beginning of that week. They include Jesus' responses to the religious hierarchy's series of trick-questions in the temple precincts, his denunciation of the scribes and Pharisees, his lament over Jerusalem, his overview of world history from that point of time until his Second Coming, and three

[63] 'Caretaker' is being used here in its American sense of what, in the U.K., we would call 'a caregiver'. The German word is 'Pfleger'.
[64] See also Matthew 7:28, 11:1, 13:53 and 19:1.

significant parables concerning readiness for his future return (Matthew 21:22 – 25:46). So, the time is now, in all probability, the Tuesday evening of Jesus' final week of ministry, as indicated by the mention of 'two days' before the Passover. In the Jewish system of reckoning time, 'Wednesday' would have begun at sunset on the Tuesday.

There is deliberate irony in the way Matthew sets the scene, which highlights for us the sovereign control of God over all the events of the next three chapters. The chief priests and the elders of the people imagine that they are in charge as they draw up their plans to have Jesus arrested and killed. Their intention is *not* to do so during the Passover festival, but rather to wait until afterwards, in order to avoid an uproar among the people. Many Jewish people lived in cities and towns across the whole Roman Empire, and large crowds came to Jerusalem for such occasions as the Passover. It is reckoned that the population of Jerusalem would have been up to five times larger than normal. So, we can understand that the authorities would have great difficulty in getting rid of Jesus unobtrusively in such circumstances. However, we know that the opposite of what the religious leaders intend is what will happen: Jesus *will* be arrested and killed during the Passover festival.

This irony leads to another irony concerning the forthcoming death of Jesus, which again underlines God's sovereign control. There was a divine necessity that Jesus should die at the time of the Passover, because he is the fulfilment of all that Passover signified – he is the true Passover lamb. We shall return to this when we look at the verses concerning Jesus' institution of the Lord's Supper in the discussion of the next scene.

Jesus is not only the Passover lamb. Two other roles of his are flagged up at the beginning of Matthew 26. One is indicated only indirectly from the immediate context, namely the previous verses in Matthew 25:31-46 which concern the Final Judgement, when Jesus comes in his glory, gathers all mankind before him and decides who shall inherit the kingdom and who shall be consigned to eternal fire. Jesus is the

Judge, and yet he himself is willing to allow himself to be subjected to the unjust judgement of wicked men.

The other title for Jesus, this one stated explicitly, is the 'Son of Man'. Jesus has chosen, throughout his ministry, not to be known as 'the Christ' (or 'Messiah'), even though that title is rightfully his, because expectations of political and military leadership had become associated with the Old Testament anticipations of the Messiah. Instead, he has repeatedly referred to himself as the 'Son of Man'. While the title could refer to an ordinary human being (this is the way the phrase is used many times, for example, in the Book of Ezekiel),[65] Jesus clearly had in mind its use in Daniel 7:13-14, which speak of a human figure who exercises divine authority and kingship for ever. Later in this study we shall find Jesus, while on trial before Caiaphas and the Council, quoting from these verses with reference to himself.[66] But Jesus also, on a number of occasions, uses this title with reference to himself in connection with his sufferings and death, in a way that links his role with the Suffering Servant of the Book of Isaiah, who will suffer an atoning death for sinners.[67] 'Son of Man', therefore, points to Jesus' suffering and to his divine authority.

A word of explanation will be helpful in connection with the reference to 'chief priests' and 'high priest' in v 3. The Greek word used for both is the same, and this is reflected in the German translation in the Luther Bible. Pamela Dellal, therefore, consistently translates the term as *high priest,* in both the singular and the plural uses of the word, while English translations by and large distinguish between 'high priest' in the singular (the one individual with the supreme priestly authority in the role first held by Aaron, the brother of Moses), and 'chief priests' in the plural (referring to the hierarchy, made up of the current high priest and any who had formerly occupied this post). Herod the Great had made frequent changes in the high priesthood. Caiaphas is named in v 3 as the current high priest. He was in office AD 18 – 36 and was the son-in-law of Annas, a former high priest (AD 6 – 15). Judging from

---

[65] See, for example, Ezekiel 2:1.
[66] Matthew 26:64. See also Matthew 16:27-28.
[67] See, for example, Matthew 17:9-12 and Isaiah 52:13 – 53:12.

a number of New Testament references, Annas was clearly still a powerful figure. John 18:13 and 24 mention the role of Annas in the trials of Jesus.

While Matthew 26:1–2 set the scene, vv 3–16 deliberately draw our attention to a contrast between two responses to Jesus. There is a 'sandwich' structure to these verses. The 'outer layers' (vv 3–5 and 14–16) focus on hostility to Jesus, while the 'filling' of the sandwich (vv 6–13) has to do with an act of devotion. The account of Jesus being anointed at Bethany is placed here for thematic reasons. Chronologically, this event took place earlier. Matthew's reference to 'two days' before the Passover is in connection with Jesus' statement in v 2, not with the incident at Bethany. John, in his Gospel, specifically places the anointing of Jesus at Bethany as 'six days before the Passover' (John 12:1), which means the Saturday of the previous week, but beginning on the Friday evening. There are enough similarities between John's account and the account found here in Matthew 26 (and in Mark 14:3–9) for us to be confident that they are recording the same incident.[68]

Vv 3–5 (the top layer of the sandwich) show us the hostility towards Jesus from the religious authorities. Opposition from that direction had been mounting for some time. Within this same Gospel, Matthew 12:14 gives evidence of the Pharisees wishing to destroy Jesus and Matthew 21:45–46 tells of the intention of the chief priests and Pharisees to arrest him. Vv 14–16 (the lower layer of the sandwich) tell of Judas Iscariot's decision to betray Jesus. All four Gospels identify Judas as the betrayer but none of them clearly indicates the motive for his action. The most obvious inference is that his avarice led him to inform on Jesus. John says this of Judas: 'he was a thief, and having charge of the money bag he used to help himself to what was put into it.' (John 12:6) This was not apparent at the time, of course, but would have become evident later on. John also identifies Judas as one who particularly voiced a protest about the extravagance involved in Jesus' anointing (John 12:4). Matthew tells us that other disciples too, and not

---

[68] The anointing of Jesus that Luke records (Luke 7:36-50) is a different incident that took place at an earlier stage in Jesus' ministry in Galilee.

just Judas, were indignant at the woman's act of devotion (vv 8–9). But for Judas, Jesus' approval of what he regarded as a waste of money seems to have been the last straw.

Vv 6–13 (the filling of the sandwich) focus on the act of devotion by an unnamed woman at a meal in Bethany, which was about two miles from Jerusalem. Clearly, if this incident is the same as the one recorded in John 12:1–8 (which is being claimed in this study), we know that this woman is none other than Mary, the sister of Martha and Lazarus. Why she should not be named in Mathew's account (or Mark's) cannot be stated with certainty, but it is possible that the identity of Mary and her family needed to be kept confidential at the time of the writing of Matthew's and Mark's Gospels (perhaps for their safety), while John – writing at a later date – knew that secrecy was no longer an issue. That, however, is purely speculative. Matthew tells us that the woman's action was costly: John says that the perfume was worth 300 denarii (John 12:5). Jesus' assessment of the action was significant. He described her deed as 'beautiful', and that is connected with the fact that it was performed for Jesus ('For she has done a beautiful thing *to me'*, he says – my italics). Jesus also declared that the pouring of the ointment on his body was preparation for his burial. Whether this was Jesus' own interpretation of the act, or whether the woman herself recognised what lay ahead for him, is not clear. Jesus' final comment about the woman's act of devotion is that her deed would 'be told in memory of her.' Not only has that prophecy been fulfilled time and time again down the centuries, not least at every performance of this *Passion*, but also Jesus envisages the proclamation of the 'gospel' throughout 'the whole world'. We have here an anticipation of the Great Commission which will appear as the conclusion of this Gospel (Matthew 28:16–20).

Application

MOVEMENT 1

- This is an expression of *lament*. We are urged to listen and respond in a spirit of penitence.
- Jesus is the *Bridegroom*. This title goes back to Old Testament references to God himself and reminds us that, in God's

purpose of salvation, the goal is that the church for whom Christ has died will be his Bride.[69]

- Jesus is the *Lamb.* This word is rich in Old Testament allusions. Throughout the Old Testament era, lambs were sacrificial animals. Particularly significant are the lamb (or ram) provided by God for Abraham, to be sacrificed in place of Isaac; the Passover lamb (more will be said about this in the discussion of the following scene), and the lamb of Isaiah 53, led to the slaughter for the sins of God's people.[70]
- Jesus' *patience, love, graciousness,* and his *innocent* person are contrasted with our *guilt* and *sins,* which he has *borne* in our place. This is the Bible's own teaching of what is meant by the penal substitutionary atonement that Jesus accomplished on the cross: he took our punishment in our place.[71]

MOVEMENT 3

- We are challenged concerning our love for Jesus. 'Do you love me?' Jesus asked Peter three times.[72]
- Jesus is the Righteous One, yet he has been judged in our place.

MOVEMENTS 9 and 10

- These two movements are a prayer that we may be like Mary of Bethany: that we may not count the cost in our devotion to him, and that our sorrowful *repentance* may be accompanied by heart-felt love and thankfulness.

MOVEMENT 12

- We note here the appropriate sense of revulsion that a close friend of Jesus should choose to betray him. The text picks up on an image which originates in one of Aesop's fables, namely of nursing a viper in one's bosom. The picture in the text of this aria is of someone, like a nurse, who lovingly cares for a young child and discovers that she has been 'taking care' of a

---

[69] See, for example, Isaiah 62:5.
[70] Genesis 22:8, 13; Exodus 12; Isaiah 53:4-7.
[71] See, for example, 1 Peter 3:18.
[72] John 21:15-17.

venomous snake, which then viciously turns on her. Implicitly, we are urged to pray that our discipleship of Jesus may be pure.

What to Listen out for in the Music of Part I Scene 1

There will not be a musical comment on every movement of the oratorio.

Movement 1: Chorus and Chorale

Listen out for the massive dimensions of this impressive opening chorus and chorale. There are three groupings among the choral singers. Two of these are the two choirs for the chorus. While the two choirs do at times sing with each other, effective use is made of an antiphon between the two choirs. That means that, for a large part of the movement, one choir sings a question (*Whom? How? What? Where?*) which is answered by the other choir. The third grouping is a *ripieno* group of sopranos. *Ripieno* normally refers to a supplementary group of performers. This *ripieno* group of sopranos sings the words of the chorale (a Good Friday chorale which was well-known to the original listeners), divided into separate lines with a break between each, at the same time as the two choirs are singing their chorus. The chorale acts as a *cantus firmus,* a fixed melody to which the other voices are added. The overall effect is powerful.

Listen out for the contrast in rhythms between, on the one hand, the two choirs and the orchestra and, on the other hand, the *cantus firmus* of the chorale sung by the *ripieno* group of sopranos. While there are four beats in the bar for all the musicians, the music for the two choirs and the orchestra reflects the fact that each beat consists of a dotted crotchet (in other words a triplet of three quavers) – this is sometimes called 'compound time' ('Greensleeves' is a good example of a piece in compound time). The pattern is set by the orchestral introduction, which is driven by a persistent crotchet-plus-quaver rhythm in the bass instruments. By contrast, the music for the *ripieno* group of sopranos consists usually of one note per beat.

Listen out for the minor key of the movement, which firmly establishes a mournful atmosphere.

Movement 2: Recitative

Listen out for the so-called 'halo' effect in the accompaniment to the sung words of Jesus, which was referred to in the above Introduction. In addition to the continuo providing the accompaniment, the entire string section also play long sustained notes and highlight certain words. (This will happen throughout the oratorio and will not normally be commented on again.)

Movement 3: Chorale

Listen out for, and enjoy, the expressive quality of this, the first chorale for the full choir. What makes Bach's chorales so effective is the simplicity of the tune, coupled with interesting harmonization. Many listeners will find the chorales, which occur throughout the work, to be some of the most engaging items within the whole work. Some, like this one, appear in the oratorio as separate items. Some are embedded within other movements, as in Movement 1. (Further chorales will not necessarily be commented on, but there will be a note about the chorales of Movements 21, 23, 53, 63 and 72, which are all based on the same chorale tune – the main note about this sequence of chorales will be found in the musical comment on Movement 72.)

Listen out for the final chord being a major chord, despite the movement as a whole being set in the minor key. This is known as a 'tierce de Picardie', a device often used in Bach's time.

Movement 5: Chorus

Listen out for the use of the double choir in this movement. With each choir singing the words independently of the other, the impression is given of the Sanhedrin's deliberations.

Movement 9: Recitative (Contralto)

Listen out for the two flutes providing a lovely *obbligato* in this movement.

Movement 10: Aria (Contralto)

Listen out for the two flutes providing an *obbligato* in this item too.

Listen out for the ternary structure of the movement: its shape is A-B-A. Often, such a piece is written with just 'A' and 'B' sections but with the letters D.C. (or *da capo*) at the end. This means that the music goes back to the beginning and repeats the 'A' section. Listen out for the contrast of mood between the 'A' sections and the middle 'B' section.

Listen out for the way the flutes' accompaniment to the words, 'die Tropfen meiner Zähren' (*the drops of my tears*), might be described as resembling the fall of raindrops.

Movement 12: Aria (Soprano)

Listen out, again, for the two flutes' *obbligato* and for the ternary structure of the movement.

Listen out for this movement being another example of a ternary structure.

Listen out for the way the word 'Schlange' (*serpent*), at the end of the middle section, is set with a suitably twisting melody.

SCENE 2: The Lord's Supper *(PART I of the oratorio)*

13. RECITATIVE
(Evangelist) *But on the first day of unleavened bread the disciples came to Jesus and said to him:*

14. CHORUS
Where do you want us to prepare to eat the Passover lamb?

15. RECITATIVE
(Evangelist) *He said:*
(Jesus) *Go into the city to a certain person and say to him: The Master says to you: My time is here; I will hold Passover in your house with my disciples.*
(Evangelist) *And the disciples did as Jesus had commanded, and prepared the Passover lamb. And in the evening he sat at dinner with the twelve. And as they ate, he said:*
(Jesus) *Truly I say to you: one of you will betray me.*
(Evangelist) *And they were very troubled and began, each one among them, to say to him:*
(Chorus) *Lord, is it I?* (Matthew 26:17-22)

16. CHORALE
It is I, I should atone,
bound hand and foot in hell.
The scourges and the bonds
and what you endured,
my soul has earned.

17. RECITATIVE
(Evangelist) *He answered and said:*
(Jesus) *He who has dipped his hand in the bowl with me will betray me. The Son of Man will indeed pass away as it stands written of him; yet woe to the man through whom the Son of Man is betrayed! It would be better for him if this had not been born.*
(Evangelist) *Then Judas, who betrayed him, answered and said:*
(Judas) *Is it I, Rabbi?*
(Evangelist) *He said to him:*
(Jesus) *You say it.*

(Evangelist) *While they ate, however, Jesus took bread, and blessed and broke it and gave it to the disciples, and said:*
(Jesus) *Take, eat; this is my body.*
(Evangelist) *And he took the cup, and blessed it, gave it to them and said:*
(Jesus) *Drink from this, all of you; this is my blood of the new covenant, which is poured out for many for the forgiveness of sins. I say to you: From now on I will not drink again from this fruit of the vine until the day when I drink it again with you in my Father's kingdom.* (Matthew 26:23-29)

18. RECITATIVE (Soprano)
Although my heart is swimming in tears,
since Jesus takes leave of me,
yet his Testament brings my joy:
his flesh and blood, O preciousness,
he bequeaths to my hands.
Just as in the world, among his own,
he could not wish them harm,
just so he loves them to the end.

19 ARIA (Soprano)
I will give you my heart,
sink within, my Saviour!
I will sink into you;
although the world is too small for you,
ah, you alone shall be for me
more than heaven and earth.

Matthew 26:17-29

Matthew wastes no time in taking us on to the Lord's Supper, giving no explanation as to who the *certain person* is, whom the disciples are to contact, or how Jesus had arranged for this individual's house to be made available to him at such a busy time in Jerusalem, when so many visitors to the city would be seeking somewhere to celebrate the Passover. The meal had to be eaten after sunset, which is when the new day was reckoned to begin. Verse 20 tells us that the evening had come, and the day in question is the Thursday of this significant final week of Jesus' ministry.

The Passover has been referred to a few times already during the discussion of the previous scene. It was the most important of the annual Jewish festivals, commemorating the Exodus-deliverance of the Hebrew people from slavery in Egypt in the time of Moses. Pharaoh had repeatedly hardened his heart against God and refused to let the people depart from Egypt, despite the clear evidence of God's power displayed in a series of plagues. The tenth (and last) plague was God passing in judgement through the whole land. He would be taking the life of the firstborn of every household as an act of judgement. As Exodus 12 tells us, the only way the Hebrew households were spared that judgement was if a lamb was killed, one for every household, and the blood of that lamb was daubed on the lintels and doorposts of each Hebrew household. When God saw that blood he would 'pass over' those homes and his people would be saved from judgement.

The Passover lamb of Exodus 12 was an anticipation of Jesus as the true Passover lamb. Firstly, it was a lamb of *substitution*. The instruction was that there should be one lamb per household, to meet the needs of each household, so that the lamb died in the place of (or as a substitute for) the firstborn of that Israelite family. Similarly, Jesus was to die as our substitute.[73] Secondly, the Passover lamb was a lamb of *propitiation*, which means turning away the righteous wrath of God. As explained above, when God passed through the land of Egypt in judgement, there was no danger for those who sheltered beneath the blood of the propitiatory lamb. Similarly, Jesus' blood was to be shed for our propitiation.[74] Thirdly, the Passover lamb was a lamb of *nourishment*. The eating of that Passover meal would sustain the Israelites for the journey ahead. Similarly, Jesus is the bread of life, so that coming him and believing in him we may never hunger or thirst on our pilgrimage through this life.[75]

---

[73] See, for example, 1 Peter 3:18, referred to in an earlier footnote.
[74] See, for example, 1 John 4:10.
[75] John 6:35.

The above comments set the scene for us. As we turn now to the content of Matthew's account of the institution of the Lord's Supper, we discover that Jesus did three things.

First, *he deliberately centred the supper on betrayal.* This is the very first topic recorded in the dialogue at the meal. Jesus announced in v 21: 'Truly, I say to you, one of you will betray me.' Most probably, we are meant to recognise the echo of an Old Testament verse which is being fulfilled at this very point in time: 'Even my close friend in whom I trusted, who ate my bread, has lifted his heel against me.' (Psalm 41:9) Although Jesus knew all about Judas's treachery, he allowed all the disciples to ask the question, 'Is it I, Lord?' Possibly, he wanted them to recognise their common weakness: all of them, within their hearts, had the capacity to carry out such a deed. When we today share the Lord's Supper in a church-fellowship, we need to be aware that it is a supper for sinners who do not deserve to be partakers of the Lord's grace. When Judas, in v 25, asked the question, 'Is it I, Rabbi?' Jesus' reply to him was: 'You have said so' – literally, 'You have said' – *you say it* in the translation of the verse in the Luther Bible. While it is an affirmative, the meaning is not altogether clear-cut, and the sense of the phrase really depends on the intonation of the voice. So, the other disciples need not, at this moment, have recognised that Jesus was naming Judas as his betrayer. Jesus' words in v 24 are significant: 'The Son of Man goes as it is written of him, but woe to that man by whom the Son of Man is betrayed! It would have been better for that man if he had not been born.' Jesus combined in this statement the twin truths of divine sovereignty and human responsibility. The Scriptures themselves reveal that the Messiah's betrayal was a divine necessity, as the above-quoted verse from Psalm 41 shows, but in the most solemn terms imaginable Jesus spelt out the truth that Judas was personally accountable for his choices and actions. We find these two major biblical truths difficult to reconcile, but it is in the events leading up to the cross that we most clearly see them come together.[76] Some people may express their sympathy for Judas in view of his act of betrayal being foretold by Scripture. But we should take note of a comment by John

[76] See also Acts 4:24-28.

Calvin, when he wrote, 'Judas may not be excused on the ground that what befell him was prophesied, since he fell away not through the compulsion of prophecy but through the wickedness of his own heart.'[77]

Second, *Jesus wove the supper into the Passover.* As will be clear from the explanation above, the Passover meal focused on the lamb: its death and its flesh. But the Passover was also a sharing of unleavened bread and wine. While Jesus himself would be the true Passover lamb when he died on the cross, the items that Jesus chose to take at this supper, as the signs and tokens of all that the Passover signified, were bread and wine. So, in v 24, he said, 'Take, eat; this is my body.' And in v 27, 28, he said, 'Drink of it, all of you, for this is my blood of the covenant, which is poured out for many for the forgiveness of sins.' In this way, Jesus was spelling out the finality and fulfilment of the true meaning of the Passover: it all pointed to the death of himself, the Lamb of God, on Calvary.

Third, *Jesus explained the supper as a covenant.* Referring again to v 28, we notice that Jesus said: '... for this is my blood of the covenant, which is poured out for many for the forgiveness of sins.' Some ancient manuscripts include the word 'new' before 'covenant' – the Luther Bible follows this reading, as will be seen from the translation of the text above. The textual evidence for each of the two readings in this verse of Matthew 26 is evenly divided, while Luke certainly includes the word 'new' in his Gospel (Luke 22:20), as also does Paul in his account of Jesus' institution of the Lord's Supper (1 Corinthians 11:25). Whether or not the word 'new' should be included in Matthew's account, the meaning is, unmistakably, that the wine represents Jesus' blood of 'the new covenant'. Jesus was clearly alluding to Jeremiah's prophecy of the new covenant: 'Behold, the days are coming, declares the LORD, when I will make a new covenant with the house of Israel and the house of Judah' (Jeremiah 31:31). That 'new covenant' included the blessings of God's law written on his people's hearts (i.e., an

---

[77] J. Calvin, *The Acts of the Apostles,* ed. D.W. and T.F. Torrance (Edinburgh: Oliver and Boyd, 1965-6), Vol. I, 40 (originally published in 2 volumes, 1552 and 1554).

internal working of the Holy Spirit in the lives of his people); a relationship between himself as his people's God and them as his people; a personal, intimate knowledge of God to be enjoyed by his people, and complete forgiveness of sins. Jesus was saying to his disciples in that house in Jerusalem that 'the new covenant', promised six hundred or so years earlier, was about to come into effect through his 'blood', meaning his imminent death.

Application

MOVEMENT 16

- The words of this chorale go to the heart of the meaning of the cross. It is indeed *I* who *should atone* for all that *my soul has earned.* But the price would be beyond calculation. The good news of the Gospel, however, is that Jesus has provided full atonement by his once-for-all death in my place on the cross.

MOVEMENTS 18 and 19

- The combination of *tears* and *joy* is highly appropriate. Believers should weep over their sins AND be profoundly glad that our Lord's *Testament* (or Covenant) assures us of forgiveness.
- Jesus *loves them* (i.e., *his own*) *to the end.* Here we have a quotation of John 13:1, the first verse in John's Passion narrative: 'Now before the Feast of Passover, when Jesus knew that his hour had come to depart out of this world to the Father, *having loved his own* who were in the world, *he loved them to the end.'* (John 13:1, my italics)
- The soloist echoes the apostle Paul's assessment of the priceless value of having a personal relationship with the Lord Jesus Christ: 'Indeed, I count everything as loss because of the surpassing worth of knowing Christ Jesus my Lord.' (Philippians 3:8)

What to Listen out for in the Music of Part I Scene 2

Movement 15: Recitative

Listen out for the repeated question from the choir towards the end of the movement, 'Herr, bin ichs?' (*Lord, is it I?*). The word, 'Herr' (*Lord*), comes eleven times, one for each disciple except Judas Iscariot.

Movement 17: Recitative

Listen out for Jesus' words of institution of the Lord's Supper. This is an impressive section within the movement.

Movement 18: Recitative (Soprano)

Listen out for the expressive tone to this recitative for the soprano – and for the *obbligato* for the two oboes d'amore.

Movement 19: Aria (Soprano)

Listen out for a further *obbligato* for the two oboes d'amore – and for the ternary shape of this aria for the soprano.

SCENE 3: Gethsemane
(PART I of the oratorio)

20. RECITATIVE
(Evangelist) *And when they had spoken the benediction, they went out to the Mount of Olives. Then Jesus said to them:*
(Jesus) *Tonight you will all be angry at me. For it is written: "I will strike the shepherd, and the sheep of the flock will be scattered." When, however, I rise again, I shall go before you into Galilee.* (Matthew 26:30-32)[78]

21. CHORALE
Acknowledge me, my Guardian,
my Shepherd, take me in!
From you, source of all goodness,
has much good come to me.
Your mouth has nourished me
with milk and sweet sustenance;
your spirit has lavished on me
much heavenly joy.

22. RECITATIVE
(Evangelist) *Peter answered, however, and said to him:*
(Peter) *Even though everyone will be angry at you, yet I will never be angry.*
(Evangelist) *Jesus said to him:*
(Jesus) *Truly, I say to you: Tonight, before the cock crows, you will deny me three times.*
(Evangelist) *Peter said to him:*
(Peter) *Even if I must die with you, I will not deny you.*
(Evangelist) *And all the other disciples said the same.* (Matthew 26:33-35)

---

[78] ... *you will all be angry at me* (v 31 and v 33) is an accurate rendering of the German, but Luther may not have handled this part of the text quite correctly. The word in the Greek means 'to be caused to stumble'. Luther has selected a word which emphasizes the inward *feelings* of the disciples (i.e., their indignation, or sense of being offended, at Jesus' total lack of resistance at the moment of his arrest), while English translations have correctly gone for wording which expresses their *action*, namely, to fall away and desert Jesus.

23. CHORALE
I will stay here with you,
do not scorn me!
I will not leave you,
even as your heart breaks.
When your heart grows pale
at the last stroke of death,
then I will hold you fast
in my arm and bosom.

24. RECITATIVE
(Evangelist) *Then Jesus came with them to a garden, which was called Gethsemane, and spoke to his disciples:*
(Jesus) *Sit here while I go over there and pray.*
(Evangelist) *And he took with him Peter and the two sons of Zebedee, and began to mourn and despair. Then Jesus said to them:*
(Jesus) *My soul is troubled even to death: stay here and watch with me!*
(Matthew 26:36-38)

25. RECITATIVE (Tenor) and CHORALE
O pain!
Here the tormented heart trembles;
how it sinks down, how his face pales!
– What is the cause of all this trouble?
The Judge leads him before judgment.
No comfort, no helper is there.
– Alas! My sins have struck you down;
he suffers all the torments of hell,
he must pay for the crimes of others.
– I, alas, Lord Jesus, have earned this,
– that you endure.
Ah! Could my love for you,
my Saviour, diminish or bring aid
to your trembling and your despair,
how gladly would I stay here!

26. ARIA (Tenor) and CHORUS
I will watch with my Jesus,
– So our sins fall asleep.

My death Is atoned for by his soul's anguish;
His sorrow makes me full of joy.

– Therefore his deserved suffering
– Must be truly bitter and yet sweet to us.

27. RECITATIVE
(Evangelist) *And he went away a bit, fell down on his face and prayed and said:*
(Jesus) *My Father, if it is possible, let this cup pass from me; yet not as I will it, rather as you wish.* (Matthew 26:39)

28. RECITATIVE (Bass)
The Saviour falls down before his Father;
through this he lifts up himself and everyone
from our fall to God's grace again.
He is ready to drink the cup of death's bitterness,
in which the sins of this world are poured and which stink horribly,
since it is pleasing to our loving God.

29. ARIA (Bass)
Gladly will I force myself
to take on the Cross and the chalice,
yet I drink after the Saviour.
For his mouth,
which flows with milk and honey,
has sweetened the grounds
and the bitter taste of sorrow
through his first sip.

30. RECITATIVE
(Evangelist) *And he came back to his disciples and found them sleeping, and said to them:*
(Jesus) *Couldn't you then remain awake with me one hour? Stay awake, and pray, so that you do not fall into temptation! The spirit is willing, but the flesh is weak.*
(Evangelist) *For a second time he went away, prayed and said:*
(Jesus) *My Father, if it is not possible that this cup pass away from me, then I will drink it; thus may your will be done.* (Matthew 26:40-42)

31. CHORALE
What my God wills always occurs,
his will is the best;
he is ready to help those
who believe firmly in him.
He gives aid in need, this righteous God,
and punishes with measure.
Who trusts in God, relies upon him firmly,
God will never abandon.

32. RECITATIVE
(Evangelist) *And he came back and found them sleeping nevertheless, and their eyes were full of sleep. And he left them and went away another time and prayed for the third time, and spoke the same words. Then he came back to his disciples and said to them:*
(Jesus) *Alas! Do you wish to sleep and rest now? Behold, the hour has come, when the Son of Man is to be handed over into the hands of sinners. Get up, let us go: see, he who betrays me is here.*
(Evangelist) *And as he was speaking, behold, there came Judas, one of the twelve, and with him a large troop from the high priests and the elders of the people with swords and spears. And the betrayer had given them a sign and said: 'The one that I will kiss is him; seize him!' And just then he stepped forward to Jesus and said:*
(Judas) *Greetings to you, Rabbi!*
(Evangelist) *And kissed him. However, Jesus said to him:*
(Jesus) *My friend, why did you come?*
(Evangelist) *Then they stepped forward and laid hands on Jesus and seized him.* (Matthew 26:43-50)

33. ARIA (Soprano and Contralto) and CHORUS
Thus my Jesus is now captured.
    – Leave him, stop, don't bind him!
Moon and light
for sorrow have set,
since my Jesus is captured.
    They take him away, he is bound. **Are lightning and thunder**
    – extinguished in the clouds?
    – Open the fiery abyss, O hell,
    – crush, destroy, devour, smash – with sudden rage

– the false betrayer, the murderous blood!

34. RECITATIVE
(Evangelist) *And, behold, one of those who were with Jesus stretched out his hand and struck a servant of the high priest, and cut off his ear. Then Jesus said to him:*
(Jesus) *Put your sword back in its place; for whoever takes the sword will perish through the sword. Or do you think that I could not ask my Father to send me more than twelve legions of angels? How would the scripture be fulfilled then? It must happen thus.*
(Evangelist) *At the time Jesus said to the crowd:*
(Jesus) *You have come out as if to a murderer, with swords and spears to take me; yet I have daily sat among you and have taught in the temple, and you did not arrest me. However, all of this has happened in order to fulfil the writings of the prophets.*
(Evangelist) *Then all the disciples deserted him and fled.* (Matthew 26:51-56)

35. CHORALE
O mankind, mourn your great sins,
for which Christ left his Father's bosom
and came to earth;
from a virgin pure and tender
he was born here for us,
he wished to become our Intercessor,
he gave life to the dead
and laid aside all sickness
until the time approached
that he would be offered for us,
bearing the heavy burden of our sins
indeed for a long time on the Cross.

Matthew 26:30-56

The first part of this section of the narrative concerns Jesus' foretelling of Peter's denials.

It makes sense to divide the biblical text into separate scenes, determined by location or focus (as explained earlier). So, a new scene begins at v 30, where we are told that Jesus had now left the house to go to the Mount of Olives. But if we ignore that division for a moment, we notice how Matthew has bracketed his account of the institution of the Lord's Supper between two accounts of human sin and weakness. Immediately before the verses about the Lord's Supper we have the focus on Judas's betrayal (v 20-25), and immediately following it the spotlight falls on the defection of all the disciples and, in particular, Peter's failure to stand firm in the time ahead (v 30-35).

Just as Jesus had known about Judas's treachery, he knew also that his friends would desert him and that he would be quite alone. Announcing this shocking truth, he quoted Zechariah 13:7, words about God striking the shepherd (namely Jesus) and the sheep of the flock (namely the disciples) being scattered. What may not be immediately apparent, without turning to that chapter of Zechariah, is that the context shows that the purpose of this striking and scattering is that God's people may be purified and a remnant saved. Jesus clearly sounded one positive note concerning his resurrection and that he would 'go before' them to Galilee. That expression ('go before') must have been chosen deliberately, since it expresses the action of a shepherd. In other words, he (the shepherd) will be struck and they (the sheep) will be scattered, but he will not cease to be their shepherd and they will not cease to be his flock.

Peter responded typically to Jesus' prediction that he would deny his Master three times that night. He was sincere in his protestations of loyalty, but he had not yet learned to distrust his own resources of courage. Similarly, all the disciples promised never to desert Jesus.

The most striking aspect of Jesus' time of prayer in the garden which we know as Gethsemane is his horror and revulsion at the prospect of his forthcoming death. The experience that lay before Jesus was unique. What lay before him was not just physical suffering, namely scourging and crucifixion, both of which were extremely barbaric. Nor was it just the physical suffering plus psychological or emotional suffering, namely desertion by his friends and rejection by the nation. Jesus undoubtedly felt the bitter pain of this suffering. But what was reserved for Jesus alone was the spiritual suffering, which is described in this part of Matthew 26 as drinking from 'this cup' (v 39 and v 42).

The 'cup' being referred to here is the cup of God's wrath, the carrying out of God's judgement on the sin of the world which Jesus would bear on his shoulders while hanging on the cross. One of several Old Testament verses which speak of this cup of judgement is Psalm 75:7. The previous verse tells us, 'it is God who executes judgement,' and then comes verse 7 of the psalm:

> For in the hand of the LORD there is a cup with foaming wine, well mixed, and he pours out from it, and all the wicked of the earth shall drain it down to the dregs.

It is beyond our comprehension to take in what it would have meant for the sinless Son of God, who had enjoyed unbroken intimacy with his Father from eternity, to be abandoned by his Father and to endure the punishment merited by the whole human race. We shall return to this reflection in connection with Jesus' crucifixion itself. But we can be sure that it was this terrible prospect which Jesus had in mind when he asked Peter and James and John to watch and pray with him. It explains too why Jesus spoke of his soul being 'very sorrowful, even to death'. It is also beyond our comprehension to fathom the depths of Jesus' prayer: 'My Father, if it be possible, let this cup pass from me; nevertheless, not as I will, but as you will.'" Jesus knew that he had come into the world to die on the cross as the Saviour of the world. But that did not hold him back from praying that prayer. Furthermore, his prayer did not stop with the request to be spared the spiritual ordeal. It continued with his willing submission to his Father's will.

In passing, we should note that Jesus modelled his own teaching on prayer, because he had taught his disciples that they should pray, 'Your will be done' (Matthew 6:10). Matthew gives us the central words of Jesus' prayer, but we should notice that Jesus' prayer was anything but brief and rushed – rather, according to v 40, it lasted a whole hour, and yet, according to v 44, it was the same words that Jesus prayed in each of his three times of prayer. Jesus' prayer in the garden of Gethsemane stands in total contrast to what happened in a different garden. The garden of Eden, in Genesis 3. Adam and Eve acted according to the principle, '"Not your will, but mine' – whereas Jesus prayed, 'Not my will, but yours'. It was here in the garden, as Jesus wrestled in prayer, that the battle of the cross was won. Adam and Eve failed in their moment of testing, while Jesus (the last Adam, as Paul describes him in 1 Corinthians 15:45) stood firm against the temptation to by-pass the suffering that lay before him. When Jesus left the garden, there was no wavering from his purposeful journey to the cross.

Another amazing thing about Jesus' time in Gethsemane is his concern for his friends, who – three times – failed to provide him with any support but fell asleep. At this crucial time, he urged them to watch and pray so that they might not enter into temptation. It was for their benefit that he gave them this command. Even while his ordeal was approaching, he was thinking of the much lesser trial that they would face, and his words were spoken with compassion. It is a common experience in the Christian life to find that our spiritual eagerness is accompanied by carnal weakness: 'the spirit indeed is willing, but the flesh is weak.'

Judas arrived with a large crowd, who were armed. Those accompanying Judas are described as being 'from the chief priests and elders', but it is possible that some Roman soldiers were present with Pilate's authorisation. It was dark, so Jesus needed to be identified for the benefit of those arresting him. This was done by Judas's treacherous kiss, accompanying his grimly ironic words, 'Greetings, Rabbi!' There is some uncertainty as to whether Jesus' words were a question ('Why have you come?') or a command ('Do that for which you have come'). Both translations are possible. But Jesus called Judas, his betrayer, 'Friend' – there was an unexpected tone of open-heartedness in his address. Peter was the disciple who drew his sword and wildly cut off the ear of one of the high priest's servants, as John tells us (John 18:10). However, Jesus healed the servant's ear. Ineffective as Peter's impetuous gesture was, he should be given the credit of showing some courage. What Matthew particularly turns his attention to is Jesus' complete control of the situation. This is shown firstly in Jesus' rejection of violence. He knew that heavenly forces were available to him at an instant, should he wish, but he affirmed the divine necessity of his arrest: 'But how then should the Scriptures be fulfilled, that it *must* be so?' (my italics). Secondly, Jesus' control is clear from the way he questioned the need of the arrest-party to carry out their duty with such a show of force, when he had been available each day teaching in the temple. In complete contrast to Jesus's control, the disciples lost their nerve and fled under the cover of darkness, just as Jesus had foretold.

Application

MOVEMENT 21

- This chorale picks up on Jesus' reference to himself as the *shepherd*. The believer longs to be included in his flock. There may well be a hint here of Isaiah 40:11:

  He will tend his flock like a shepherd;
  he will gather the lambs in his arms ...

  and of Psalm 23:1-3:

  The LORD is my shepherd; I shall not want.
  He makes me lie down in green pastures.
  He leads me beside still waters.
  He restores my soul.
  He leads me in paths of righteousness for his name's sake.

MOVEMENT 23

- The protestations of loyalty from Peter and the other disciples are still echoing in our minds as we hear this chorale. Knowing, as we do, that Peter will deny Jesus and all of them will desert Jesus, we are challenged concerning the reality of our instinctive pledge of devotion.

MOVEMENT 25

- This movement reflects on the reasons for Jesus' words *My soul is troubled even to death.*
  - He faces the prospect of *judgement* and *all the torments of hell* from *the Judge* (i.e. God).
  - He must face the ordeal alone, with *no comfort, no helper*.
  - It is *the crimes of others*, including *my sins*, that have brought this about.

- In view of all this, we are challenged to express our love and loyalty.

MOVEMENT 28

- We reflect on Jesus' prayer to his Father and his submission to the Father's will that he should *drink the cup of death's bitterness,* foul as it is with *the sins of this world.*
- Why was Jesus prepared to accept the Father's will and make it his own? To do so *is pleasing to our loving God.*

MOVEMENT 29

- We are challenged about our willingness *to take on the cross and the chalice.* Jesus had announced earlier in his ministry, 'If anyone would come after me, let him deny himself and *take up his cross* and follow me.' (Matthew 16:24, my italics) James and John had claimed to be willing to drink Jesus' 'cup' and Jesus had said that they would indeed drink it (Matthew 20:2223). But there is a difference between the way Jesus would take up his cross and drink the cup of God's wrath the very next day (Good Friday), and the way his followers are called to take up their cross and drink the cup. This difference is indicated in the aria by the phrase, *yet I drink after the Saviour* (my underlining) – and this difference truly sweetens the bitterness of Christian suffering. Jesus would carry his cross and drink the cup in a unique way, providing a once-and-for-all penal substitutionary atonement for the sins of the world. His followers are called to expect the possibility of suffering for Christ's sake, and to count it as a privilege, but to do so in the assurance that Jesus has risen from the dead. This gives us a guarantee for the *past*: he has paid the price for sin in full and has drawn the sting of death. Jesus' victory gives us a guarantee for the *present:* he is with us today and every day by his Spirit, so that we will never face adversity on our own. His triumph gives a guarantee for the *future:* beyond this life, whatever we may experience on earth, Christians can look forward to the solid joys of heaven.

MOVEMENT 31

- This chorale could be taken as a sung comment on Paul's words in Romans 8:28: 'And we know that for those who love

God all things work together for good, for those who are called according to his purpose.' In the light of that truth from God's word, Christians can indeed affirm with confidence: *What my God wills always occurs, his will is the best; he is ready to help those who believe firmly in him.*

MOVEMENT 33

- The confident assertions in the comments on the two movements above make sense in the full light of Easter Day. But at this stage in the drama, it is still Maundy Thursday, and Good Friday lies in the future. So, in this aria and chorus, we are plunged once again into an expression of horrified outrage that Jesus should be betrayed, arrested, and led away to be put on trial.

MOVEMENT 35

- This chorale rounds off the whole of Part One of the oratorio and therefore reflects on Jesus' incarnation, ministry, and atonement. It traces Jesus' laying aside of his heavenly glory, his humble birth as a human being, his compassion for people in need, his healing of the sick and his raising of the dead – all leading to his death on the cross when he would bear *the heavy burden of our sins*. There is much here to ponder and to move us to heart-felt wonder and thanksgiving.

What to Listen out for in the Music of Part I Scene 3

Movement 21: Chorale

This is the first of five movements in the oratorio to make use of a chorale tune, known as 'O Haupt, voll Blut und Wunden' or 'Befiehl du deine Wege', both by Paul Gerhardt. The other four movements to make use of this chorale tune are 23, 53, 63 and 72. Each time, the chorale is set in a different key. The musical comment on Movement 72 will refer to features concerning Bach's handling of the whole sequence.

Movement 23: Chorale

See the musical comment on Movements 21 and 72.

Movement 25: Recitative (Tenor) and Chorale

Listen out for the tortured tone of the tenor recitative, most appropriate for singing about the deeply troubled and sorrowful feelings of the Lord Jesus in the garden.

Listen out also for way the choir's singing of a chorale intersperses with the soloist's part, radiating a sense of calm in contrast with the mood of the soloist's music. In the context of the musical effect of the movement, the chorale possibly represents the prayer that the three disciples should have been engaged in.

Listen out for the use of two recorders in this piece, together with the oboes da caccia, if it is performed as Bach intended.

Movement 26: Aria (Tenor) and Chorus

Listen out for the oboe *obbligato* in this movement.

Listen out for the choir's repeated lines interspersing with the tenor soloist's part.

Movement 33: Aria (Soprano and Contralto) and Chorus

Listen out for the duet for the soprano and contralto soloists in the first part of this movement.

Listen out for the staccato commands from the choir, urging Jesus' captors to unbind him and let him go.

Listen out for the second part of the movement, with its sudden switch to a faster tempo, as the full choir sing dramatically of the possibility of the elements intervening and halting the arrest of Jesus. The dramatic effect is heightened by each voice making its initial entry in turn, which constitutes a fugal effect, and by an unexpected silent bar occurring in the middle.

Movement 35: Chorale

Listen out for this large, impressive movement, which brings Part One of the work to a conclusion. It is scored for both choirs. All the sopranos are scored as a *ripieno* section, not just some of them as in Movement 1. They sing the chorale – another well-known tune for the first listeners – as a *cantus firmus* (as happened also in Movement 1).

Part Two

SCENE 1: The Trial before Caiaphas

36. ARIA (Contralto) and CHORUS
Alas, now my Jesus is gone!
– ***Where, then, has your beloved gone,***
– *O most beautiful among women?*
Is it possible, can I behold it?
– ***Which way has your beloved turned?***
Alas! My lamb in the claws of a tiger;
Alas! Where has my Jesus gone?
– ***We will seek him with you.*** (Song of Solomon 6:1)
Alas! What shall I say to the soul,
when she asks me anxiously:
Alas! Where has my Jesus gone?

37. RECITATIVE
(Evangelist) *But after they had arrested Jesus, they brought him to the High Priest Caiaphas, where the scribes and the elders had gathered. Peter, however, followed him from afar to the palace of the high priest, and went inside and sat with the servants, so he could see how it came out. The high priests, however, and the elders, and the entire council sought false witness against Jesus, so that they could put him to death, and found none.* (Matthew 26:57-60a)

38. CHORALE
The world has judged me deceitfully,
with lies and false statements,
many traps and secret snares.
Lord, perceive me truthfully
in this danger;
protect me from malicious falsehoods!

39. RECITATIVE
(Evangelist) *And although many false witnesses came forward, they found none. Finally, two false witnesses came forward and said:*

(Witnesses) *He has said: I can destroy the temple of God and in three days build it up again.*
(Evangelist) *And the high priest stood up and said to him:*
(High Priest) *Do you answer nothing to this, that they say against You?*
(Evangelist) *But Jesus was silent.* (Matthew 26:60-63a)

40. RECITATIVE (Tenor)
My Jesus is silent at false lies,
in order to show us
that his merciful will
is bent on suffering for us,
and that we, in the same trouble,
should be like him
and keep silent under persecution.

41. ARIA (Tenor)
Patience, patience!
When false tongues pierce.
Although I suffer, contrary to my guilt,
shame and scorn,
indeed, dear God shall
revenge the innocence of my heart.

42. RECITATIVE
(Evangelist) *And the high priest answered and said to him:*
(High Priest) *I abjure You by the living God to tell us whether You are the Christ, the Son of God!*
(Evangelist) *Jesus said to him:*
(Jesus) *You say it. Yet I say to you: from now on it will come to pass that you will see the Son of Man sitting at the right hand of Power, and approaching in the clouds of heaven.*
(Evangelist) *Then the high priest tore his garments and said:*
(High Priest) *He has blasphemed God; what further witness do we need? Behold, now you have heard his blasphemy. What do you think?*
(Evangelist) *They answered and said:*
(Chorus) *He is worthy of death!*

43. RECITATIVE
(Evangelist) *Then they spit in his face and struck Him with fists. Some of them, however, struck Him in the face and said:*
(Chorus) *Prophesy to us, Christ, who is it who strikes You?*
(Matthew 26:63b-68)

44. CHORALE
Who has struck you thus,
my Saviour, and with torments
so evilly used you?
You are not at all a sinner
like us and our children,
You know nothing of transgressions.

Matthew 26:57-68

Verses 57 and 58 announce the agenda of the remainder of Matthew 26. Verse 57 informs us that Jesus was taken to Caiaphas's house, and the trial before Caiaphas will be related in verses 59-68. Verse 58 tells us that Peter followed Jesus 'at a distance' – we might describe this as a halfway point between courage and cowardice – and prepares us for the account of Peter's denials in verses 69-75.

The travesty of justice in Jesus' trial is evident in so many ways. We are told immediately that the chief priests and the whole Sanhedrin were deliberately seeking *false witness* in order to be able to condemn Jesus to death. Remarkably, they were unable to do this, until two witnesses came forward with their garbled account of Jesus' words about being able to destroy the temple and rebuild it in three days. According to John, Jesus made such a statement early on in his ministry when he had visited Jerusalem and cleared the temple of traders and money-changers – and we shall return in a moment to Jesus' actual words and what he meant by them. Matthew, along with Mark and Luke, had chosen not to record that incident, but instead to provide a record of Jesus' cleansing of the temple during his final week of ministry – while John had chosen not to include an account of that later incident. A strong case can be made for Jesus having cleared the temple of traders and money-changers on two occasions – an *early* incident (recorded by John) and a *later* incident (recorded by Matthew, Mark and Luke). For their own editorial reasons, the four Gospel writers made their decisions about which parts of Jesus' ministry they would include and which parts they would exclude. One of the arguments which support this view is the silence by Matthew, Mark and Luke concerning Jesus' statement about destroying and rebuilding the temple. If Jesus made that statement early on in his ministry (as is being argued here), but they had chosen not to include an account of Jesus' visit to Jerusalem early in his ministry, they could not record Jesus' actual words. When we examine John's Gospel to find what Jesus had actually said about the temple, his statement was: 'Destroy this temple, and in three days I will raise it up.' (John 2:19) So, Jesus had not said that he would destroy the temple. In addition, John goes on to explain that Jesus was not talking about the Jerusalem temple: 'But he was speaking about the temple of his body.' (John 2:21) In case there is still any confusion, John then explains that it was much later that the disciples realised Jesus had been speaking about his resurrection (John 2:22).

Initially, Jesus remained silent before all his accusers, as he would also do before Pilate (Matthew 27:12). This should be seen as a fulfilment of the Suffering Servant of Isaiah 53: 'He was oppressed, and he was afflicted, yet he opened not his mouth; like a lamb that is led to the slaughter, and like a sheep that before its shearers is silent, so he opened not his mouth.' (Isaiah 53:7)

One of the further instances of the illegal nature of Jesus' trial before Caiaphas is the high priest's leading question to Jesus: 'I adjure you by the living God, tell us if you are the Christ, the Son of God.' (verse 63) Out of order as such a challenge clearly was, Jesus was bound (by the use of the oath) to give an answer. Jesus' reply was: 'You have said so. But I tell you, from now on you will see the Son of Man seated at the right hand of Power and coming on the clouds of heaven.' The first part of Jesus' answer was deliberately ambiguous, just like Jesus' earlier reply to Judas's hypocritical question whether he was the betrayer (Matthew 26:25). However, the second part of Jesus' reply was totally unambiguous. Jesus' use of the title 'Son of Man' was referred to in the earlier comments on Part I Scene 1, and his use of it here at his trial was particularly noted. His reply to the high priest indicates that Jesus claimed to be the individual in Daniel 7:15-16 who exercises divine authority and kingship for ever. This, unmistakably, amounted to a claim to be the Christ, the Son of God. Jesus went on to tell the high priest and the Sanhedrin that 'from now on' (i.e. in the future) they would no longer see him as their prisoner but in his true role as Judge of all. The high priest tore his robes to signify that what Jesus had spoken was blasphemy. They not only condemned Jesus to death but also inflicted gratuitous abuse and humiliation on Jesus. They mocked him for being a self-styled prophet, striking him while presumably blindfolded and demanding that he should 'prophesy' who it was that administered the blow.

We should not miss the irony of the situation. The religious hierarchy believed that they had achieved what they intended, without considering the terrifying possibility that what Jesus had said was the truth. In reality, it was not Jesus who was on trial but they themselves. They had provided irrefutable evidence of their own guilt, and it was they themselves who stood condemned.

Application

MOVEMENT 36

- This is the only movement in the entire oratorio that makes direct use of a biblical passage other than Matthew 26 and 27. The words sung by the chorus, which intersperse with the soloist's aria, are taken from The Song of Solomon 6:1. This Bible book celebrates the joy of love and sex within marriage but also speaks of God's love for his people and the intimacy that he seeks with believers. There is a connection between the two, because God designed marriage to be a picture of Christ's love for the church. This same connection is made in Ephesians 5:22-32.
- At this point in the Bible book, 'the bride' is conscious of 'Christ's' temporary absence: '... my beloved had turned and gone ... I sought him, but found him not ...' (Song of Solomon 5:6). In chapter 6 verse 1, others speak to 'the bride' and offer to help in seeking him.
- The application of this Old Testament verse within the oratorio is provided by the words of the soloist's aria. These challenge

us as individuals in our response to *my Jesus* being taken away, and finding himself like a *lamb in the claws of a tiger* – and he is *my lamb* (my underlining).

- We should take to heart the phrase, only two verses later in this Bible book: 'I am my beloved's and my beloved is mine' (Song of Solomon 6:3).
- We should notice the way Bach has skilfully bound together the openings of both parts of the oratorio by means of the 'wedding' theme. In the opening movement of Part One, Jesus was referred to as the 'Bridegroom'. Here, in the opening movement of Part Two, 'the bride' feels sorrow at the absence of her beloved. This is more than a mere artistic device: we are reminded that the Lord's Passion has to do with him bringing about the deepest imaginable relationship between himself and his people. We shall return to this theme of relationship in the Conclusion at the end of the study.

MOVEMENT 38

- The text for this chorale consists of the imagined thought, or unspoken words, of Jesus, who is suffering as the innocent victim of *the world's* plots and *malicious falsehoods.*
- Like the psalmist, he prays for God's vindication and protection.[79]

MOVEMENTS 40 and 41

- These two items reflect on Matthew 26:63a: Jesus' silence before the accusations of the false witnesses. I take the phrase, in Movement 41, *contrary to my guilt* (German: 'wider meine Schuld') to mean in effect 'although I am innocent' – i.e., as a parallel phrase with *the innocence of my heart.* With possibly a reference to the teaching of Peter's First Letter, we are urged to pray that, like Jesus, we may *keep silent under persecution.*[80] We can leave it to God to act in vengeance.

---

[79] See, for example, Psalm 5.

[80] See, for example, 1 Peter 2:18-23; 4:12-19.

MOVEMENT 44

- This chorale picks up on the ill-treatment that Jesus received at the end of his trial before Caiaphas. We should be filled with wonder that the innocent Saviour should receive such abuse, while we, who are sinners, should benefit from his kindness.

What to Listen out for in the Music of Part II Scene 1

Movement 36: Aria (Contralto and Chorus)

Listen out for the contrast between the opening movement of Part Two of the oratorio with the opening movement of Part One. This movement is more restrained.

Listen out for the choir singing the words of The Song of Solomon 6:1. These are interspersed with the words of the contralto soloist's aria, as she laments the loss of her Jesus.

Listen out for the way each vocal line makes a separate entry, thus creating another short fugue, as in Movement 33. This gives the impression of a large number of people joining in the search.

Movement 40: Recitative (Tenor)

Listen out for the striking accompaniment in this movement. It consists throughout of quaver chords, suggestive of the incessant suffering that Jesus was enduring. The chords are marked as staccato for the oboes and as 'rolled' chords for the continuo instruments and organ. Both these features, in different ways, accentuate the sharp, throbbing effect.

Movement 42: Recitative

Listen out for the very last line of this movement, where the members of the Sanhedrin shout that Jesus is worthy of death. This line is sung by both choirs, so that there are eight vocal lines. This gives the impression of a large crowd shouting out the same thing but at slightly different times.

Movement 43: Recitative

Listen out for something similar to what was mentioned in the previous comment. The full choir again acts as the members of the Sanhedrin, mocking Jesus by demanding that he should 'prophesy' who is hitting him. Again, there are eight vocal lines, with words being sung by different vocal lines at different times, in order to intensify the effect of a large body of people.

Movement 44: Chorale

Listen out for the arresting juxtaposition of the last phrase of the previous movement with the first words of this movement. At the end of Movement 43 we hear (in the English translation) the words, *Who is it who strikes you?* – sung mockingly and harshly. The first words of Movement 44 are: *Who has struck you thus?* – sung tenderly and lovingly. Given that the full choir are made to change their role in the space of two seconds (from hostile Sanhedrin to devoted worshippers) and sing virtually the same words, the effect is striking. One thought that immediately comes to mind, here, is that in our relationship to the Lord Jesus there can be no neutrality – no middle-ground of polite indifference. We are either his enemies, or we are his friends.

SCENE 2: Peter and Judas
(PART II of the oratorio)

45. RECITATIVE
(Evangelist) *Peter, however, sat outside of the palace; and a maid came up to him and said:*
(First Maid) *And you were also with that Jesus of Galilee.*
(Evangelist) *He denied it however before them all and said:*
(Peter) *I don't know what you are saying.*
(Evangelist) *As he was going out of the door, however, another one saw him and said to those who were near:*
(Second Maid) *This one was also with that Jesus from Nazareth.*
(Evangelist) *And he denied again, and swore to it:*
(Peter) *I do not know the man.*
(Evangelist) *And after a little while people standing around came up and said to Peter:*
(Chorus) *Truly, you are also one of them; your speech gives you away.*

46. RECITATIVE
(Evangelist) *Then he began to curse and swear:*
(Peter) *I do not know the man.*
(Evangelist) *And just then the cock crew. Then Peter remembered the words of Jesus, when he said to him: 'before the cock crows, you will deny me three times.' And he went out and wept bitterly.* (Matthew 26:69-75)

47. ARIA (Contralto)
Have mercy on me, my God,
for the sake of my tears!
Look here, heart and eyes
weep bitterly before you.
Have mercy, have mercy!

48. CHORALE
Although I have been separated from you,
yet I return again;
even so your Son set the example for us
through his anguish and mortal pain.
I do not deny my guilt,
but your grace and mercy

is much greater than the sin
that I constantly discover in me.

49. RECITATIVE
(Evangelist) *The next day, however, all the high priests and the elders of the people held a council about Jesus so that they could put him to death. And they bound him, led him out and turned him over to the Governor, Pontius Pilate. When Judas, who betrayed him, saw that he was condemned to death, he felt remorse and brought back the thirty silver pieces to the high priests and the elders and said:*
(Judas) *I have done evil by betraying innocent blood.*
(Evangelist) *They said:*
(Chorus) *How does that concern us? See to it yourself!*

50. RECITATIVE
(Evangelist) *And He threw the silver pieces into the temple and left, and went away and hanged himself. However, the high priests took the silver pieces and said:*
(High Priests) *It will not do to put them into the coffers of God, since it is blood money.*
(Matthew 27:1-6)

51. ARIA (Bass)
Give me my Jesus back!
See the money, the murderer's fee,
tossed at your feet by the lost son!

52. RECITATIVE
(Evangelist) *They held a council, however, and bought a potter's field with them for the burial of pilgrims. Therefore, this same field is called the Field of Blood to this very day. Thus was fulfilled what was spoken through the Prophet Jeremiah, who said: 'They have taken thirty silver pieces, the price of Him who was bought from the children of Israel, and have given them for a potter's field, as the Lord has commanded me.' Jesus, however, stood before the Governor; and the Governor questioned him and said:*
(Pilate) *Are you the King of the Jews?*
(Evangelist) *Jesus, however, said to him:*
(Jesus) *You say it.*
(Evangelist) *And to the accusations from the high priests and the elders he answered nothing. Then Pilate said to him:*

(Pilate) *Do you not hear how harshly they accuse you?*
(Evangelist) *And he answered him not even one word thus, to which even the Governor was greatly amazed.* (Matthew 27:7-14)

53. CHORALE
Commit your path,
and whatever troubles your heart,
to the most faithful caretaker,
he, who directs the heavens,
who to the clouds, air, and winds
gives path, course, and passage,
he will also find ways
for your feet to follow.[81]

Matthew 26:69 – 27:10

We have already had evidence of Matthew's skilful craftsmanship in his narration of the events of the Passion. He juxtaposes and interleaves his paragraphs, leaving us to take note of contrasts or comparisons in the text. The account of Peter's denials in the last paragraph of chapter 26 is a particularly striking example of this, because Matthew places it at this point in his text for two reasons – quite apart from the obvious fact that this is where it belongs chronologically. First, he intends his readers to compare and contrast Jesus' trial before Caiaphas with Peter's denials of Jesus in the courtyard. As was noted earlier, verses 57-58 set the agenda for the rest of the chapter. Verse 57 prepares us for Jesus' appearance before Caiaphas and the Sanhedrin (verses 59-68), and verse 58 anticipates Peter's experiences in the courtyard (verses 69-75). Second, the account of Peter's denials at the end of chapter 26 are followed almost immediately at the beginning of chapter 27 by the account of Judas's remorse and suicide. It is true that the first two verses of chapter 27 are

[81] An earlier footnote commented on the American use of the word 'caretaker', which in the U.K. is better expressed as the one who cares or provides care. In fact, the German text, translated literally, says: 'Commit your path...to the most faithful care of him who directs the heavens...' The phrase 'of him who' is not the most elegant of phrases, so the translation in the text above makes good sense for an American audience.

concerned with Jesus being sent to Pilate, but the verses about Judas follow on from the verses about Peter very quickly. The text deliberately invites us to compare and to contrast the failures of both disciples. (Chapter and verse divisions do not belong to the original text, and we must therefore make sure that we do not set up barriers and boundaries where they do not belong.)

We focus first, therefore, on the contrast between Jesus' trial and Peter's denials. It was not only Jesus who was on trial – Peter was effectively on trial too, but realised this too late. Jesus was opposed by the whole Sanhedrin, but Peter was challenged initially by just one servant girl, then by another servant girl, and only then by a number of bystanders. Jesus stood firm before a large number of powerful, hostile men and spoke nothing but the truth, while Peter fell at the first hurdle, let alone the other two, and each time told lies. Jesus was confronted with rigged evidence, but Peter was faced with true allegations – so, the honesty of Peter's 'trial' stands in contrast to the hypocrisy of Jesus' hearing. Jesus stood alone and was ill-treated by his accusers, while Peter was making himself comfortable among the crowd in the courtyard – and no doubt warming himself by the fire, which Luke mentions in his account (Luke 22:55). It was noted in the earlier comments about Gethsemane that, while Jesus had prayed three times in the garden, Peter had slept three times. Futhermore, it was three times that Peter denied Jesus, just as Jesus had predicted (verse 34). The intensity of his denials increased each time. First, it was a straightforward denial. The second denial was accompanied by an oath. The third time, Peter began to invoke a curse on himself and to swear. It was at that point that the cock crowed and Peter remembered Jesus' words of earlier on. The paragraph ends poignantly: 'And he went out and wept bitterly.' (verse 75) Here are tears of repentance, which alone can prepare the way for restoration. That, however, is not included in Matthew's narrative. This is the last time that Peter is mentioned in this Gospel. The account of Peter's restoration is to be found in John 21:15-19.

Before Matthew moves on to tell us about Judas, verses 1 and 2 prepare us for Jesus' trial before Pilate, which Matthew will record very soon.

This is typical of Matthew's narrative technique. He gives us a series of panels, which record the sequence of events, and from chapter 26 verse 57 to chapter 27 verse 31 every second panel has to do with Jesus. So, we have:

Jesus taken to Caiaphas (26:57),

Peter following at a distance (26:58),

Jesus on trial before Caiaphas (26:59-68),

Peter denying Jesus (26:69-75),

Jesus taken to Pilate (27:1-2),

Judas's remorse and suicide (27:3-10),

Jesus on trial before Pilate (27:11-31).

At the same time as Matthew is preparing to draw his readers' attention to a comparison of Judas with Peter, he reminds us of the central thread of his narrative: Jesus' journey towards the cross.

The second major focus in this section is Judas's story following his betrayal of Jesus – and, as noted above, we are invited to compare Judas with Peter in their failure as disciples of Jesus. Jesus' condemnation by the Sanhedrin led to Judas being overcome with remorse and to his decision to return the thirty pieces of silver to the chief priests and elders. What exactly was going through Judas's mind is impossible to fathom. The suggestion that Judas had intended to force Jesus to take decisive political action by arranging for him to be arrested, and subsequently realised that he had totally miscalculated, can be nothing more than a guess. There is no direct evidence to indicate that Judas was politically motivated. All we can say is that Judas betrayed Jesus and 'changed his mind', which in the Luther Bible comes over as *felt remorse.* From his words to the chief priests and elders, it is clear that he now – too late – recognised Jesus' innocence. Remorse, however, is not the same as repentance. The Jewish leaders' indifference to Judas's concerns was totally hypocritical: if Judas had betrayed innocent blood, they were the ones who had condemned innocent blood.

The important contrast between the accounts of the failure of two disciples, Peter and Judas, concerns the nature of the 'remorse' that each felt. There is one kind of remorse that leads to genuine repentance – what the apostle Paul calls 'a repentance that leads to salvation without regret' and 'godly grief' (2 Corinthians 7:10-11). In the mercy of God, this was Peter's experience, but the assurance of his forgiveness did not come until something like two weeks later.[82] But there is another kind of remorse, which Paul describes as 'worldly grief', which produces death (2 Corinthians 7:10). This was Judas's experience. While he acknowledged his sin to the chief priests, there is no sign that he sought the forgiveness of the one who alone can forgive sins. His guilt led to despair, not to repentance. The 'death' that Paul had in mind is a spiritual one, but tragically in Judas's case it led also to physical death, because he went and hanged himself. There is a mystery here about what constituted the difference of outcome in the spiritual journey of each of these two disciples. Divine sovereignty and human responsibility were both involved. One disciple's story stands as a cautionary tale, the other's as a testimony of God's grace.

As is often the case in this Gospel, Matthew wants his readers to be aware that Scripture is being fulfilled in the events surrounding Jesus' ministry. He does this here with reference to Judas's death. The verses that he quotes seem to be a rough rendering of Zechariah 11:12-13, but he attaches the name of Jeremiah (not Zechariah) as the Old Testament writer whose word has been fulfilled. The best way to approach this puzzle is to see a reference here to *two* Old Testament passages, not just one. While Zechariah 11:12-13 is directly quoted (albeit in Matthew's wording), Jeremiah 19:1-13 also seems to be in Matthew's mind. This passage includes a number of words and ideas that are relevant here: for example, a 'potter', 'the blood of innocents', 'the Valley of the Son of Hinnom' (see the comment below on the traditional site for Judas's death), and 'place to bury'. Jeremiah's name

[82] John 21 begins with the words 'after this', which relates to the last incident recorded in chapter 20, namely Jesus' second appearance to the disciples, including Thomas, a week after Easter Day. In addition, the events of John 21 took place in Galilee, not in Jerusalem. So, something like a fortnight would have elapsed between Maundy Thursday and the events of John 21.

alone is mentioned, possibly because he was the more important of the two prophets.

A brief comment may be helpful about the apparent differences between Matthew's account of Judas's death and the account provided by Luke at the beginning of Acts (Acts 1:18-20). There are two apparent differences: one is the manner of Judas's death, the other is, who was reponsible for purchasing the field where Judas died, so that it should be used as a burial ground? Both Matthew and Luke were committed to truth, and for that reason we should expect to find reasonable grounds for harmonizing their separate, independent accounts. In connection with *the manner of Judas's death,* Matthew writes simply that Judas hanged himself, while Luke says: 'falling headlong he burst open in the middle and all his bowels gushed out.' The traditional site for Judas's death is the Hinnom Valley, where trees grow out of the steep cliffs that form the side of the valley. It is not difficult to imagine that it was from one of these trees that Judas chose to hang himself. Nor is it difficult to imagine that his body remained suspended for some time, until the collapse of the tree-branch or the rope and the partial decomposition of the body brought about the circumstance that Luke describes. What Luke records is so singular that only such an explanation as this can account for it. Matthew, writing primarily for a Jewish audience, may well have considered that a simple record of Judas's death by hanging was enough to establish the thought that he had died under a divine curse. This is what the Old Testament says: '... a hanged man is cursed by God.' (Deuteronomy 21:23) Luke, writing primarily for a Gentile audience who might be less familiar with the Old Testament, may well have felt that he needed to highlight other gory details of Judas's demise, in order to convey that same sense of Judas dying under a curse.[83]

In connection with *the purchase of the field,* Matthew tells us plainly that it was the chief priests who bought it. Luke says that Judas 'acquired a field with the reward for his wickedness'. He does not say that Judas purchased the field – rather, he is saying that the end-result of Judas's treachery was this field.

It makes best sense to regard this scene as ending at Matthew 27:10, the end of the section of verses concerning Judas. Matthew 27:11 begins the account of Jesus' trial before Pilate and of Pilate's further actions, which we will look at as the next scene. However, Bach has made one single recitative of verses 7-14 of this chapter (Movement 52), which has been included in the text for this scene, as set out above. Comments on verses 7-10 have been included in the discussion of this scene, while comments on verses 11-14 will be held over to the discussion of the following scene.

Application

MOVEMENT 47

- These words come immediately after the statement of Peter's bitter weeping, as he realises that he has denied Jesus three times, just as Jesus had said he would do. The challenge to us is to imagine ourselves as Peter, and by implication to bring to mind the times when we have in effect denied our Lord. So, in our *heart* and not just with our *eyes,* we *weep bitterly* before God and ask for *mercy.*

---

83 In mentioning 'bowels' and 'falling headlong', Luke is possibly suggesting a parallel with the demise of Antiochus IV Epiphanes, a Seleucid king, who reigned from 175 to 164 B.C. He carried out appalling atrocities against the people of Judah and desecrated the Jerusalem temple. The apocryphal book 2 Maccabees (9:5-9) records how he was struck with a disease of the bowels, which resulted in a terrible death from internal putrefaction. Those verses also record that he fell headlong from his chariot.

MOVEMENT 48

- The previous movement was sung by a soloist, while this chorale is sung by the chorus. It is therefore a collective plea for mercy (even though it is couched in the first person singular). We ackowledge our sin (*separated from you*) and we repent (*return again*). We give thanks that God's *grace and mercy* are greater than our sin.
- '... but where sin increased, grace abounded all the more.' (Romans 5:20)

MOVEMENT 51

- Here we imagine ourselves as Judas, expressing his remorse, conscious of his horrendous sin: he asks, *Give me my Jesus back!*
- Judas is compared to *the lost son* (i.e., the prodigal son) of Luke 15. We are reminded that all sinners can say to God, 'Father, I have sinned against heaven and before you. I am no longer worthy to be called your son.' (Luke 15:21)
- If only Judas had asked for forgiveness, instead of letting self-pitying remorse lead him to despair!

MOVEMENT 53

- This chorale follows on after the account of the first part of Jesus' appearance before Pilate. It connects with Jesus' refusal to mount any defence against his accusers. In the light of this, we are encouraged – like Jesus, committing himself to his Father's *most faithful care* – to bring all our concerns to our Sovereign God, who will direct our paths.

What to Listen out for in the Music of Part II Scene 2

Movement 46: Recitative

Listen out for the end of this recitative, when we hear the words following Peter's denials, *And he went out and wept bitterly*. The soloist's vocal line gives an amazingly tortured expression of Peter's sense of shame and dejection.

Movement 47: Aria (Contralto)

Listen out for the violin *obbligato* in this movement, which reflects the mournful tone of the piece.

Listen out for the matching sorrowful mood of the contralto's air, most appropriately expressing Peter's utter dejection following his denials of Jesus. One feature which enhances this effect is the rising diminished seventh arpeggios on the second and third instances of the word 'erbarme' (*have mercy*) – it happens again with two further occurrences of this word. Bach makes use of diminished seventh arpeggios a number of times in the oratorio, but it makes sense to highlight them in connection with this movement.

Movement 51: Aria (Bass)

Listen out for the violin *obbligato* in this movement.

Movement 53: Chorale

See the musical comment on Movements 21 and 72.

SCENE 3: The Trial before Pilate
(PART II of the oratorio)

54. RECITATIVE
(Evangelist) *At the festival, however, the Governor had a custom of releasing a prisoner to the people, whichever they wanted. He had, however, at the time a most unusual prisoner named Barabbas. And as they were gathered together, Pilate said to them:*
(Pilate) *Which one do you want me to release to you? Barabbas or Jesus, of whom it is said, He is the Christ?*
(Evangelist) *For he knew well that they had handed him over out of envy. And while he sat upon the judgment seat, his wife sent to him and her message said:*
(Pilate's Wife) *Have nothing to do with this righteous man; I have suffered much in a dream today on his account!*
(Evangelist) *But the high priests and the elders convinced the people that they should ask for Barabbas and convict Jesus. So when the Governor answered and said to them:*
(Pilate) *Which one between the two do you want me to release to you?*
(Evangelist) *They said:*
(Chorus) *Barabbas!*
(Evangelist) *Pilate said to them:*
(Pilate) *What shall I do then with Jesus, of whom it is said, He is the Christ?*
(Evangelist) *They all said:*
(Chorus) *Let him be crucified!* (Matthew 27:15-22)

55. CHORALE
How strange is this punishment!
The Good Shepherd suffers for the sheep.
The Lord, the Righteous One, atones for the crime
on his servant's behalf.

56. RECITATIVE
(Evangelist) *The Governor said:*
(Pilate) *What evil has he done then?* (Matthew 27:23a)

57. RECITATIVE (Soprano)
He has done good things for all of us;
he gave sight to the blind,

he made the lame to walk,
he told us His Father's word,
he drove out the devil,
he has strengthened the troubled.
He took sinners in and embraced them,
other than that, my Jesus has done nothing!

58. ARIA (Soprano)
Out of love my Saviour wants to die,
he knows nothing of a single sin,
so that the eternal destruction
and the punishment of judgment
would not remain upon my soul.

59. RECITATIVE
(Evangelist) *They screamed even more and said:*
(Chorus) *Let him be crucified!*
(Evangelist) *When Pilate saw, however, that he achieved nothing, rather that a much greater riot occurred, he took water and washed his hands before the people and said:*
(Pilate) *I am innocent of the blood of this righteous man, see to it yourselves!*
(Evangelist) *Then all the people answered and said:*
(Chorus) *Let his blood be on us and on our children.*
(Evangelist) *Then he released Barabbas to them; but Jesus he had scourged and handed him over to be crucified.* (Matthew 27:23b-26)

60. RECITATIVE (Contralto)
Forgive this, God!
Here stands the Saviour bound.
O scourging, o blows, o wounds!
You hangmen, stop!
Doesn't the soul's anguish,
the sight of such horror soften you?
Alas indeed! You have such hearts
that are like the whipping posts themselves
and even much harder.
Have mercy, stop!

61. ARIA (Contralto)
If the tears on my cheeks
can do nothing,
o then take my heart as well!
    Yet let it, for the flow,
    when the wounds gently bleed,
    be the offering-bowl as well.

62. RECITATIVE
(Evangelist) *Then the soldiers of the Governor took Jesus with them into the courthouse and gathered around him the entire troop; and undressed him and put a purple mantle on him; and they wove a crown of thorns and set it upon his head, and a reed in his right hand, and they bowed before him and mocked him, saying:*
(Chorus) *Hail to you, King of the Jews!*
(Evangelist) *And they spat on him and took the reed and struck his head with it.* (Matthew 27:27-30)

63. CHORALE
O Head, full of blood and wounds,
full of suffering and shame!
O Head, bound in mockery
with a crown of thorns!
O Head, once beautifully adorned
with the highest honour and beauty,
now rather supremely defiled:
be greeted by me!

You,[84] noble countenance,
before which rather should tremble and cower
the great powers of the world,
how spat upon are You,
How ashen You have become!
Who has treated the light of Your eyes,

---

[84] 'You noble countenance' is not a misprint for 'your ...'. The two stanzas are parallel to each other: the first addresses the head of Jesus, while the second addresses the countenance (or face). This, of course, is a poetic way of addressing Jesus himself.

which is like no other light,
so shamefully?

Matthew 27: 11-30

The Jewish leaders had already taken Jesus to Pilate, the Roman governor (verses 1-2). Although they had found Jesus guilty, they were not legally authorised to carry out the death penalty. This lay in the hands of the Roman administration. Pilate would not have been interested in a charge of blasphemy, so we can infer from Pilate's initial question to Jesus ('Are you the King of the Jews?') that they had changed the charge to one of insurrection or sedition. In a sense, Jesus' claim to be the Messiah was – in their eyes – evidence of both blasphemy and sedition. It is ironic that, in order to have Jesus killed, the Jewish leaders had to accuse Jesus of being a political Messiah, which was the very thing that Jesus refused to be. In reply to Jesus' question, Jesus answered with the same words that he had used on two earlier occasions: 'You have said so.'[85] 'King of the Jews' would be the inscription on the cross (verse 37), but Jesus' acceptance of that title was in a different sense from the one that Pilate would have understood. In the more detailed account of the conversation between Jesus and Pilate, recorded by John, Jesus said, 'My kingdom is not of this world.' (John 18: 36)

Pilate is said to have been 'amazed' at Jesus and clearly found no evidence of crime. He evidently took no notice of the 'many things' that the chief priests had testified against Jesus. He was well aware that Jesus had been handed over to him 'out of envy'. Pilate's wife knew what was going on, and used her influence to try and persuade her husband to release Jesus. We do not know whether or not her dream concerning Jesus, as someone who was 'righteous', was a supernatural one like those that Matthew recorded in connection with Jesus' birth and infancy. Pilate in fact made some attempt to have Jesus released. There was a tradition that, at the Passover, the governor would release one prisoner whom the crowd asked for, and he hoped that he might have Jesus released in that way. But the chief priests and elders stirred

[85] Matthew 26:25 and 64.

up the crowd to ask for Barabbas to be released, and to demand that Jesus be crucified. Barabbas was 'a notorious prisoner'. Mark describes him as a murderer (Mark 15: 7); very possibly he was an insurrectionist, guilty of the very crime with which the Jewish leaders had falsely charged Jesus. This makes the guilt of the whole people all the greater, in that they demanded the release of such a man instead of Jesus. It also points implicitly to the key Bible truth of substitution: Jesus was to die the death that sinners should die. It is very appropriate that we might imagine Barabbas possibly saying, 'Jesus died for me. He died in my place. I can live, because Jesus died.'

For a moment, let us develop that last point. Who was responsible for the death of Jesus? Matthew's account lists a number of agents that led to Jesus being crucified. *The chief priests and elders* plotted to have Jesus arrested and unjustly condemned. *Judas* betrayed Jesus to the Jewish authorities. *The whole crowd* demanded Jesus' crucifixion and acknowledged their responsibility in horrific terms. *Pilate* condemned Jesus to death – and more will be said about his guilt in the next paragraph. But there are two other far more significant agents in bringing about the death of Jesus. The first of these is *God himself.* Matthew repeatedly emphasizes that Jesus died in fulfilment of all that Scripture had foretold. 'The LORD has laid on him (the Suffering Servant figure, who is none other than Jesus) the iniquity of us all.' (Isaiah 53:6b) And Jesus, God the Son, actively and willingly accepted that role: 'I said, "Behold, I have come to do your will, O God"' (words of Psalm 40:8, which in Hebrews 10:5-7 are attributed to Christ). The second of the fundamentally significant agents in the death of Jesus is *the whole human race, which includes each one of us, personally and individually.* This too is the consistent Bible message, and the arias, recitatives, choruses and chorales in this oratorio keep reminding us of it. Earlier on, the words of 1 Peter 3:18 have been referred to: 'For Christ also suffered once for sins, the righteous for the unrighteous, that he might bring *us* to God' (my italics).

We return to Pilate. Despite his attempts to have Jesus released, he failed to act as a just leader. He gave up on Jesus and 'delivered him to be crucified.' His guilt is immortalized in the words of the Apostles'

Creed, 'suffered under Pontius Pilate.'[86] His decision to take water, wash his hands before the crowd and declare his innocence, has to be regarded as a cynical action. This was not a Roman custom but rather a contemptuous imitation of a Jewish rite (Deuteronomy 21:6). To this he added the gratuitous cruelty of having Jesus scourged. Matthew does not dwell on the excruciating details of what this entailed, since, in company with the other Gospel writers, he wants to focus on the spiritual suffering that Jesus endured as our Saviour. But we should be aware that scourging, or flogging, was barbaric and brutal. The ends of the strands of the lash had bits of bone on them, which tore the flesh off the back of the victim. As if that was not enough, Jesus was also subjected to beating and spitting by the Roman guard. Matthew mentions the humiliating mockery of being arrayed in a purple cloak and a crown of thorns, with the soldiers kneeling before him – all this as a parody of homage to royalty.

At the end of these comments, we would do well to ponder the truth that Jesus is indeed the King. Far from there being any contradiction between Jesus' humiliation and his royal majesty, the New Testament consistently affirms that his sufferings represent his divinely appointed route to his supreme position of honour and glory throughout the whole universe. One of the clearest instances of this comes in Paul's letter to the Philippians, where the apostle reminds us that God's purpose, as a result of Jesus' death and resurrection, is that 'at the name of Jesus every knee should bow, in heaven and on earth and under the earth, and every tongue confess that Jesus Christ is Lord, to the glory of God the Father.' (Philippians 2:10-11) This 'every' includes Roman soldiers and Pilate and Caiaphas. Not all who will bow the knee to Jesus will do so willingly and gladly – but how great will be the praise and adoration of those who do love and honour the Son!

---

[86] *Common Worship* (London: Church House Publishing, 2000), 141.

Application

MOVEMENT 55

- This item picks up on the theme of penal substitution, suggested by the way Jesus, who is sinless, is condemned to die in the place of Barabbas, who is a guilty sinner. Indeed, *How strange is this punishment!*
- There is an echo here of Isaiah 53:6, part of which was quoted in the comments above. In full the verse reads: 'All we like sheep have gone astray; we have turned – every one – to his own way; and the LORD has laid on him the iniquity of us all.'
- There is an echo too of Jesus' words in John 10:11: 'I am the good shepherd. The good shepherd lays down his life for the sheep.'

MOVEMENT 57

- Pilate has responded to the crowd's demand for Jesus to be crucified with the question, 'Why, what evil has he done?' This aria focuses on the *good things* that Jesus has done for us during his earthly ministry – not least, welcoming sinners.

MOVEMENT 58

- This item focuses movingly on Jesus' loving willingness, despite his sinlessness, to bear the full weight of judgement on himself, so that we might go free.

MOVEMENTS 60 and 61

- These two items reflect on Jesus' scourging and expresses the believer's amazement that Jesus should go through this for us.

MOVEMENT 63

- The choice of this chorale at this point in the oratorio is most appropriate. We have just heard how the soldiers *struck his head* with the reed (to be understood as a solid staff). Now, in this chorale, we focus on the *Head, full of blood and wounds.*
- Readers may be familiar with classical paintings entitled *Ecce Homo* (Latin for 'Behold the man!'), showing Jesus on trial before Pilate and clothed in the purple robe and crown of thorns, as mentioned in Matthew 27:28-29. Pilate's words 'Behold the man!' are taken from John 19:5, when Pilate

mockingly shows Jesus to the crowd after his scourging.[87] This is the way we are to imagine the Lord Jesus in this chorale.

- We are invited to echo these words of praise and adoration. Despite the mockery he received on this occasion, he is the King – and he went through all the Passion for us!

[87] One such painting is to be found in All Souls Church, Langham Place, London, situated prominently behind the communion table in the central position at the eastern end of the church. It is the work of Richard Westall (1765 - 1836) and was probably presented to All Souls Church by King George IV.

WHAT TO LISTEN OUT FOR IN THE MUSIC OF PART II SCENE 3

Movement 54: Recitative

Listen out for the words sung by the full choir: first, a loud cry of *Barabbas!* (demanding that Pilate release this prisoner); and secondly, the repeated demand concerning Jesus, *Let him be crucified!* – each vocal line enters separately, forming a mini-fugue.

Movement 57: Recitative (Soprano)

Listen out for the slow, contemplative mood of this item for the soprano soloist.

Listen out for the two oboes da caccia used in the accompaniment.

Movement 58: Aria (Soprano)

Listen out for the slow tempo of this piece, allowing time to focus on the words. Occasional pauses, for the soloist and for the instrumentalists, reinforce the mood of contemplation.

Listen out for some striking chromatic progressions in the soloist's vocal line.

Listen out for the flute *obbligato,* playing over the two oboes da caccia.

Movement 60: Recitative (Contralto)

Listen out for the dotted rhythm throughout the accompaniment of this movement, suggestive of the scourging.

Movement 61: Aria (Contralto)

Listen out for the ternary structure (A-B-A) of this movement.

Movement 63: Chorale

See the musical comment on Movements 21 and 72.

SCENE 4: The Crucifixion *(PART II of the oratorio)*

64. RECITATIVE
(Evangelist) *And when they had mocked him, they took off the mantle and put his clothes back on; and led Him out to be crucified. And as they were going out, they found a man from Cyrene named Simon; they compelled him to carry his cross for him.* (Matthew 27:31-32)

65. RECITATIVE (Bass)
Yes, willingly are flesh and blood
compelled to the Cross;
the better it is for our souls,
the bitterer it feels.

66. ARIA (Bass)
Come, sweet Cross, this I want to say:
My Jesus, give it always to me!
If my suffering becomes too heavy one day,
you yourself will help me bear it.

67. RECITATIVE
(Evangelist) *And when they had come to the place named Golgotha, which is translated the place of the Skull, they gave him vinegar to drink mixed with gall; and when he tasted it, he would not drink it. When they had crucified him, however, they divided up his clothing and tossed lots over them, so that what was spoken through the Prophets was fulfilled: 'They have divided my clothing among them, and over my robe they have cast lots.' And they sat around and kept watch. And over His head they lifted up a written sentence of death, namely: 'This is Jesus, the King of the Jews'. And there were two murderers crucified with him, one to his left and one to his right. But those who passed by cursed at him and shook their heads, saying:*
(Chorus) *You who destroy the temple of God and build it up again in three days, help yourself! If you are the Son of God, climb down from the Cross!*
(Evangelist) *In the same way the high priests also mocked him, together with the scribes and the elders, saying:*
(Chorus) *He has helped others and he cannot help himself. If he is the King of Israel, let him climb down now from the Cross, and we will believe in him. He has trusted in God to rescue him now; he lied, because he has said: 'I am the Son of God.'*

68. RECITATIVE

(Evangelist) *In the same way He was reviled by the murderers who were crucified with Him.* (Matthew 27:33-44)

69. RECITATIVE (Contralto)

Alas, Golgotha, unhappy Golgotha!
The Lord of glory
must shamefully perish here,
the blessing and salvation of the world
is placed on the Cross as a curse.
From the Creator of heaven and earth
earth and air shall be withdrawn.
The innocent must die here guilty;
this touches my soul deeply;
Alas, Golgotha, unhappy Golgotha!

70. ARIA (Contralto) and CHORUS

Look, Jesus has stretched out his hands
to embrace us,
come! – where? – in Jesus' arms
seek redemption, receive mercy,
seek it! – where? – in Jesus' arms.
Live, die, rest here,
you forsaken chicks,
stay! – where? – in Jesus' arms.

71. RECITATIVE

(Evangelist) *And from the sixth hour there was a darkness over the entire land until the ninth hour. And at the ninth hour Jesus cried out loudly and said:*
(Jesus) *Eli, Eli, lema sabachthani?*
(Evangelist) *That is: 'My God, my God, why have you forsaken me?' Some of those, however, who were standing by, when they heard this, said:*
(Chorus) *He is calling Elijah!*
(Evangelist) *And some of them quickly ran, took a sponge and filled it with vinegar, and put it on a reed for him to drink. But the others said:*
(Chorus) *Stop! Let's see whether Elijah comes and helps him.*
(Evangelist) *But Jesus cried out loudly once again and died.*
(Matthew 27:45-50)

72. CHORALE
**When I must depart one day,
do not part from me then,
when I must suffer death,
come to me then!
When the greatest anxiety
will constrict my heart,
then wrest me out of the horror
by the power of your anguish and pain.**

73. RECITATIVE
(Evangelist) *And behold, the veil of the temple was torn in two pieces from top to bottom. And the earth shook, and the cliffs were rent, and the graves opened up, and many bodies of saints arose, who were sleeping, and came out of their graves after his resurrection and came into the Holy City and appeared to many people. The Captain, however, and those with him who were guarding Jesus, when they saw the earthquake and what happened then, they were terrified and said:*
(Chorus) *Truly, this was the Son of God.* (Matthew 27:51-54)

Matthew 27:31-54

Crucifixion is undoubtedly the cruellest means of execution that has ever been devised by man. It amounted to a slow death by torture. The victim suffered the pain of being nailed to a cross through the ankles and hands, and the accompanying shock and loss of blood that this and the earlier flogging would have caused. Then there was the humiliation of being stripped naked. When the cross was raised up vertically, the victim was forced to lift himself repeatedly in order to breathe. This process came to an end only when the victim no longer had the strength to push up on his legs and died of suffocation. Often a victim might hang on the cross for hours before death. In the case of the two robbers crucified with Jesus, their legs were broken by the soldiers so as to ensure their deaths before the sabbath (John 19:31-32). In Roman law, crucifixion was reserved for criminals and lower classes – no Roman citizen was crucified, except on the rarest of occasions. Among Jews, the horror of the cross was even greater because, according to Deuteronomy 21.23, 'a hanged man is cursed by God.' This was noted earlier in connection with Judas. Because this verse (together with the preceding verse) refers to being hanged on a tree, the curse was reckoned to apply to anyone crucified. Paul refers to this Old Testament verse when he spells out the significance of Jesus' death on the cross: 'Christ redeemed us from the curse of the law by becoming a curse for us – for it is written, "Cursed is everyone who is hanged on a tree"' (Galatians 3:13).

The awful physical details of crucifixion are hardly referred to by any of the Gospel writers. While the first readers would have been familiar with the process, the major concern in each Gospel in recording the crucifixion was – as also in the earlier reference to Jesus being scourged – the spiritual, rather than the physical, ordeal.

This section of the Passion narrative, involving Jesus' final hours leading up to his death, cannot fail to convey a sense of awe and wonder. We have to recognise our own inability to comprehend the full meaning of the cross. Ambrose, who was one of the greatest preachers in the history of the church and lived some 1600 years ago, preached in the cathedral of Milan one Good Friday.[88] He said: 'I find it impossible to speak to you today. The events of Good Friday are too great for human words. Why should I speak while my Saviour is silent and dies?'[89]

The significance of Simon of Cyrene being compelled to carry Jesus' cross is that it shows that Jesus was already weakened and exhausted from his earlier ordeal.

Jesus was offered wine to drink, mixed with gall. Presumably it was the soldiers who did this. Almost certainly this was not a gesture of compassion but of torment. Mark describes the substance added to the wine as 'myrrh' (Mark 15:23), which tastes bitter. So, a large quantity of myrrh mixed with the wine would make it undrinkable. It is probable that Matthew uses the word 'gall' in order to describe the taste and to link this action with Psalm 69:21: '... for my thirst they gave me sour

---

[88] Ambrose, bishop of Milan (c.340 – 397)

[89] Quoted in J.M. Drescher, *Testimony of Triumph* (Grand Rapids: Zondervan, 1980), 7.

wine to drink.' Jesus was thirsty but refused to drink the wine when he tasted its bitterness.

The soldiers' division of Jesus' clothes between them by casting lots was a fulfilment of Psalm 22:18. Matthew would expect his readers to be aware of the Old Testament link without it being made explicit.

The tablet with the statement of Jesus' 'crime', attached to the cross, was referred to in an earlier comment. John tells us that it was written in Hebrew, Greek and Latin. Although the wording was intended to be cruel mockery, the irony is that it declared the truth, and did so in the three major languages of the known world. Jesus is indeed King, not just of the Jews but of all nations.

Two sets of insults were hurled at Jesus. The first group came from passers-by. They taunted Jesus concerning his alleged claim to rebuild the temple. This charge was brought against him at his trial before Caiaphas, but – as was noted earlier – Jesus' words, rightly understood, pointed to his resurrection to come. The second part of this taunt ('If you are the Son of God ...') is another echo, not only of Jesus' trial, but also of the devil's words, 'If you are the Son of God ...,' when he had tempted Jesus to side-step the way of the cross, and instead choose easier ways of exercising his role as Messiah (Matthew 4:3, 5).

The second group of insults came from the chief priests, scribes and elders. They accused Jesus of being able to save others but unable to save himself. The word 'save' can mean both 'heal' and 'redeem'. They used the word in the first sense. But the truth was that the only way he could truly 'save' (and 'redeem') his people was by *not* saving himself, and instead dying a sacrificial death and bearing God's wrath in man's place. The religious leaders mocked him, telling him to come down from the cross, so that they might believe in him. They fulfilled Scripture by using virtually the same words as appear in Psalm 22:8: 'He trusts in the LORD; let him deliver him. Let him rescue him, for he delights in him.' But the supreme sign that men and women needed to see, in order to believe, was not Jesus coming off the cross 'now', but Jesus staying on it to die. Atonement for sinful men and women has only been made possible because Jesus did not come down from the cross. General William Booth, the founder of the Salvation Army, is reported to have said, 'If Jesus had come down they might have believed on him for a while. But the centuries have believed in him because he stayed up.'[90] The religious leaders thought that Jesus was too weak to save himself, but in reality his divine power was demonstrated by his refusal to save himself.

The two robbers, crucified with Jesus, also joined in with the insults. Matthew does not include what Luke tells us about one of these two men, who turned to Jesus, acknowledging the rightness of his own condemnation but recognizing Jesus as sinless and as King; he asked Jesus to remember him when he (Jesus) came into his kingdom. Jesus assured that man that he would be with Jesus that very day in Paradise (Luke 23:39-43).

The verses concerning the death of Jesus represent the high point of Matthew's Gospel. In verses 45 and 46, the focus is on God the Father forsaking his Son. First, there was the supernatural darkness from midday until 3.00 p.m. We might describe it as a visual aid from God. In the Old Testament, darkness in the day-time symbolized God's wrath. The supreme instance of this was the ninth of the ten plagues in Exodus 10. It preceded the final plague, which consisted of God passing in judgement over the whole land of Egypt and taking the life of the firstborn in every home, except where he saw the blood of the Passover lamb on the doorposts and lintels. So, what we have here in the Gospel account is the fulfilment of the ninth and tenth plagues, as God covered 'all the land' with darkness and carried out his judgement on his own 'firstborn'.

Secondly, following the darkness (and explaining it), there is Jesus' loud cry, which was so memorable that Jesus' Aramaic words are recorded: 'Eli, Eli, lema sabachthani?' Matthew explains that those words mean, 'My God, my God, why have you forsaken me?'. We sometimes call this Jesus' cry of dereliction (or desolation). Jesus was quoting from Psalm 22:1, and that explains why Jesus' cry is a question: Psalm 22:1 is itself a question. But it was a real cry from the very depth

---

90 Quoted in Drescher, *Testimony of Triumph*, 90.

of his being, not a mere intellectual quotation of a verse of Scripture. Jesus was clearly meditating on this psalm as he hung on the cross, and Psalm 22:1 expressed exactly what he experienced.[91] It would be wrong to suggest that Jesus only *felt* forsaken but was not forsaken, because his Father was with him all the time. The point is that Jesus *was* forsaken by his Father. That is what the three hours of darkness signified: God the Father was turning the light of his face away from his own beloved Son. Here was the reality of the prospect that Jesus contemplated when he wrestled in prayer in the garden of Gethsemane. Jesus was taking upon himself the full weight of the sin of the world and he was receiving in his own person the full, undiluted penalty and wrath of the judgement of God that our sin deserves. If hell can be defined as 'where God is not', Jesus was experiencing hell during those three hours of darkness, so that we might *not* have to experience hell – Jesus was being punished in *our* place. Sin is so serious that there was no other way for men and women to be saved. The cross is both the demonstration of God's wrath and of God's mercy.

Some bystanders misunderstood Jesus' words and thought he was calling for Elijah. There was an old Jewish tradition that Elijah would come to the rescue of those in distress. Wine was again offered to Jesus, but it is not clear if this was further mockery, together with a desire to prolong his life and agony, or whether the act this time was one of compassion. Matthew almost certainly intends his readers to think again of the mention of wine in Psalm 69:21.

Jesus' loud cry in verse 50 may be his words, 'It is finished' (John 19:20), but we are certainly shown Jesus' sovereignty over the exact moment of his death. Jesus had said on an earlier occasion, 'No one takes it (i.e., his life) from me, but I lay it down of my own accord' (John 10:18), and that promise is fulfilled in the words 'Jesus ... yielded up his spirit.'

---

[91] It will be noted that Psalm 22 is referred to a number of times in this section. We might describe this psalm as a psalm of the cross, since many of its details anticipate the circumstances of Jesus' crucifixion.

At this point in the narrative, Matthew chooses immediately to take his focus off the hill of Calvary and redirect it onto what was happening inside the Jerusalem temple: 'the curtain of the temple was torn in two, from top to bottom.' We are being shown exactly what the death of Jesus has achieved. The curtain referred to here hung between the Holy Place and the Holy of Holies. It was a thick curtain, about three inches thick, rather like a luxury carpet, and it hung all the way down from ceiling to floor for something like thirty feet. The curtain served as a massive 'No entry' sign. It spoke of the huge divide between the holiness of God and the sinfulness of men and women. No one was allowed to enter the Holy of Holies except the High Priest, and he could do so only once a year on the Day of Atonement, taking with him sacrificial blood to be sprinkled on the ark of the covenant. But when the curtain was torn miraculously at the moment of Jesus' death ('from top to bottom' indicates that it was a divine action), God was in effect saying, 'Come in!' He was announcing that the way was open for men and women to enter into his presence, because the price for sin had been paid by what Jesus did on the cross.

We sometimes use the phrase, 'the finished work of Christ', which helpfully summarises what was achieved by Jesus' death on the cross. It was this phrase which led to the conversion of Hudson Taylor, the pioneer missionary to China, in 1849, when he was 17. Years later he wrote about what had happened, when he came across a tract which used the phrase, 'the finished work of Christ'.

> "Why does the author use this expression?" I questioned. "Why not say the atoning or propitiatory work of Christ?" Immediately the words "It is finished" suggested themselves to my mind. "What was finished?" And I at once replied, "A full and perfect atonement and satisfaction for sin. The debt was paid for our sins, and not for ours only, but also for the sins of the whole world." Then came the further thought, "If the whole work was finished and the whole debt paid, what is there left for me to do?" And with this dawned the joyful

> conviction, as light flashed into my soul by the Holy Spirit, that there was nothing in the world to be done but to fall down on one's knees and, accepting this Saviour and His salvation, praise Him for evermore.[92]

Matthew has more to say about what happened following on from Jesus' death. He records an earthquake and rocks being split. The description is dramatic. This key moment in salvation history is being marked by an earthquake, a symbol, in the Bible, of God's judgement and revelation.[93]

Then Matthew records the resurrection of 'saints' (or holy people) who entered Jerusalem and appeared to many.[94] Matthew is the only Gospel writer to include this. It makes best sense to understand this event as happening after Jesus' own resurrection, as Matthew describes, and not immediately after Jesus' death. In other words, we should understand that there is a full stop after the words, *opened up,* so that the next phrase, *and many bodies of saints arose ...,* begins a new sentence – which is how the ESV understands it. The phrase, *after his resurrection,* goes not only with their entry into the city and their appearances but also with *their* being raised. After all, it would be strange if these Old Testament believers were to experience resurrection immediately after Jesus died, while Jesus himself had to wait until the Sunday for his own resurrection, which Paul calls 'the firstfruits of those who have fallen asleep.' (1 Corinthians 15:20)

It may be asked why, then, does Matthew mention the resurrection of the 'saints' at this point? There are probably two reasons. One is that, if he were to record their resurrection in chapter 28, which would place it in its chronologically correct position (after Jesus' own resurrection),

---

[92] Dr and Mrs Hudson Taylor, *Biography of James Hudson Taylor* (London: Hodder and Stoughton, 1965), 17.

[93] Notable earthquakes in the Old Testament include Exodus 19:18, 1 Kings 19:11 and Isaiah 29:6.

[94] There will be a comment on the expression 'who had fallen asleep' (Matthew 27:52) in the discussion on 1 Corinthians 15:51-52 in the third part of this study on Brahms' *Requiem.*

it could intrude on the emphases that Matthew had in mind for the closing section of his Gospel. What Matthew wanted to focus on there was three things: Jesus' own resurrection; the soldiers being bribed to tell a false story concerning Jesus' resurrection, and the Great Commission.

The other reason is that it can be argued that Matthew's decision to record those resurrections here in chapter 27 makes good sense. The death and resurrection of Jesus belong closely together. Jesus' death marks the climax and completion of his work of salvation. When Jesus died, he dealt decisively with sin. The tearing down of the curtain is evidence that there is now open access to God. The writer to the Hebrews tells us that Jesus' purpose was that 'through death he might destroy the one who has the power of death, that is, the devil, and deliver all those who through fear of death were subject to lifelong slavery.' (Hebrews 2:14-15) While the message of Good Friday might have appeared to be "Jesus defeated" (in the sense that Jesus was defeated), Matthew wants his readers to understand that the true message of the cross is 'Jesus defeated sin and death and hell.' The clear light of Easter Day enables us to understand that Good Friday was a day of victory for the Lord Jesus and all those who belong to him. That is what Matthew is telling us in verses 52b-53 of chapter 27: his reference to those resurrected 'saints' flags up for us that a new age has dawned at the moment of Jesus' death, even though their rising again would not in fact happen until a little later.

Matthew brings the focus of his narrative back to the cross, as he records the reaction of the centurion and his squad of soldiers in charge of the crucifixions. We are told that they had been keeping watch over Jesus and had been witnesses of the earthquake and everything else that had taken place. Matthew writes, 'They were filled with awe and said, "Truly this was the Son of God!"' Evidently we are meant to understand that some degree of understanding had reached the minds of these Roman soldiers. With their pagan background, their grasp of spiritual reality would have been limited, and they would probably have known little about the God of the Jews. But, having served in Palestine for a while at least, they must have been aware of Jesus' story and why he was condemned to death. They must have known that 'Son of God' was a messianic title. It is ironic, therefore, that at Jesus' death the first people to articulate a statement of Jesus' true identity were Gentiles. How appropriate this is, in view of the Great Commission coming soon in this Gospel – the commission to go and make disciples 'of all nations' (Matthew 28:19).

Application

MOVEMENTS 65 and 66

- These two items reflect on Simon of Cyrene being compelled to carry Jesus' cross. The mental image of this incident, as in Movement 29, points to Jesus' own words: 'If anyone would come after me, let him deny himself and take up his cross and follow me.' (Matthew 16:24)
- We must avoid the popular tendency to trivialize the idea of carrying our cross. Rightly understood, taking up our cross may mean persecution and any kind of physical, mental or emotional suffering which we endure because we follow Christ.
- We are encouraged willingly to take up our cross and follow Jesus.

MOVEMENT 69

- We reflect on Jesus being crucified for us. He endured the *curse* of God for us (Galatians 3:13), so that we might receive the *blessing and salvation.*

MOVEMENT 70

- Some readers may well feel that to interpret the outstretched hands of Jesus on the cross as his willingness to embrace is somewhat sentimental, when the reality is that Jesus' outstretched arms and hands were forced on him as part of the cruel torture he suffered.
- While this criticism makes a valid point, we should look beyond the imperfections of the poetic expression to the underlying reality: the wonderful truth of Jesus' love and compassion displayed on the cross.

- The reference to *forsaken chicks* is an echo of Jesus' words of lament over Jerusalem:

  > 'O Jerusalem, Jerusalem, the city that kills the prophets and stones those who are sent to it! How often would I have gathered your children together as a hen gathers her brood under her wings, and you were not willing! See, your house is left to you desolate. For I tell you, you will not see me again, until you say, "Blessed is he who comes in the name of the Lord."' (Matthew 23:37-39)

MOVEMENT 72

- This chorale is placed just after the account of Jesus' cry of dereliction.
- We can look ahead to our own death with confidence: because Jesus was forsaken for us on the cross in his once-for-all sacrifice of himself, we will never be forsaken.

What to Listen out for in the Music of Part II Scene 4

Movement 66: Aria (Bass)

Listen out for the viola da gamba (or cello) *obbligato* accompanying the bass soloist.

Movement 67: Recitative

Listen out for the two parts sung by the full choir, representing first the crowd of onlookers, and then the religious leaders, hurling their insults at Jesus. In the first part, there are eight vocal lines, creating a large crowd-effect. The second part begins as eight vocal lines but reduces to four, finishing with an emphasis on Jesus' claim to be the Son of God.

Movement 69: Recitative (Contralto)

Listen out for the chromatic leaps and progressions, which create a mood of mournfulness. This is enhanced by the accompaniment from the oboes da caccia.

Movement 70 Aria (Contralto)

Listen out for the combination again of the contralto soloist and the oboes da caccia. The movement is punctuated by occasional questions from the choir.

Movement 71 (Recitative)

Listen out for the absence of the 'halo' effect (from sustained strings) at the moment of Jesus' cry of dereliction. Clearly, this is intended to accentuate this moment of forsakenness.

Movement 72 (Chorale)

Listen out for this fifth and final use of the chorale tune, which has previously appeared in Movements 21, 23, 53 and 63. As indicated in the comment on Movement 21, Bach has deliberately arranged the sequence with a change of key each time. He has gradually 'emptied' the key signature of each subsequent setting in terms of the key signature's number of sharps or flats. So, the sequence of the five occurrences of this chorale tune is: E major (5 sharps), E flat major (4 flats), D major (2 sharps), D minor (1 flat), A minor (no sharps or flats). This sequence is clearly deliberately planned by Bach. While the details of this progression will not be immediately apparent to listeners, it will be obvious that the chorale tune (very well known to earlier audiences, even more so than today) is being repeated, and that there are subtle differences each time. The change of key is not the only difference within the sequence. While the first two occurrences of the chorale do have the same harmonization (albeit in different keys), the third occurrence introduces differences in the harmonization of the third and fourth lines. The fourth occurrence has another different harmonization. The fifth occurrence – the one here in Movement 72 – is different yet again and makes use of an unusually chromatic setting. This is particularly appropriate at the high point of intensity at the death of Jesus.

Movement 73: Recitative

Listen out for the dramatic runs in the lower strings, accompanying the words in the first part of this recitative about the curtain in the temple being torn in two, the earthquake and the holy people rising from the dead.

Listen out for the lovely short chorus with the words of the centurion and the other Roman soldiers, '*Truly, this was the Son of God*'.

SCENE 5: The Burial *(PART II of the oratorio)*

73 (cont.)
(Evangelist)
And there were many women there, watching from a distance, who had followed him from Galilee and had served him, among whom were Mary Magdalene, and Mary the mother of James and Joseph, and the mother of the sons of Zebedee. In the evening, however, came a rich man from Arimathea, named Joseph, who was also a disciple of Jesus; he went to Pilate and asked him for Jesus' body. Then Pilate ordered that it be given to him.
(Matthew 27:55-58)

74. RECITATIVE (Bass)
In the evening, when it was cool,
Adam's fall was made apparent;
in the evening the Saviour bowed himself down.
In the evening the dove came back,
bearing an olive leaf in its mouth.
O lovely time! O evening hour!
The pact of peace with God has now been made,
since Jesus has completed his Cross.
His body comes to rest,
Ah! dear soul, ask,
go, have them give you the dead Jesus,
O sacred, O precious remembrance!

75. ARIA (Bass)
Make yourself pure, my heart,
I want to bury Jesus myself.
For from now on he shall have in me,
forever and ever,
his sweet rest.
World, get out, let Jesus in!

76. RECITATIVE
(Evangelist) *And Joseph took the body, and wrapped it in a pure shroud, and laid it in his own new tomb, which he had carved out of a single rock, and rolled a large stone before the opening of the tomb and went away. But Mary Magdalene and the other Mary were there, and they sat opposite the*

tomb. On the next day, that followed after the Sabbath day, the high priests and Pharisees came all together to Pilate and said:
(Chorus) *'Lord, we have remembered that this deceiver said, when he was still alive: "I will rise again after three days." Therefore, order that the tomb be guarded until the third day, so that his disciples do not come and steal him, and say to the people, "He has arisen from the dead," and the newest fraud would be worse than the first one!'*
(Evangelist) *Pilate said to them:*
(Pilate) *'You have guards there; go and guard it as you see fit!'*
(Evangelist) *They went forth and protected the tomb with guards and put a seal on the stone.* (Matthew 27:59-66)

77. RECITATIVE (Bass, Tenor, Contralto and Soprano) and CHORUS
Now the Lord is brought to rest.
    – My Jesus, good night!
The weariness is over, that our sins have given him.
    – My Jesus, good night!
O blessed bones,
see, how I weep over you with repentance and regret,
since my fall has brought such anguish upon you!
    – My Jesus, good night!
Lifelong, thousand thanks to you for your suffering,
since you held my soul's salvation so dear.
    – My Jesus, good night!

78. CHORUS
We sit down with tears
and call to you in the grave:
rest gently, gently rest!
    Rest, you exhausted limbs!
    – Rest gently, rest well.
    Your grave and headstone
    shall, for the anxious conscience,
    be a comfortable pillow
    and the resting place for the soul.
    – Rest gently, gently rest!
    Highly contented,
    there the eyes fall asleep.

Matthew 27:55-66

Matthew wants his readers to know that Jesus was truly dead. While he does not record, as Mark does, that Pilate checked out the report that Jesus had died (Mark 15:44), the fact that Pilate was willing to release the body for burial indicates his certainty on this point. Also, Matthew wants his readers to know that Jesus was given a proper burial, unusual as this was for someone who had been condemned to death as a criminal.

Matthew mentions the women who witnessed Jesus' crucifixion and his death, standing at a distance. They were from Galilee and had provided for the material needs of Jesus and his disciples. The three who are specifically mentioned by name are Mary Magdalene, Mary, the mother of James and Joseph, and the mother of the sons of Zebedee (i.e., James and John). Mary Magdalene is best known from John's Gospel as the first witness of Jesus' resurrection (John 20:15-16). It is very possible that the second Mary is Jesus' own mother, since Matthew 13:55 lists Jesus' half-brothers as *James, Joseph,* Simon and Judas (my italics). Two of the women were witnesses to the burial (verse 61).

There was some urgency to have Jesus buried, because it had to be done before the sabbath began, which would be reckoned as sunset on the Friday. Joseph of Arimathea undertook to have Jesus buried in his tomb, which was very near, hewn out of the rock. We are told that Joseph was a rich man, probably as a deliberate echo of Isaiah 53:9: "And they made his grave with the wicked and with a rich man in his death." Jesus had fulfilled the first part of that by being crucified alongside two robbers, and now he was fulfilling the second part by being buried in a rich man's tomb. It is Mark who tells us that Joseph was a member of the Sanhedrin (Mark 15:43), but Matthew informs us that he was a disciple of Jesus. It was a courageous act by Joseph to nail his colours to the mast in this way. He would have needed help to have the body of Jesus taken to his tomb. We know that Nicodemus, another member of the Sanhedrin, stepped forward to assist Joseph (John 19:39-40), and no doubt they had servants to help too. We are told about the large stone that was rolled across the entrance of the tomb. No mourning was allowed for those who had been executed, so the burial would have taken place quietly as well as quickly.

Matthew records the concern of the chief priests and the Pharisees in connection with Jesus' claim to rise from the dead after three days. No doubt, Judas had informed them of Jesus' earlier words to the disciples (e.g., Matthew 16:21). 'Three days' is to be understood as an example of inclusive counting (i.e., Friday to Sunday). Their concern was not that Jesus might really come to life again on the Sunday, but that the disciples might try to steal the body from the tomb and make it look as if Jesus had risen from the dead. We know, of course, that the disciples did not believe Jesus' words about rising again and were now totally despondent in the wake of Jesus' death.

So, they came to Pilate the next day, even though it was the sabbath, and asked for the tomb to be made secure. ESV translates Pilate's reply as 'You have a guard of soldiers' and a footnote points out that this could equally well be a command: 'Take a guard.' The former might be regarded as the more likely. It would be typical of Pilate to respond with cynicism. The Jewish leaders had wanted Jesus to be killed, and he wanted to have nothing more to do with it. Now that Jesus was dead, they must take responsibility for any further action. This would explain why, when the tomb was discovered to be empty on the Sunday, the guard reported to the chief priests and not to Pilate (Matthew 28:11). But Pilate did also authorize the sealing of the tomb.

The sequel to this incident is reported in the next chapter. After the tomb was found to be empty on the Sunday, the Jewish leaders bribed the soldiers to spread the false story of the disciples coming by night and stealing the body (Matthew 28:11-15). Matthew tells us that this cover-story was still in circulation at the time when he wrote this Gospel. This is very likely to have been the reason that Matthew, who was writing primarily for a Jewish readership, wanted to expose the lie and explain the truth.

The *St Matthew Passion* ends on a cliff-hanger. We might almost call it an anti-climax. We finish the narrative with the religious hierarchy's request for proper security on the tomb of Jesus. We are left waiting for the account of the resurrection, the glorious confirmation that Jesus had won the victory of the cross (Matthew 28:1-10), and for the important closing verses of the Gospel. In the last few lines of this Gospel, Jesus assures his disciples of his authority over the whole universe, sends them out to evangelise and teach people of all nations, and promises his continuing presence with them to the end of the age (Matthew 28:16-20). We may well wish that this oratorio ended with a chorus of triumphant praise in the style of the Hallelujah Chorus from Handel's *Messiah.* The fact is, of course, that all *Passions,* whether those written by Bach or by other composers, were designed for use on Good Friday, and not for general use throughout the year. The first audiences of worshippers in Leipzig would have looked forward to Easter Day to enter into joyful celebration of Christ's resurrection. We, who listen to Bach's *St Matthew Passion* today, must ensure that we move on in our minds and hearts from the focus on Jesus' death to the focus on Jesus' resurrection. However, we need most certainly to grasp the truth that our Christian rejoicing can only be based on the fact of Jesus' Finished Work on the cross. In the words of the apostle Paul, we need to be able to say, 'But far be it from me to boast except in the cross of our Lord Jesus Christ" (Galatians 6:14). It is only via the sufferings and death that Jesus endured on the first Good Friday that we can enter into the joy and celebration of Easter.

Application

MOVEMENT 74

- This item reflects on three biblical evenings. We take them in chronological order:
    - The first is the evening of the fateful day of the Fall in Genesis 3, when Adam and Eve had disobeyed God and sin had entered the world that God had created to be perfect. It was 'in the cool of the day' – i.e., the evening – when Adam and Eve hid from God (Genesis 3:8).
    - The second is the return of the dove in the evening to Noah in the ark, carrying in its mouth an olive leaf as a sign that, following the flood of judgement, there was hope of a new beginning (Genesis 8:11).

- The third is the evening of Good Friday, when Jesus had died and had finished the work of atonement. *The pact of peace with God has now been made, since Jesus has completed his Cross.*

MOVEMENT 75

- We place ourselves in the role of Joseph of Arimathea, and pray that our devotion too may be such, that we would be willing to do whatever is required for Jesus in his service.

MOVEMENTS 77 and 78

- These two items are sung as the conclusion to the whole oratorio. They therefore reflect on all that Christ has endured and achieved by his suffering.
- He has taken *our sins,* and we respond *with repentance and regret* and with *lifelong, thousand thanks.*
- He has achieved *my soul's salvation.*
- Tears are appropriate as we focus on the cross of Jesus, at the same time as we give thanks for all that Jesus has done.
- Our hearts express our penitence and a deepening understanding of what our salvation cost Jesus.
- The chorus focuses on Jesus' *rest* after his suffering. We know that the 'rest' of *the grave* would be only a temporary experience for Jesus, since he had already conquered sin and death.
- We can legitimately view this *rest* in a number of ways:
    - We should see a parallel between the 'rest' that God enjoyed on the seventh day after the completion of his work of creation (Genesis 2:1-3) and the 'rest' into which Jesus entered when he finished his work of salvation.
    - We should equate Jesus' 'rest' with his sitting down in heaven, as a sign of the work being completed. 'After making purification for sins, he sat down at the right hand of the Majesty on high' (Hebrews 1:3).
    - The Letter to the Hebrews uses the word 'rest', or the expression 'God's rest', to mean heaven, to which all Christian believers look forward. This theme will be developed further in the third part of this study, on Brahms' *Requiem.*

What to Listen out for in the Music of Part II Scene 5

Movement 74: Recitative (Bass)

Listen out for this quiet, slow, meditative piece, reflecting on three important biblical evenings.

Movement 75: Aria (Bass)

Listen out for the gentle beauty of this piece for the bass soloist. It is striking how simple, and at the same time how effective, is the soloist's opening phrase, twice repeated. It consists of three notes descending the scale, followed by five notes ascending.

Listen out for the ternary structure of the movement (A-B-A).

Listen out for the oboes da caccia in this piece.

Movement 77: Recitative (Bass, Tenor, Contralto and Soprano) and Chorus

Listen out for the simplicity of this quiet movement. Four soloists (bass, tenor, contralto and soprano) each sing a line or two, with the chorus singing their line after each. While the chorus sing the same words each time, each arrangement is different from the others – but there is a subtle similarity in each of the four: each time one of the vocal lines begins one beat before the others.

Movement 78: Chorus

Listen out for this magnificent final chorus, which rounds off the whole oratorio. It is set for both choirs. There is a large amount of antiphonal use of the two choirs, particularly on the phrases 'Sanfte ruh, ruhe sanfte' (*Rest gently, gently rest*) and 'Ruhet sanfte, ruhet wohl' (*Rest gently, rest well*), sung by the second choir in gaps between the first choir's phrases or while the first choir are holding a unison note for a couple of bars.

Listen out for the ternary shape of the chorus – another example of the A-B-A structure.

Listen out for the repeat of the lines *We sit down with tears and call to you in the grave* in each of the 'A'. sections. While the shape of the phrases is very similar each time, the second occurrence of the lines each time is in fact set at a different pitch with changes in the harmonization.

Listen out for the quiet ending of the central "" section on the words *there the eyes fall asleep.* Bach has indicated a *piano* (soft), then a *piu piano* (softer), and then a *pianissimo* (very soft). But there is an affirmative *forte* (loud) ending to the movement.

Part 3: Everlasting Rest

Brahms' *Requiem*

Introduction

Introducing Johannes Brahms

Johannes Brahms was born in Hamburg, Germany, in 1833. His father was a double-bass player, proficient also on several other instruments, who worked his way up from playing in local taverns to being a member of the Hamburg Philharmonic Orchestra. He gave the young Johannes an excellent musical training and arranged for him to study the piano with a good local teacher. Brahms also began composing at an early age. At the age of 20, he came to the notice of the violinist and composer Joseph Joachim and the composer and pianist Franz Liszt, both of whom helped Brahms in his musical progress.

That same year, 1853, after Joachim gave Brahms a letter of introduction to Robert Schumann, the composer, Brahms travelled to Düsseldorf and was welcomed into the Schumann family. Schumann was amazed by the young man's talent, as both a composer and a virtuoso pianist, and wrote in highly favourable terms about him in his musical journal 'Neue Zeitschrift für Musik' ('New magazine for Music'). Following Robert Schumann's attempted suicide and his subsequent confinement in a mental sanatorium, Brahms provided great support, both as a help to Schumann's wife Clara and their eight children and as a visitor to Robert, whom Clara was unable to visit until two days before his death in 1856. Brahms and Clara, who was 14 years older than him, maintained a close but unusual lifelong friendship. They had great affection but also there was respect for one another. For a time, Brahms had a position in Detmold, in the Principality of Lippe, as court music-teacher and conductor. He finally settled in Vienna in 1862 and spent the rest of his life there until his death in 1897.

Brahms is normally described as a German Romantic composer, who worked in the German classical forms. In other words, he was both a traditionalist and an innovator in his style of composition. Brahms' compositions include four symphonies, two piano concertos, a violin concerto and a double concerto for violin and cello – and much else besides. For example, he also produced much excellent chamber music and piano music, many songs and choral music. The *Requiem,* first performed in its entirety in 1869, established his reputation throughout Europe. As a result, his financial situation greatly improved, but despite his wealth he lived simply and is known to have been generous to friends and to musical students. His popularity and influence as a composer were considerable and he continues to be regarded as one of the greatest composers in history.

He was a perfectionist and is known to have destroyed some of his works and to have left others unfinished. He did not produce his first official symphony until 1876, when he was in his early 40s. One factor in this was the pressure of high expectation put on him by Schumann's early announcement of Brahms' capability. Also, for a long time he felt overawed by Beethoven, whom he greatly admired, and was fearful of being compared unfavourably with that great master.

Introducing Brahms' *Requiem*

What is a Requiem? – and how did Brahms approach it?

The full title of the work is 'A German Requiem, to words of the Holy Scriptures' and it is listed as Op. 45.[95] It will be helpful to explain what is normally understood by the word 'Requiem'; readers who are already familiar with the concept of a 'Requiem' may well have their misgivings about it. As we shall see, Brahms' *Requiem* differs from most other Requiems in two important respects.

The Requiem Mass has long been associated with the liturgy of the Roman Catholic Church – the fuller term used is 'Mass for the Dead' ('Missa pro Defunctis' in Latin); it is usually set in the context of a funeral. Musical settings are known as 'Requiems', the word 'Requiem' being the first word of the introit for the liturgy: 'Requiem aeternam dona eis, Domine' ('Give them eternal rest, O Lord').[96] So, the liturgical form focuses on praying for those who have died, that they may have rest and be spared the torments of judgement to come. A major part of the liturgy is the 'Dies Irae' ('Day of Anger' – i.e., the Day of Judgement).

No passage in the Old or New Testaments gives any basis for the practice of praying for the dead. The Bible tells us that the Christian who dies goes to be 'with Christ' (Philippians 1:23 – and implied also in 2 Corinthians 5:8), and on the cross Jesus assured the penitent criminal crucified with him that he would be with Christ in Paradise 'today' (Luke 23:43). The time to decide for or against Christ is in this life only: 'it is appointed for man to die once, and after that comes

[95] The title in German is 'Ein deutsches Requiem, nach Worten der heiligen Schrift'.

[96] 'Requiem' is the accusative case of the Latin word 'requies' (= 'rest'). The wording of the introit derives from the Latin translation of two verses in the Apocrypha: 2 Esdras 2:34-35. In the context of that chapter, those words are not used as a prayer for the dead (whereas that is what they do become in the Roman Catholic liturgy). Rather, they are a promise of what will happen for the nations who hear and understand the Lord's commandment.

judgement' (Hebrews 9:27).[97] The assurance of the Christian gospel is that whoever trusts in Christ 'does not come into judgement, but has passed from death to life.' (John 5:24) If those two Bible verses appear to be contradicting each other on the subject of coming into judgement, the point is that Christian believers can know *now*, concerning the final judgement, that the verdict *then* will be 'not guilty – forgiven'. Therefore, prayers for the dead are, at best, irrelevant and unnecessary. In the history of the Christian church, the apostolic fathers do not mention prayers for the dead. The custom seems to have arisen in the church at the end of the second century. But in the Protestant tradition, following the Bible's guidelines, prayers for the dead have no rightful place.

A good number of musical composers have produced their versions of the Requiem Mass. Opinions may vary concerning the appropriateness of such works, but it would seem to be perfectly proper to take delight in the music of all of them, and to do so with thankfulness to God, 'who richly provides us with everything to enjoy' (1 Timothy 6:17), while at the same time keeping clear in our minds that some of the words of the Requiem do not have a biblical foundation. Readers may be familiar with Requiems from the 18th and 19th centuries, for example those of Mozart (1791), Berlioz (1837), Bruckner (1849), Verdi (1874), Saint-Saëns (1878), Dvorak (1890) and Fauré (1887-90) – or, from the 20th century, Requiems by Britten (his 'War Requiem', 1961-62), Lloyd Webber (1985) and Rutter (1985), and, from this century, one by Jenkins (2005).

As indicated above, Brahms departs from the traditional pattern of the Requiem Mass in two ways. First, the words of his oratorio are in German, not Latin, which is why the proper title of the work is 'A German Requiem'. Secondly, Brahms does not use the words of the Roman Catholic liturgy at all. Instead, he has made use of his own selection of Bible verses. He also incorporates two verses from the Apocrypha, and that will be discussed a little later. No part of the

---

97 Furthermore, the Bible is clear that not deciding for Christ in this life is the same as deciding against him: 'Whoever is not with me is against me' (Matthew 12:30).

content of the *Requiem* conforms in any way to the normal pattern of a Requiem. Instead of being a liturgy for the dead, it is a liturgy for the living. Bible verses are chosen and arranged to direct listeners from present sorrow to eternal certainties of joy to come. More will be said below about this central theme of the oratorio. We today accept this *Requiem* as it is, almost certainly without thinking too much about Brahms' radical approach. But audiences of the 1860s would have been taken by surprise. Those from a Lutheran tradition, as Brahms was himself, would certainly have warmly welcomed Brahms' innovative re-invention of the Requiem as a musical form. And, as mentioned above, the oratorio met with great acclaim.

Composition of the work

Brahms worked on the *Requiem* during three periods of his life.

First, he composed an early version of what later became the second movement in 1854, not long after Robert Schumann's attempted suicide.

Next, most of the *Requiem* (movements 1-4 and 6-7, as they became in the final version) was composed after his mother's death in 1865 and completed by August 1866. A partial première, consisting of the first three movements, took place in Vienna in 1867. This was not a success, because the timpanist misunderstood Brahms' markings of *pf* as *f* or *ff* in parts of the third movement, with the result that he drowned out the rest of the orchestra.[98] The first performance of the six movements of the work was performed the following year in Bremen Cathedral on Good Friday. This performance was a great success.

Finally, an additional movement, which became the fifth movement, was inserted soon afterwards, and that item was first performed later in 1868. The complete seven-movement version of the *Requiem* was premièred in Leipzig in February 1869 and the work was published that year. The first British performance was in 1871 in London in the

[98] The dynamics marking *pf* means *poco forte* (slightly loud), whereas *f* means *forte* (loud) and *ff* means *fortissimo* (very loud).

home of Lady Thompson, formerly known as Kate Loder, a celebrated pianist.

Looking at the content and structure of the work

The *Requiem* is the longest of all Brahms' compositions, lasting about 65 minutes. The singing parts are scored for two soloists (a soprano and a baritone) and a chorus. The orchestra consists of a standard combination of instruments: strings and 1 or 2 harps; woodwind (piccolo, 2 flutes, 2 oboes, 2 clarinets, 2 bassoons and an optional contrabassoon); brass (4 horns, 2 trumpets, 3 trombones and a tuba); timpani, and an optional organ.

In contrast to a Baroque oratorio (Handel's *Messiah,* for example), the soloists do not sing any arias. Their parts fit into the overall structure of the movements.

The seven movements of the *Requiem* have a symmetrical shape around the central Movement 4, which is the well-known item 'How lovely are thy dwellings' (to give it its English title). This is often sung as an anthem on its own. Movements 1 and 7 both begin with the words 'Selig sind ...' ('Blessed are ...') and these two movements are both slow. The final word of the work, in Movement 7, is 'selig' ('blessed') – mirroring the very first word of Movement 1. This deliberate repetition of such a key word intensifies the sense of the rounded nature of the whole work. Movements 2 and 6 (i.e., the second and second to last) can both be described as having a dramatic nature. There is a deliberate contrast between the dominant mood of each of these movements: the funeral-march mood of Movement 2 is balanced by the triumphant resurrection-theme of Movement 6. Movements 3 and 5 (i.e., the third and third to last) both begin with a solo voice (the baritone and the soprano respectively).

The unity of the composition is further strengthened by the use of recurring musical features. More will be explained about this in the musical comments on each of the movements, although not all of them will be identified in these pages. Such features are not meant necessarily to be heard consciously, but on a subconscious level they do reinforce a sense of the work's unity.

Both the symmetry and the unity of the *Requiem* provide solid evidence of Brahms' characteristic craftsmanship and perfectionism.

The theme of the work as 'Everlasting Rest'

The Bible-texts that Brahms has selected seem to be designed to draw a series of contrasts between life on earth (what we might call the 'here and now') and life in heaven (which we might call the 'there and then'). Throughout the oratorio, we are shown two completely opposite scenarios. On the one hand, there are things that make this life a burden or, at the very least, detract from the possibility, in this life, of complete satisfaction. On the other hand, there are the future certainties and joys of heaven to come for Christian believers. While this contrast is made more explicitly in some movements than in others, each movement sets up an antithesis, expressed by the heading formulated for each movement. In the discussion of each movement, a case will be made for the appropriateness of each heading. (The present writer has devised these headings; Brahms did *not* use them, nor did he suggest any headings at all. The text of the oratorio alone that has prompted these headings.) The meanings of the words chosen for the 'here and now' category overlap with each other, as do the meanings of those chosen for the 'there and then' category.

It may be helpful to set out, in the following table, the contrasts in the seven movements:

	Here and now	*There and then*
1.	Sorrow	Joy
2.	Transience	Permanence
3.	Mortality	Security
4.	Longing	Fulfilment
5.	Sadness	Comfort
6.	Time	Eternity
7.	Toil	Rest

As mentioned in the Preface to this study, an explanation will be given as to why the words 'Everlasting Rest', chosen for this part of the study, provide an apt description for the theme of Brahms' *Requiem*. The words come from the title of a book by the 17th century Puritan pastor and writer, Richard Baxter, *The Saints' Everlasting Rest*, written in 1649.[99] Baxter wrote it in his mid-30s, when he thought he was on his deathbed, and the book catapulted him to prominence as a writer on spiritual issues.

Importantly, as the title suggests, Baxter's book centres on the hope of glory that strengthens the believer's heart, giving him energy and direction for purposeful living in the 'here and now'. The word 'rest" is chosen as the last in the 'there and then' category in the table above, because the word appears in the Bible verse for Movement 7, Revelation 14:13: '"Blessed are the dead who die in the Lord from now on." "Blessed indeed," says the Spirit, "that they may *rest* from their labours, for their deeds follow them!"' (my italics). Jesus promises 'rest' in his well-known words of Matthew 11:28: '"Come to me, all who labour and are heavy laden, and I will give you *rest*"' (my italics). The Christian who responds to Jesus' invitation receives rest 'here and now' – but the full measure of that rest belongs to the 'there and then'.

Brahms has produced an oratorio that directs listeners to the true Everlasting Rest of heaven.

Brahms' religious beliefs

It is well known that Brahms' religious views tended to be humanistic and agnostic. This may come as a surprise to many listeners to the *Requiem*, in view of Brahms' use of the Bible in the oratorio. To speak of a contradiction between what Brahms believed and what he produced in this work may be overstating the case, but there is certainly a tension between orthodoxy and scepticism in Brahms' outlook and musical composition that we need to be aware of. Some commentators have come to the conclusion that Brahms' attitude to the Bible and to the Christian faith was cultural rather than something personal and existential. That may well be correct.

---

99 R. Baxter, *The Saints' Everlasting Rest* (Bellingham: Regent College Publishing, 2004).

It may help to draw up a list of the evidence in connection with the *Requiem* that should alert us to Brahms' less than wholehearted commitment to a vibrant Christianity. This will be followed by a few comments which should encourage listeners, nevertheless, to continue coming to the *Requiem* with a real expectation of being fed spiritually.

First, then, the evidence that points towards Brahms' agnostic views:

ITEM 1: Brahms told Carl Martin Reinthaler, director of music at Bremen Cathedral, where the first performance of the six-movement version of the work took place in 1868, that he would have gladly called the oratorio 'ein menschliches Requiem' ('a human Requiem').[100] To put that comment in its best light, there is genuine human compassion and warmth in the text of the work. It speaks directly to the human heart. But, at the same time, Brahms seems to have been distancing himself from a personal statement of Christian faith.

ITEM 2: There is no direct reference in the oratorio to the Lord Jesus Christ. While the Bible verses inevitably point us to his Person and Work, he is not mentioned at all.

ITEM 3: Correspondence took place between Reinthaler and Brahms on precisely this point. Reinthaler expressed concern that there were no references to 'the redeeming death of the Lord', such as John 3:16. But Brahms refused to make any changes.[101] Apparently, at the Bremen performance of the *Requiem*, Reinthaler took it upon himself to insert the aria 'I know that my Redeemer liveth' from Handel's *Messiah* into the programme, in order to satisfy the clergy.

ITEM 4: Brahms' inclusion in the *Requiem* of a couple of verses from the Apocrypha may well cause some concern. It was mentioned earlier that this issue would be considered further. The Apocrypha (meaning 'things hidden') refers to certain additional books to the Old Testament Canon, which are included by some parts of the Christian church and

---

[100] M. Steinberg, *Johannes Brahms: A German Requiem* (Oxford: Oxford University Press, 2005), 70.
[101] M. Musgrave, *The Music of Brahms* (Oxford: Routledge & Kegan Paul, 1985), 80.

excluded by others. They were rejected from the Hebrew Canon. Christian usage and opinion about them were somewhat fluid until the 16th century, when twelve apocryphal works were included in the Canon of the Roman Catholic Church by the Council of Trent – while Protestant churches excluded them, on the grounds that they are not part of the inspired word of God. They admitted them only for private edification. This is, for example, the official position of the Church of England and the Lutheran Church – and of Jerome's impressive *Vulgate* translation of the Bible into Latin in the 5th century AD. There is nothing heretical or wrong in the two apocryphal verses incorporated in the *Requiem,* but the full title of Brahms' work, it will be remembered, is 'A German Requiem, to words of the Holy Scriptures'. Why, then, did Brahms feel it necessary to select material from outside the Holy Scriptures, when those same Scriptures would have adequately provided for all his needs as a composer?

That, then, is what may be described as the 'case for the prosecution'. However, while all those '"charges' (to use another court-room expression) may be true, there is also a 'case for the defence'. It may not be powerful enough to exonerate Brahms from the 'charges', but it will at least set out mitigating circumstances and cause us to consider our verdict carefully.

ITEM 1: Brahms' decision to recast the mould of the traditional model of the Requiem may not have been the result of doctrinal conviction but of cultural and artistic reasons. Nevertheless, many people since the late 1860s will be delighted that they can listen to a Requiem that is not conveying unbiblical beliefs.

ITEM 2: While Brahms seems to have avoided Bible texts that mention Jesus Christ directly, and those that might have seemed to him too focused on salvation-issues, so many of the Bible texts that he does use *do* point to Jesus – perhaps not directly, but indirectly and certainly. Two of his Bible texts, including the very first one in the work, are words of Jesus himself. There is an intriguing verse in Mark's Gospel: '... And he (Jesus) entered a house and did not want anyone to know, yet he could not be hidden.' (Mark 7:24). Let's leave to one side the first part of that verse, telling us that Jesus wanted to keep a low profile –

that is not relevant here. But, instead, let's focus on the last part of the verse, telling us that Jesus 'could not be hidden'. That phrase is an apt comment on Brahms' *Requiem*. Jesus Christ is certainly *not* hidden in this work. What we have in this oratorio is a selection of verses which, individually and collectively, point to Jesus. This is a reminder of the main theme of the Bible, which is Jesus. It is impossible to read the Bible and understand its underlying message, without seeing that the focal point of the Bible's Big Picture is Jesus and salvation in him. My hope is that, in the discussion in the following pages, we shall see that perspective on Jesus emerging from the text again and again.

ITEM 3: Similarly, the Bible texts that Brahms has chosen point us again and again away from the sadness and transience of life on earth, and towards the solid joys and eternal security of heaven to come. An earlier part of this Introduction has already put forward the case for regarding heaven as a major theme of the oratorio – hence the title for the third part of this study being 'Everlasting Rest'.

ITEM 4: The selection of Bible verses that Brahms has made for this work is amazingly insightful, and the connections which often emerge very naturally from one to another are most instructive. There may be places where we would want to quibble with Brahms – for example, in choosing two apocryphal verses when he could have stuck with the Bible, or one or two passages where he might have included the whole rather than the part. But there are many occasions when we will we be thrilled at the choices that he did make. In the discussion that follows, we must accept that we cannot know whether these choices were made deliberately by Brahms, with that wider perspective in mind, or whether they happened fortuitously – but I for one am willing to give him the benefit of any doubt, and to thank God for the inspiring oratorio that has been composed for us.

A short comment on the Bible texts used in this study

The German text of Brahms' *Requiem*, which is based on Martin Luther's translation of the Bible, will be found in an Appendix,[102] together with a translation into English. That translation is my own. It aims to follow familiar English versions as far as possible. But it deliberately aims to adopt modern usage and, at the same time, to translate the Luther version accurately.

The German text will be referred to several times in the comments on 'What to listen out for in the music', together with the relevant words from the translation in the Appendix. This seems to be the sensible thing to do, since most performances will use the German words.

However, in the discussion of the message of each movement in the following pages, the ESV translation is used. The relevant Bible verses will be given at the beginning of the discussion of each movement. The two apocryphal verses are taken from the Revised Standard Version Apocrypha (1957).

---

[102] Luther's New Testament was published in 1522, and the whole Bible in 1534.

The Message of Brahms' *Requiem* and What to Listen out for in the Music

Movement 1: Sorrow and Joy

Blessed are those who mourn, for they shall be comforted. (Matthew 5:4)

Those who sow in tears shall reap with shouts of joy!
He who goes out weeping, bearing the seed for sowing, shall come home with shouts of joy, bringing his sheaves with him. (Psalm 126:5-6)

The two Bible extracts that form Movement 1 are held together by the contrast described in the heading: 'sorrow and joy'. Both Bible extracts speak of a progression from the first to the second.

Matthew 5:4: a promise of comfort

Matthew 5:4 is the second verse in our Lord's Sermon on the Mount, which occupies almost the whole of **Matthew 5 – 7**. The opening section of the Sermon is known as The Beatitudes (Matthew 5:3-12), deriving from the Latin word for 'blessed', and in these verses Jesus declares those who exhibit certain qualities to be 'blessed'. Sometimes, this second Beatitude ('Blessed are those who mourn, for they shall be comforted') is regarded as a promise addressed to those who have suffered a major loss, particularly the death of a loved one. Those familiar with the Church of England's more recent liturgies, whether the Alternative Service Book or Common Worship, will know that Matthew 5:4 is one of the verses to be used at the beginning of the

Funeral Service.[103] However, what is being described in this verse is not the sorrow of a bereavement but the sorrow of repentance.

In order to demonstrate this point, it may be helpful to present the text of the first four of the Beatitudes (i.e., Matthew 5:3-6), with verse 4 printed in bold:

3. Blessed are the poor in spirit, for theirs is the kingdom of heaven.

4. **Blessed are those who mourn, for they shall be comforted.**

5. Blessed are the meek, for they shall inherit the earth.

6. Blessed are those who hunger and thirst for righteousness, for they shall be satisfied.

The whole Sermon is addressed to those who are already Jesus' disciples, as verses 1-2 of Matthew 5 explain. In modern-day terms, therefore, we can say that these verses apply to Christian believers, not to mankind in general. In the Beatitudes Jesus is describing aspects of Christian character. They are not listed randomly but are presented in a logical order. The starting point is poverty of spirit (v 3), which means that I acknowledge that I have nothing in myself to qualify me for salvation. Toplady's famous hymn 'Rock of ages' expresses this strikingly:

> Nothing in my hand I bring, / Simply to Thy cross I cling:
> Naked, come to Thee for dress; / Helpless, look to Thee for grace;
> Foul, I to the fountain fly: / Wash me, Saviour, or I die![104]

Being willing to own up to my poverty of spirit will lead me to grieve and mourn over my sin (v 4). The Bible gives many examples of people

---

[103] *The Alternative Service Book 1980* (London: SPCK, 1980), 307; *Common Worship: Pastoral Services* (London: Church House Publishing, Second Edition 2005), 259.

[104] A. Toplady, 'Rock of Ages', written in 1763, first published in *The Gospel Magazine* in 1775.

mourning over their own sin or that of others. The writer of Psalm 119 prayed, 'My eyes shed streams of tears, because people do not keep your law.' (Psalm 119:136) A large part of Ezra 9 contains a prayer of Ezra in which he publicly confessed his people's sin, and Ezra 10:1 – referring to this prayer – tells us that he 'prayed and made confession, weeping' and that also 'the people wept bitterly.' The Lord Jesus wept over the sins of Jerusalem (Luke 19:41-44), and the apostle Paul wrote in Philippians 3:18: 'For many, of whom I have often told you and now tell you even with tears, walk as enemies of the cross of Christ.'

The sequence of thought in Matthew 5:3-6 leads from admitting that I am 'poor in spirit' (v 3) and mourning over sin (v 4), to meekness (v 5) and to hungering and thirsting for righteousness (v 6). Being 'meek' means that I will not only confess my spiritual need to God but will be willing for others to know it too – and I will not retaliate when they point out my failings. But at the same time, I will 'hunger and thirst for righteousness', because I want to show the fruits of repentance in the way I live. The remaining Beatitudes continue this progression, as they spell out some of those fruits. So, in v 7 I shall want to show mercy to others; in v 8 I shall aim for purity in heart; in v 9 I shall seek to be a peacemaker, and in vv 10-12 I shall count it as joy when I suffer for being a disciple of Christ.

Each of the Beatitudes gives a reason for these aspects of Christian character to be described as 'blessed'. Each time the blessing is what we might call a reward, provided we recognise the 'reward' as a gift from God rather than something to be earned. The promised blessing, each time, is stated either as a present spiritual reality for the Christian believer ('for theirs is the kingdom of heaven', v 3 and v 10), or as a future one (as in each of the Beatitudes apart from the first and the last). However, it makes sense to regard all the promised blessings as both present and future; the certainty of all of them is to be enjoyed here and now, and the full experience of all of them will be enjoyed perfectly hereafter, in the Everlasting Rest of heaven.

Here we focus on the promise attached to v 4, the verse which is included in the *Requiem*. The promise is that 'those who mourn ... shall be comforted.' In terms of the sequence of thought within the

Beatitudes, this comfort must be understood as forgiveness. 'Comfort' is an echo of an Old Testament promise, namely Isaiah 40:1: 'Comfort, comfort my people, says your God.' – which leads into the assurances of v 2 of that chapter, namely that Jerusalem's 'warfare is ended' and that her iniquity is 'pardoned'. From chapter 40 onwards, the Book of Isaiah consists of prophecy concerning the return of God's people from exile in Babylon. This prophecy is particularly remarkable because the exile would not take place for another century, and the return would not be until seventy years beyond that. But it is a fact of history that the exile did take place, and so too did the promised return. The reason for that exile was as a punishment for the people's sin: their persistent disobedience to the Lord God. Therefore, when the very first two verses of the section of Isaiah announcing the return from exile focus on 'comfort' and 'pardon', the impact of those words is extremely forceful. The sin of disobedience has been dealt with.

When Jesus deliberately echoed that Old Testament promise in Matthew 5:4, he was in effect declaring that he was bringing about the end of the exile. This implies that the true exile for mankind was the exile that resulted from Adam and Eve's disobedience in Genesis 3, and their expulsion from the Garden of Eden. It is this exile which he in person, as the promised Messiah, had come to release people from. The Babylonian exile was a small-scale version of the Big Picture. Jesus was pointing to the Bible truth that the 'comfort' (and therefore also the pardon), promised in Isaiah 40:1-2[105], would come to all those who would 'mourn' for their sin and put their trust in him.[106] As mentioned

---

[105] Those familiar with Handel's *Messiah* will be aware that the very first vocal item of that oratorio is a setting of Isaiah 40:1. The reason is the same as is being discussed here – namely, that Jesus is the Messiah who, by his coming into the world and his substitutionary death, brings about the true end of exile for God's people. The Old Testament exile is, by comparison, only a pale reflection of this.

[106] In Luke 2:25 the aged Simeon is said to be 'waiting for the *consolation* of Israel' (my italics). When he is privileged to meet Mary, Joseph and the infant Jesus in the Jerusalem temple, he realises that Jesus is the promised Christ. This seems to be another echo of Isaiah 40:1 – 'consolation' meaning 'comfort'. Here, then, was a godly man who believed that the end of the exile would be brought about by the coming of the Messiah.

above, each of the promises attached to the Beatitudes has both a present and a future reality. That applies to the 'comfort' of Matthew 5:4. Now, in this life, the believer can know the reality of forgiveness of sin, and one day, in the life to come, he or she will experience complete release from the sorrow that sin causes. In the words of Revelation 7:17, 'God will wipe away every tear from their eyes.'

Before we move on from Matthew 5:4, the question may arise in our minds: Did Brahms himself recognise that this verse has to do with the sorrow of repentance rather than the sorrow of a bereavement? As noted in the introductory comments above, the death of his mother was a major factor leading him to compose this *Requiem*. That might lead us to assume that Brahms was using this verse for the wrong reasons. We shall never know the answer to this with certainty. However, as we proceed with the discussion of further texts (particularly the next one and Isaiah 35:10 in Movement 2), there is evidence that Brahms may well have had an awareness of the Bible theme of exile and restoration, to which these verses point.

Psalm 126:5-6: tears now, but joy to come

As we come now to the second Bible extract in Movement 1, Psalm 126: 5-6, it will be helpful again to display the text of the whole psalm, with verses 5-6 printed in bold:

> 1. When the LORD restored the fortunes of Zion, we were like those who dream.
> 2. Then our mouth was filled with laughter, and our tongue with shouts of joy; then they said among the nations, "The LORD has done great things for them."
> 3. The LORD has done great things for us; we are glad.
> 4. Restore our fortunes, O LORD, like streams in the Negeb!
> 5. **Those who sow in tears shall reap with shouts of joy!**

6. **He who goes out weeping, bearing the seed for sowing, shall come home with shouts of joy, bringing his sheaves with him.**

It will be evident that the psalm falls into two halves. The first half looks back to an amazing restoration in the fortunes of God's people, culminating in v 3: 'The LORD has done great things for us; we are glad.' The second half looks forward with a prayer to God, asking him to do the same again. While it is not possible to be certain, a very plausible background for this psalm is the return of Jewish exiles to their homeland at the end of their captivity. The NIV commits itself to this interpretation and translates v 1 of the psalm as 'When the LORD brought back the captives of Zion, we were like men who dreamed.' Placing this psalm at the time of the first return to the Jewish homeland makes it easy to understand both the past and the future perspectives of the psalm. The Books of Ezra and Nehemiah record both the initial return of Jewish people to their land, when King Cyrus of Persia issued his decree, and the subsequent waves of returnees from Babylon in Persia. They also record (to borrow the well-known phrase of Churchill) the 'blood, toil, tears and sweat'[107] involved in the rebuilding of the temple and the walls, and in dealing with serious troubles, the external opposition from hostile neighbours and the internal problem of sin against God's law. As the first group of Jews returned to Judah, they would praise God for what he had already done for them, and they would pray that he would continue to prosper them in the tough times ahead.

If this is the correct understanding of the background of Psalm 126, the inclusion of two verses from it at this point in the *Requiem* is most appropriate. The theme of exile and return reinforces the message that has already been suggested by Matthew 5:4 – again, with the understanding that the Old Testament record of exile and return is to be viewed as pointing to the Bible's Big Picture. As explained above, that Big Picture can be spelt out as this: mankind is exiled from God

---

[107] W. Churchill, *House of Commons Hansard*, 13 May 1940, volume 360, column 1502.

because of sin, but in Jesus we meet the one whose coming into this world, in order to die on the cross as the Saviour of the world, brings about the true end of exile for those who believe in him.

Brahms makes use of only the last two verses of Psalm 126, but the context of those verses gives the attentive listener the framework required for a more complete understanding. These two verses present the contrast between present 'sorrow' and future 'joy' by means of a farming image. (Brahms will make use of another Bible verse with a reference to farming in Movement 2.) The present situation for believers is – with reference again to Churchill's famous words – 'blood, toil, tears and sweat'. Farming can be a most heart-breaking experience; all its joys are hard-won and long-awaited. The same is true of the Christian pilgrimage. But there *is* a certain future prospect, namely the harvest to come. Our focus must be on the Everlasting Rest of heaven to come.

What to Listen out for in the Music of Movement I

The shape of this movement is A – B – A, with the Bible verse Matthew 5:4 being sung at both the beginning and the end of the movement, with Psalm 126:5-6 coming in the middle.

The chorus sing this item without soloists.

Listen out for the lyrical quality of the movement, which derives from the slow, expressive phrasing and the beauty of the harmonization.

Listen out for the absence of the violins in this opening movement. The violas are the leaders in the string material here. This gives a deep, sombre mood at the beginning of the whole work.

Listen out for the opening phrase in the violas, consisting basically of three ascending notes of the scale, followed by four descending notes of the scale. This phrase is repeated three times in succession, each time pitched slightly higher. It creates a sense of mounting expectancy. We will hear this phrase again within the movement, as will be explained a little later.

Listen out for a particularly important motif that Brahms employs in every movement of the work. It makes sense, therefore, to label it as the 'unifying motif' (or the U.M. for short). It is a major building-block of the whole work and appears in various guises (i.e., upside-down and back-to-front) and not always in its basic form as it is in this movement. The U.M. makes its first appearance in the soprano line of the chorus's first entry. The motif consists of an upward leap of a major third, usually followed by a semitone (i.e., a half-step) in the same direction. This motif in its basic form can best be understood by humming or singing the first three notes of the Christmas carol 'Once in royal David's city'. It will be heard in the soprano voice on the three syllables of the opening words 'Selig sind' ('Blessed are').

Listen out for the way the orchestra twice stop playing when the chorus make their entry. First the chorus sing the opening word 'Selig' unaccompanied. Then, after a further instance of the U.M. from the orchestra, the orchestra stop again for a few bars, as the chorus sing the words of Matthew 5:4 in full, again unaccompanied. It is as if they stop in order to listen, and are inviting us to do the same.

Listen out for prominent phrases in various places throughout the movement from the oboe, flute and horn, all the more striking for their simplicity.

Listen out for the tenors and basses introducing the central section (B – the setting of the words of Psalm 126:5-6), before they are joined first by the contraltos and then by the sopranos.

Listen out for the appropriate change of mood in the music with the words 'werden mit Freuden ernten' ('shall reap with joy'). The dynamics marking is *forte* (= loud) and the chorus, for the first time, are given several quavers to sing – up to this point, their parts have consisted almost exclusively of longer notes. This intensification of sound and a sudden sense of movement make the expression of joy all the more powerful. Also, at this point the harps provide a rippling accompaniment.

Listen out, in the setting of the second part of the central section B (i.e., verse 6 of Psalm 126), for the return of that earlier motif, first heard on the violas (the three ascending notes, followed by the four descending notes). This time it is sung by the chorus: first the tenors, then the contraltos, and then the sopranos. As before, the motif is repeated three times.

Listen out for the third section of the movement, the return to a setting of Matthew 5:4. We again hear the motif of ascending and descending notes from the violas and the U.M. from the soprano voice of the chorus, first in a modified form and then in its original form.

Listen out for the harp accompaniment towards the end of this movement.

Movement 2: Transcience and Permanence

for "All flesh is like grass and all its glory like the flower of grass. The grass withers, and the flower falls, ..." (1 Peter 1:24)

Be patient, therefore, brothers, until the coming of the Lord. See how the farmer waits for the precious fruit of the earth, being patient about it, until it receives the early and the late rains. (James 5:7)

"... but the word of the Lord remains forever." (1 Peter 1:25a)

And the ransomed of the LORD shall return and come to Zion with singing; everlasting joy shall be upon their heads; they shall obtain gladness and joy, and sorrow and sighing shall flee away. (Isaiah 35:10)

It will be seen that Brahms makes use of two consecutive verses of 1 Peter 1 (or rather one verse plus the first half of the following verse). But he inserts another New Testament verse between them, since he clearly understands James 5:7 to be making an extra comment on the substance of 1 Peter 1:24. He completes Movement 2 with a verse from Isaiah 35. The dominant contrast here is between 'transience and permanence'. Two features link the Bible verses of Movement 2 to those of Movement 1: one is the recurrence of the farming picture, and the other, which becomes evident in Isaiah 35:10, is the theme of exiles returning home.

1 Peter 1:24: 'All flesh is grass'

In **1 Peter 1:24** we have the first part of a quotation, by the apostle, from Isaiah 40:6-8. Because Brahms does not include anything else from Peter's First letter, it makes sense to look at these verses in their context in the Book of Isaiah.[108] The whole quotation from Isaiah is this (with the parts used in the oratorio in bold):

---

[108] It is only the use of the word 'for' in the text of the oratorio, introducing the Old Testament quotation, that marks out these words as being taken from 1 Peter 1:24 rather than directly from Isaiah 40:6-8.

6: A voice says, "Cry!" And I said, "What shall I cry?" **All flesh is grass, and all its beauty is like the flower of the field.**
7: The grass withers, the flower fades when the breath of the LORD blows on it; surely the people are grass.
8: The grass withers, the flower fades, **but the word of our God will stand for ever.**[109]

Interestingly, Isaiah 40 is the same chapter that was echoed by Matthew 5:4 in Movement 1. Did Brahms have that link in mind when he chose his material? If we may assume that he did, his choice was most insightful.

The introductory verse of Movement 2 puts the spotlight on the 'transience' of mankind. It emphasises the temporary and transient nature of human existence on earth and the certainty of death. This life is not for ever and, just like the grass or the flower of the field, mankind is here today and gone tomorrow. It is not just the great and powerful of the world whose memory is forgotten by succeeding generations. It does include such people, of course, who might reckon that their stamp on the history of the world will be indelible. Shelley's poem 'Ozymandias', for example, describes a traveller finding in the middle of a desert the ruins of the statue of a man who once was a mighty ruler:

And on the pedestal these words appear:
"My name is Ozymandias, king of kings:
Look on my works, ye Mighty, and despair!"
Nothing beside remains. Round the decay
Of that colossal wreck, boundless and bare
The lone and level sands stretch far away.[110]

---

109 Comments on the use of Isaiah 40:8 in 1 Peter 1:25a will follow later in this section.

110 P. Shelley, 'Ozymandias', published in *The Examiner* (London), 11 January 1818.

The irony of the poem is that no one has ever heard of Ozymandias: far from stamping his name on the history of the world, it does not even appear as a footnote of history. 'Fading is the worldling's pleasure, all his boasted pomp and show,' as John Newton expresses it.[111] But it is not only the great and powerful who are forgotten – such is equally the lot of those who have lived their lives in obscurity. The writer of Ecclesiastes comments on the universality of death: 'It is the same for all, since the same event happens to the righteous and the wicked, to the good and to the evil, to the clean and the unclean, to him who sacrifices and him who does not sacrifice.' (Ecclesiastes 9:2) He might have included 'the great and the small' in his list of pairs which embrace the whole of humanity. Thomas Gray's famous poem, 'An Elegy in a Country Churchyard, touches on the anonymity of those now buried who, for reasons of their lowly birth, never had the opportunity to make their mark on the world. Lord David Cecil, the biographer, makes this comment about Gray's poem:

> Death, he [i.e., Gray] perceives, dwarfs human differences. There is not much to choose between the great and the humble, once they are in the grave. It may be that there never was; it may be that in the obscure graveyard lie those who but for circumstance would have been as famous as Milton and Hampden.[112]

After such a bleak and depressing description of the mortality of mankind, there *is* a positive note to be sounded – the other side of the contrast. But we must wait for that.

James 5:7: patiently waiting for the harvest to come

At this point, a verse from the Letter of James is included: **James 5:7**. The Christian believer is encouraged to be patient in waiting for the Lord's Second Coming. This is a positive counterweight to the dark reality of the preceding words in the libretto. We can be sure that the

---

[111] J. Newton, 'Glorious Things of Thee are Spoken', in *Olney Hymns*, published 1779.

[112] D. Cecil, 'The Poetry of Thomas Gray', in J. Clifford (ed.), *Eighteenth Century English Literature* (Oxford: Oxford University Press, 1959) 241.

Lord Jesus will return to take his people to himself: he himself has given many promises of this which are recorded for us in the Gospels, and every writer in the New Testament includes assurances that this will indeed be the climax of human history. But waiting is never easy, and so we are given the oratorio's second farming picture:. The farmer knows that harvest-time will come. He can do nothing to make it happen more quickly. He must simply wait patiently for the rains to come, which will enable the seed sown to produce 'the precious fruit of the earth'. 'The early and the late rains' refer respectively to the rainfall of late autumn and early spring, which were so vital for agriculture. But there is nothing passive about the farmer's waiting. He has much hard work to do as he waits. And as was noted in connection with Psalm 126:5-6 in Movement 1, this is a picture of the Christian life here and now. In practical terms, the 'hard work' of the Christian life involves what a well-known hymn describes as the call on every Christian believer to 'wrestle and fight and pray'.[113] It involves a willingness to meet opposition from the world towards all that the Christian gospel stands for. What provides the motivation to keep going is the certainty of the Lord's Return and of heaven to come.

1 Peter 1:25a: 'the word of the Lord remains for ever'

As will be explained again in the musical comment below, Brahms repeats his setting of 1 Peter 1:24 after giving us James 5:7. So, listeners should experience a real sense of relief, when eventually we are given the second part of the contrast in **1 Peter 1:25a** (quoting Isaiah 40:8) with the announcement that '"the word of the Lord endures for ever.' That might not have been what we were expecting to be the second part of the contrast. The balance to the fact of death and the transience of humanity might have been expected to be the certainty of eternal life beyond the grave, and the permanence of everything associated with heaven. We might have expected something along the lines of John Newton's words that form the contrast with the fading pleasure of the world – namely, 'Solid joys and lasting treasure none but Zion's

[113] C. Wesley, 'Soldiers of Christ, Arise' in *Hymns and Sacred Poems* (Bristol: Felix Farley, 1749)

children know.'[114] Instead, however, the apostle Peter contrasts the transience of human life and splendour with the permanence of God's word. But the contrast does point towards eternal life to come. It is only because of the truth that 'the word of the Lord endures for ever' that we can know for certain that the promises concerning the hereafter are true and trustworthy. It is only because the Lord has spoken – or, as Isaiah 40:5 puts it, 'the mouth of the LORD has spoken' – that we can be fully assured of the 'solid joys and lasting treasure' that are prepared for 'Zion's children'. To refer again to the apostle Peter, earlier in chapter 1 of this same Letter he has written:

> According to his [God's] great mercy, he has caused us to be born again to a living hope through the resurrection of Jesus Christ from the dead, to an inheritance that is imperishable, undefiled, and unfading, kept in heaven for you, who by God's power are being guarded through faith for a salvation ready to be revealed in the last time. (1 Peter 1:3-5)

Significantly, the apostle follows the first half of 1 Peter 1:25, used in the oratorio at this point, with these words which form the second half of the verse: 'And this word is the good news that was preached to you.' It is indeed 'good news'!

Isaiah 35:10: returning home with joy

Movement 2 is rounded off by **Isaiah 35:10**. It makes explicit what was implicit in Movement 1, with the echo in Matthew 5:4 of the 'comfort' promised in Isaiah 40:1 – namely the return of the exiled people of God to their homeland of Judah. 'Zion' is the name of one of the hills of Jerusalem, the one on which Solomon's temple had been built. Isaiah 35:10 is the triumphant concluding verse of a chapter that focuses on the theme of the exiles' return. As such, it sounds a clear note of confidence and praise, which contrasts with the pessimism of the beginning of Movement 1. It also reinforces most emphatically the note of joy and gladness which we saw in Movement 1. There is a marvellous

[114] J. Newton, 'Glorious things of thee are spoken'.

exuberance in this expression of glad celebration. The theme of 'permanence' should not be overlooked: '*everlasting* joy shall be upon their heads' (my italics). This is a powerful counterbalance to the 'transience' which characterizes mere earthly existence. Furthermore, 'sorrow and sighing', which belong to life on earth, are banished completely. They will have no part in the Everlasting Rest to come.

The other word particularly to note is 'ransomed', describing God's people. The word implies that a cost has had to be paid for their rescue. In the Big Picture of the Bible, that cost is nothing less than the death of God's Son, who died as their substitute on the cross, bearing their sin and their punishment. A couple of verses from the first chapter of Peter's First Letter – a chapter that has been very much to the fore in the discussion of Movement 2 – make this clear. Peter appeals to his readers to live holy lives, and tells them:

> you were ransomed from the futile ways inherited from your forefathers, not with perishable things such as silver or gold, but with the precious blood of Christ, like that of a lamb without blemish or spot. (1 Peter 1:18-19)

What to Listen out for in the Music of Movement 2

The shape of Movement 2 is A – B – A – C – D. A represents the settings of 1 Peter 1:24, and each time the Bible verse is sung twice. So, it comes four times in all, meaning that there is a strong emphasis, in the first half of the movement, on the theme of transience. B represents the setting of James 5:7, C represents the setting of 1 Peter 1:25a, and D represents the setting of Isaiah 35:10.

Like the preceding movement, Movement 2 is for the chorus without soloists.

Brahms' marking for the first part of this movement is 'Langsam, marschmäßig' ('Slow, like a march'). Interestingly, there are three beats to the bar, when a march might have led us to expect two or four. So, this march is definitely unmarchable, but it has the feeling of a slow funeral march, which underlines further, in the first half of this movement, the theme of the transience of life.

Listen out for the important U.M., which appears repeatedly and prominently throughout the first half of the movement. However, that may not be obvious at first, because this is one of the times when the motif is used in a disguised way. In this movement, we hear it upside-down and back-to-front (i.e., inverted and reversed). This modified form of the motif comes several times in the opening orchestral introduction, and is modified still further before the voices make their entry. As this orchestral phrase recurs several times, it will be evident that the motif is highly significant in Movement 2.

Listen out for the first statement by the chorus of 'Denn alles Fleisch, es ist wie Gras' ('For all flesh, it is as grass'). It is the contraltos, tenors and basses, but not the sopranos, who sing this first phrase in unison – which accentuates the sombre and bleak content of the message.

Listen out for the way this initial statement is an echo, in the minor key, of the motif of ascending and descending notes which appeared in Movement 1.

Listen out for the contrast between the first statement of 'Denn alles Fleisch, es ist wie Gras', marked *piano* (= quiet), with its second statement, this time with all four voices, which is marked *forte* (= loud).

Listen out for the timpani, whose on-going beat adds to the sombre mood.

Listen out for the change of tone when section B, the setting of James 5:7, appears. The marking is 'etwas bewegter' ('somewhat faster'). This section has a lighter feel than the funereal sections that surround it, and the contributions of the flute and harp in the accompaniment add to this.

Listen out for the repeat of section A, with the same contrast as before between a quiet first statement of 'Denn alles Fleisch ...' and its loud second statement.

Listen out for section C, the brief but authoritative statement by the chorus of

1 Peter 1:25a, telling us that the word of the Lord remains for ever. It is marked *forte* (= loud) and is in a major key, contrasting with the extensive use of a minor key throughout the first part of the movement. Both these features give a decided lift to this short interlude.

Listen out for the prominent brass contributions in this section.

Listen out for section D, the triumphant statement of Isaiah 35:10, with the announcement that God's ransomed people will return. First, it is just the basses who sing, before the rest of the chorus join in. In contrast to the time-signature so far being three beats in the bar, there is a change at this point to four beats in a bar. The different rhythm contributes to the feeling that the message has moved into a more positive mood.

Listen out particularly for the opening phrase of that section, sung by the basses, 'Die Erlöseten des Herrn' ('The ransomed of the Lord'). It is a striking motif, another one which recurs elsewhere in the work, as well as appearing a few times more in this section of Movement 2, both in the voices and in the orchestra. The most noticeable thing about it is the octave leap upwards on the words 'des Herrn'.

Listen out for the emphasis on the word 'Freude' ('joy') a number of times in this part of the movement.

Listen out for the expressive setting of the words 'und Schmerz und Seufzen' ('and sorrow and sighing').

Listen out for the dramatically staccato statements of 'wird weg müssen' ('shall have to flee away').

Listen out for a joyful restatement, shortly after this, of the first part of Isaiah 35:10. The music then takes on a calmer mood, before a final *crescendo* and *diminuendo*.

Movement 3: Mortality and Security

'O LORD, make me know my end and what is the measure of my days; let me know how fleeting I am!
'Behold, you have made my days a few handbreadths, and my lifetime is as nothing before you. Surely all mankind stands as a mere breath!
'Surely a man goes about as a shadow! Surely for nothing they are in turmoil; man heaps up wealth and does not know who will gather!'
'And now, O Lord, for what do I wait? My hope is in you.'
(Psalm 39:4-7)[115]

But the souls of the righteous are in the hand of God, and no torment will ever touch them.
(The Wisdom of Solomon 3:1)

In terms of its theme, Movement 3 of the oratorio begins with a return to the starting point of Movement 2, namely the inescapable truth of human mortality. 'All flesh is like grass,' as we heard from the apostle Peter, quoting the prophet Isaiah. Now, through the words of part of Psalm 39, written by David, we focus at greater length on the fleeting nature of life. But, as we shall see, there is also a note of hope, which points to a future security for those who trust in God. A similar contrast, or progression, can be seen in the verse selected from the Apocrypha: security in God's keeping is assured for the 'righteous'.

Psalm 39:4-7: 'O LORD, make me know my end'

Psalm 39:4-7 can be regarded as a summary of the message of the whole psalm. In the first part of the psalm (vv 1-3), David tells us that there is something he desperately wants to say, but he has decided not to speak of it openly in the presence of unbelievers. The implication is that he does not want to dishonour God's name by what might come out as impassioned words. But he cannot restrain himself indefinitely and therefore he pours out what is on his heart to God alone in the rest of the psalm (vv 4-13). This, at least, is the most natural reading of the

115 The punctuation is as used in the ESV Bible. The quotation mark after 'gather' at the end of v 6 expresses the end of a paragraph at this point, followed by the beginning of a new paragraph at the start of v 7.

psalm, and we are to assume that from verse 4 onwards David is expressing that unspoken problem hinted at in the early verses.

In his prayer, as we have it in the verses used here in the oratorio, David has clearly disciplined himself to speak calmly and thoughtfully. He approaches God with humility like a pupil willing to be taught. This is made particularly plain in the German text of the oratorio, in which David asks God to 'teach' him that his life must end.[116] As he prays for God to make him know 'the measure of (his) days' and how 'fleeting' he is, we hear an echo of another well-known psalm, attributed to Moses: 'So teach us to number our days that we may get a heart of wisdom.' (Psalm 90:12)

As David fixes his thoughts on the transience of human life, he describes human life as 'a mere breath' (v 5 – also v 11). The Hebrew word for this appears also in verse 6, where it is translated as 'for nothing' or, in the NIV, 'in vain' ('Surely for nothing they are in turmoil'). The basic meaning of this Hebrew word has to do with 'worthlessness' – hence the two ways it is translated in these verses. This same word occurs repeatedly in the Book of Ecclesiastes, where the ESV translates it as 'vanity'. The work begins with the words 'Vanity of vanities, says the Preacher, vanity of vanities! All is vanity.' (Ecclesiastes 1:2) The NIV translates that word 'vanity' as 'meaningless'. In effect, David is asking God, 'What is the point of human life when it is so brief? It is a mere breath – totally empty and meaningless.'

Another word worth commenting on briefly is 'Selah', which comes at the end of v 5, immediately following the first mention of 'all mankind' being 'a mere breath'. This word is omitted in the text of the oratorio as set out above, just as it is normally omitted in the public reading of Scripture, but it is part of the Bible text and is worth including in this discussion. The word 'Selah' is used many times in the Book of Psalms, and it appears to indicate a pause in the reading of the text, as if the

[116] The German words are 'Herr, lehre mich doch ...' ('Lord, do please teach me ...'). This is a perfectly acceptable translation of the Hebrew, which basically means 'to cause to know'. The NEB and GNB have 'tell me ...'.

reader or the worshipper is being faced with the challenge, 'Stop and reflect on what has just been said! What do you think about that?'

Before looking at the answer to David's question, which is given in this psalm, it would be helpful to notice that there is no contradiction between having faith in God and having questions about that faith in God – even big questions, as was the case with David in this psalm. The important thing is what we do with our questions. The wrong thing would be to use them as planks to build a fence between ourselves and God and in effect distance ourselves from him. The right thing to do, as David was doing here, is to use them as a springboard towards deepening one's trust in God. Another way of expressing that same truth is that we need to learn to take our problems TO God, rather than letting them drive us FROM God.

We find other examples of this wise course of action in the Bible. In both Psalms 37 and Psalm 73, the psalmist grapples with the question 'Why do the wicked seem to prosper in this life, while the godly so often seem to suffer?' In each of these psalms, the question is asked of God in a spirit of trust, despite the temptation to 'fret' about it (Psalm 37:1) or to be consumed by envy and to become 'embittered' (Psalm 73:3 and 21) – and in each of them, as a result, an answer is found, as will be discussed a little later.

A New Testament example of a man who dealt with his doubts in the right way is John the Baptist. While in prison because of speaking out against the immoral behaviour of King Herod Antipas, he began to wonder why Jesus took no action to bring about his release.[117] John had preached that Jesus was the Christ (or Messiah), and his understanding was that the Christ would bring God's judgement on evil rulers like Herod and release for the captives. He had spoken of the 'fire' with which Jesus would baptise, and had gone on to say, 'His winnowing fork is in his hand, and he will clear his threshing floor and gather his wheat into the barn, but the chaff he will burn with unquenchable fire.' (Matthew 3:11-12) After all, Isaiah 61:1-2 had promised that the Christ

---

[117] Matthew 11:2-6 (Luke 7:18-23). For the background to John's imprisonment see Matthew 14:3-4 (Mark 6:17-18) and Luke 3:19-20.

would 'proclaim liberty to the captives, and the opening of the prison to those who are bound', and that he would 'proclaim ... the day of vengeance of our God'. John, therefore, began to wonder if he was mistaken in identifying Jesus as the Christ, since what John hoped for had not happened. Wisely, John took the right action. He sent messengers to Jesus to ask him, 'Are you the one who is to come, or shall we look for another'. The immediate answer that Jesus gave to John's messengers was, 'Go and tell John what you hear and see: the blind receive their sight and the lame walk, lepers are cleansed and the deaf hear, and the dead are raised up, and the poor have good news preached to them.' (Matthew 11:2-5) Jesus was referring to Isaiah 35:5-6 and 61:1 as evidence that he was indeed performing the signs that would accompany the coming of the promised Christ.

There is another answer to John's question, and it is the same answer that is provided in Psalms 37 and 73 to the question about the wicked prospering in this life, while the godly suffer. It is also the answer to the question contained in the verses in Psalm 39 that we are considering, concerning the meaning and value of life when it is so brief. That answer can be summed up by saying that *we need to see this life in the light of eternity*. How does that answer apply to each of the examples, given above, of questions being asked in Scripture?

We take first *John the Baptist*. He failed to recognise that the Old Testament looks forward to two comings of the Christ to this world, not just one coming. Jesus had come the first time to perform acts of mercy and to bring salvation for those who put their trust in him, by dying on the cross as the Saviour of the world. But he will come a second time, at the end of the world, to take his people to himself and to bring judgement on those who have not accepted his gracious offer of salvation. If, as suggested above, John was reflecting on the content of Isaiah 61:1-2, he needed to understand that these two verses refer to both the first coming of the Christ, when he would perform healing miracles, preach the good news and 'proclaim the year of the LORD's favour', and to the second coming of the Christ – still in the future –

when he will 'proclaim ... the day of vengeance of our God'.[118] Similarly, when Jesus referred to Isaiah 35:5-6 in his answer to John's messengers, he deliberately did not quote the previous verse, which says this concerning the coming of the Christ: 'Behold, your God will come with vengeance'. The solution for John the Baptist was to have a proper perspective on this life in the light of eternity to come. Judgement and vengeance belong to the time of Jesus' return.

Next, we come to *Psalm 37*. The problem there in David's thinking, as explained above, was the apparent unfairness of this life, when wrongdoers prosper and godly people fare less well. Throughout the psalm, David counsels himself and others as he writes about the eternal destiny of wrongdoers: 'For they will soon fade like the grass and wither like the green herb.' (Psalm 37:2) It is striking that this description of transience is the same as the one used earlier in the oratorio, taken from 1 Peter 1:24 (quoting Isaiah 40:6-7). There, it was applied to 'all flesh' – here, it is applied specifically to 'wrongdoers'. In addition to recognising this, the godly, according to Psalm 37, are to wait patiently, trusting God, doing good and delighting themselves in God. One day, however, 'the meek (another word for godly people) will inherit the land' (Psalm 37:11). Again, the answer to the question raised is to see this life in the light of eternity.

Psalm 73, as we saw above, is also taken up with this question. The answer here is not provided until halfway through the psalm. Having written extensively about the wrongdoers, the psalmist then tells us of his moment of revelation: 'I went into the sanctuary of God; then I discerned their end.' (Psalm 73:17) The 'end' for those who turn their backs on God means arriving in 'slippery places': God will 'make them fall to ruin' (Psalm 73:18) and they 'shall perish' (Psalm 73:27). But there is the assurance that those who look to God have a secure future:

---

[118] See Luke 4:16-21. It is significant that, when Jesus read Isaiah 61:1-2 in the Nazareth synagogue, and applied them to himself – 'Today this Scripture has been fulfilled in your hearing.' – he deliberately stopped his reading with the phrase 'to proclaim the year of the Lord's favour.' He did not include the words 'and the day of vengeance of our God', because the fulfilment of that part of the prophecy still lay in the future.

'You guide me with your counsel, and afterwards you will receive me to glory ... My flesh and my heart may fail, but God is the strength of my heart and my portion for ever.' (Psalm 73:24-26). A right perspective on eternity changes everything.

At last, we return to *Psalm 39* and our verses in the oratorio. The answer to the problem of the brevity of life and its value in the overall scheme of things is, yet again, the eternal perspective. Life must be viewed in the light of eternity. The answer is not spelt out as explicitly as it is in the other two psalms discussed above (Psalms 37 and 73), but it is certainly implied. The last verse in Brahms' extract from the psalm is the beginning of a new paragraph, as was mentioned in an earlier footnote. This new paragraph marks a turning from the problem of human mortality to an expression of trust, and the oratorio gives us just its opening words: 'And now, O Lord, for what do I wait? My hope is in you.' (Psalm 39:7) Waiting and hoping are expressions of a deep and personal trust in the Lord himself. It is as if the psalmist is saying, 'I do not know the answer to my question, but I do know the One who does know the answer – the one who inhabits eternity and is not limited by the constraints of time and finitude. And I will trust him for now and for the future into eternity.'

The Wisdom of Solomon 3:1: security in God's hands

The Wisdom of Solomon 3:1, selected from the Apocrypha rather than from the Old or New Testament, states no more than what the canon of Scripture itself tells us – namely that 'the souls of the righteous are in the hand of God, and no torment will ever touch them.' The word 'righteous' needs to be understood, of course, in the right way. Like 'the godly,' it means those who are believers – those who, in the words of Psalm 39:7 above, can say to God, 'My hope is in you.' The fuller revelation of the New Testament, in the light of the First Coming of the Lord Jesus Christ, explains what Christian righteousness means. The apostle Paul expresses it in personal terms, but he writes for every Christian believer, when he says that to be a Christian is to:

> gain Christ and be found in him, not having a righteousness of my own that comes from the law, but that which comes through faith in

> Christ, the righteousness from God that depends on faith (Philippians 3:8-9)

Christian righteousness is not a matter of making an effort or keeping laws, but a gift from God. He takes my sin and places it on Christ, who has died once and for all to take the punishment for my sin, and he clothes me with Christ's righteousness. It is only on this basis that I, a sinner, may be reconciled to God who is holy.

This new status which is given to every Christian is a guarantee of the eternal security, which is witnessed to by this apocryphal verse. A clearer expression of it might be Jesus' own promise: 'I give them eternal life, and they will never perish, and no one will snatch them out of my hand.' (John 10:28) We may wish that Brahms had selected a clear New Testament verse such as that one – or, alternatively, the following Old Testament verse (the penultimate verse of one of the psalms discussed earlier):

> The salvation of the righteous is from the LORD;
> He is their stronghold in the time of trouble.
> (Psalm 37:39)

The Christian believer can be assured of the Everlasting Rest of a secure eternal home.

What to Listen out for in the Music of Movement 3

First, a comment about the shape of Movement 3. It is similar to that of the previous movement in that the substance of the first section reappears following the second section. This appears to be a recurring pattern in many of the movements. So, the shape can be labelled as A – B – A – C – D – E – F. With reference to the verses in their ESV and RSV Apocrypha wording (as given above), these recognisable sections within their musical setting are as follows:

A: Psalm 39:4 *('O LORD ... how fleeting I am!')*

B: Psalm 39:5ab *('Behold ... as nothing before you.')*

C: Psalm 39:5c-6 *('Surely all mankind ... will gather!')*

D: Psalm 39:7a *('And now, O Lord, for what do I wait?')*

E: Psalm 39:7b *('My hope is in you.')*

F: The Wisdom of Solomon 3:1 *('But the souls of the righteous ... touch them.')*

The double use of section A results in the theme of mortality expressed in Psalm 39:4 being given special prominence within the movement.

Listen out for the prominent role of the baritone soloist in this movement, alongside that of the chorus.

Listen out for the way the baritone soloist's initial rendering of Psalm 39:4 (section A) is followed by the chorus singing the same, but in harmony.

Listen out for the U.M. The first of its two clearly recognisable occurrences comes very near the beginning on the first three syllables of the soloist's words, 'daß ein Ende' (literally 'that an end ...'). The same happens a little later in the sopranos' vocal line, when the chorus repeat the soloist's words.

Listen out for the beginning of section B, which begins with the word 'Siehe' ('Behold'). Again, it is the soloist who sings these words first (Psalm 39:5ab), and the chorus repeat his contribution, but in harmony. The orchestral accompaniment gives this section particular urgency by the use of triplet crochets (i.e., 3 equal notes to be played in the space of 2 normal crochet beats). Some of these triplets are syncopated (i.e., there is a rest in place of the first of the three notes played). This happens particularly in the chorus's singing.

Listen out for the *crescendo* in this section on the words 'sind einer Hand breit vor dir' ('are a handbreadth before you') and on 'und mein Leben, mein Leben ist ...' ('and my life, my life is ...') in the chorus part. The *forte* (= loud) each time is matched by a *piano* (= quiet) – the first one on the words 'und mein ...' ('and my ...'), the second on 'wie nichts' ('as nothing').

In the repeat of section A, listen out for the way the chorus begin to merge with the soloist.

In section C, the soloist sings the words of Psalm 39:5c-6, before the chorus again repeat the words. Interestingly, there is a change in tonality: the soloist's line is in the key of D, while the chorus repeat in the key of F. There is no suggestion that this has any particular significance; it is simply an instance of the composer's skill in creating variations.

In section D (consisting of just half a Bible verse, Psalm 39:7a), the soloist sings the words just once, and immediately the chorus echo the question urgently, repeatedly and dramatically. This section largely consists of a fugue (which is explained in the Musical Glossary). The section slows down to a few bars of quiet music, with a suggestion of uncertainty.

There then follows, in section E, a growing sense of confidence as each voice of the chorus in turn sings, 'Ich hoffe auf dich.' ('I hope in you.'). This is another fugal passage, which leads directly into section F (The Wisdom of Solomon 3:1). Here we have yet another fugue, an amazingly elaborate one, consisting of many independent instrumental and choral lines. At this point, the U.M. makes its second significant appearance in Movement 3, with each voice in turn beginning its initial singing of 'Der Gerechten Seelen' ('The souls of the righteous') on the notes of that unifying motif. The music is loud, expansive and triumphant. Interestingly, throughout the whole of section F the bass instruments play the note D, maintaining the tonality of the music. Is there symbolism here? Possibly, the wanderings of voices and instruments represent the apparently random events of human history and personal experience, and the solid and sustained bass note represents God's sovereign rule which continues immovably. To hope in such a God is the only sensible response that any human being can make.

Movement 4: Longing and Fulfilment

How lovely is your dwelling place, O LORD of hosts!
My soul longs, yes, faints for the courts of the LORD; my heart and flesh sing for joy to the living God.
Blessed are those who dwell in your house, ever singing your praise!
(Psalm 84:1-2, 4)

This movement of Brahms' *Requiem* is deservedly very well-known and is often performed as an item on its own. Movement 4 forms the centre of the oratorio and in terms of the symmetrical shape of the oratorio, discussed earlier, it can be viewed as the climax of the work. The contrast of present longing and future fulfilment is evident from the three verses selected from Psalm 84, as reflected by the heading, and points the listener towards heaven as the goal of the psalmist's desires.

Psalm 84: a longing for heaven

It will be helpful to see **Psalm 84:1-2 and 4** in the context of the whole psalm, even though this discussion will mainly focus on those three verses. The verses that appear in the oratorio are printed in bold:

> 1: **How lovely is your dwelling place, O LORD of hosts!**
> 2: **My soul longs, yes, faints for the courts of the LORD; my heart and flesh sing for joy to the living God.**
> 3: Even the sparrow finds a home, and the swallow a nest for herself, where she may lay her young, at your altars, O LORD of hosts, my King and my God.
> 4: **Blessed are those who dwell in your house, ever singing your praise!** *Selah*
>
> 5: Blessed are those whose strength is in you, in whose heart are the highways to Zion.
> 6: As they go through the Valley of Baca they make it a place of springs; the early rain also covers it with pools.

7: They go from strength to strength; each one
appears before God in Zion.
8: O LORD God of hosts, hear my prayer; give
ear, O God of Jacob! *Selah*

9: Behold our shield, O God; look on the face
of your anointed!
10: For a day in your courts is better than a
thousand elsewhere. I would rather be a
doorkeeper in the house of my God than dwell
in the tents of wickedness.
11: For the LORD God is a sun and shield; the
LORD bestows favour and honour. No good
thing does he withhold from those who walk
uprightly.
12: O LORD of hosts, blessed is the one who
trusts in you!

Psalm 84 is a pilgrim's psalm, consisting of three stanzas of four verses each. This seems to be the most natural understanding of the structure of the psalm, despite the layout in both ESV and NIV. It will be seen that the first and the second stanzas each end with the word 'Selah', which – as was noted in the discussion of the previous movement – seems to indicate, each time, a pause for reflection on what has just been said. The psalmist has in mind a journey to the temple in Jerusalem, which – in his words addressed to God – is referred to as 'your dwelling place' (v 1), 'the courts of the LORD' (v 2) and -'your house' (v 4). In the Old Testament, the temple in Jerusalem was designated as the place where the people of Israel were to meet with God, just as had been the case with the tabernacle which preceded the building of the temple. People in Old Testament times understood, of course, that God did not really live in the temple. As Solomon prayed at the dedication of the temple, 'But will God indeed dwell on the earth? Behold, heaven and the highest heaven cannot contain you; how much less this house that I have built!' (1 Kings 8:27) Nevertheless, symbolically, the temple in Jerusalem represented God's presence among his people.

How should Christian believers today apply the Old Testament temple to their daily living? There are two answers to that question. The first has to do with the present experience of the Lord's people. Jesus is the fulfilment of the temple, because it is through him that we meet with God. He is 'the way' and he says, 'No one comes to the Father except through me.' (John 14:6). At an early stage in his ministry, Jesus had said, 'Destroy this temple, and in three days I will raise it up.' The apostle John, who records these words, goes on to explain: 'But he was speaking about the temple of his body.' (John 2:19, 21) Jesus was anticipating his death and resurrection, because it is by his work of atonement on the cross – and the evidence of his victory in the empty tomb – that we are brought into a restored relationship of intimacy with God.

But there is also a future application of the temple for Christians living in the light of Christ's First Coming, in that it represents the Everlasting Rest of heaven. So, the longing that the psalmist expresses in this psalm, particularly in verses 1,2 and 4, to be in the temple anticipates the longing for heaven that Christian believers should be experiencing. The apostle Paul, writing from prison to the Christians in Philippi, could say, 'My desire is to depart and be with Christ, for that is far better.' (Philippians 1:23) Later in the Letter, he draws the contrast between those 'with minds set on earthly things' and those with the Christian mindset: 'But our citizenship is in heaven, and from it we await a Saviour, the Lord Jesus Christ, who will transform our lowly body to be like his glorious body, by the power that enables him even to subject all things to himself.' (Philippians 3:19-21)

The selected verses from Psalm 84 express that longing for heaven with great intensity. When the psalmist describes God's dwelling place as 'lovely' (v 1), the word does not mean 'beautiful' but 'dear' or 'beloved'. It is the object of his desire. He says that his soul 'longs' for the courts of the Lord (v 2), and the word for 'to long' is used in Psalm 17:12 of a lion which is eager for its prey. In other words, the psalmist is ravenously hungry for God's presence. Then, the word which the generally reliable ESV translates as 'sing for joy' (v 2) should be understood to mean 'cry out', as in the NIV. This is a loud cry of distress, not of happiness, because his desire is not fulfilled. The Luther Bible also mistakenly understands this cry to be one of joy.

By contrast, the psalmist thinks of those who have arrived at their journey's end and are singing praises to God in the temple itself, and he has particularly in mind those who 'dwell' in God's house – they are the ones who are truly 'blessed' (v 4).

It is a pity that Brahms decided not to include verse 3 of the psalm – the only verse of this first stanza of the psalm to be omitted – because in this verse we are given a lovely picture of the 'fulfilment' aspect of the 'longing and fulfilment' contrast which Movement 4 of the oratorio seems to be seeking to provide. Having expressed his own longing for that close enjoyment of the presence of 'the living God', the psalmist feels what can only be described as envy for those who seem to experience what is denied to him. Specifically, those whom he envies are 'the sparrow' and 'the swallow', who have made nests for themselves and their young in the temple eaves and have thereby found a '*home*' (v 3) in the '*house*' of God (v 4) – the same Hebrew word is used in both verses. (We should note that the psalmist is not describing the temple as derelict, with gaping holes in the structure. Rather, we are to picture the temple's wooden eaves, which were open to the outside world.)

Our discussion of Movement 4 of the *Requiem* is rounded off with a few brief comments on the rest of Psalm 84. It is the whole of the psalm, not just the opening stanza, which expresses what we are describing as the longing for heaven. The first stanza describes what might be called *the distant home,* because the psalmist can only picture the goal of his journey from afar in his mind's eye.

The second stanza has to do with *the determined journey.* There are hints here that the pilgrim's progress is an arduous one. The 'valley of Baca' (v 6) suggests a dry terrain, because that word translates 'balsam tree', which grows in arid places, and so the NEB translates the phrase as 'the thirsty valley'. However, the eager pilgrim makes it 'a place of springs' – presumably as a result of hard digging to find sources of water, as well as by making the most of pools of water from the rain that God may be pleased to send. Most importantly, the pilgrim knows that his strength is in God, and as a result he renews his determination to reach his goal, so that 'the highways to Zion' are truly in his heart (v 5).

The third stanza concerns *the nurturing of his longing.* The psalmist feeds his mind on the glories of what lies ahead. One day in God's presence is worth a thousand elsewhere, and to stand humbly on the edge of the heavenly home is far better than anything the world could possibly offer (v 10). In addition, there is the character of God himself to fix his attention on: 'the Lord God is a sun and shield' (images of moral purity and eternal protection), and he 'bestows favour and honour' (v 11).

From the psalm as a whole, the application for Christian believers is that we should understand more clearly that our life on earth is a pilgrimage to heaven. We should have an intense longing for all that belongs to our future inheritance, above all meeting with the Lord himself and enjoying his presence for ever (vv 1-4). We should be determined pilgrims, who will turn disappointments and hardship into opportunities to experience the Lord's sufficient grace, because we have made 'highways to Zion' in our hearts (vv 5-8). We feed our longing for heaven as we focus on the character of God (vv 9-12).

What to Listen out for in the Music of Movement 4

The shape of this delightful piece for the chorus follows a pattern similar to that of the previous movements: A – B – A – C – A, with A representing verse 1 of Psalm 84, B representing verse 2, and C verse 4. The final A section consists only of the words 'Wie lieblich sind deine Wohnungen' ('How lovely are your dwellings') without the words 'Herr Zebaoth' ('Lord of hosts').

Listen out for the prominent flute part in the orchestral introduction.

Listen out for the U.M. in the soprano line on the very first words 'Wie lieblich' ('How lovely').

Listen out for the tenors singing the words of verse 1 on their own at one point, shortly before the other voices join in.

Listen out, just after that, for the four voices together singing 'Meine Seele' ('My soul') and then each voice entering in turn with an urgent 'verlanget und sehnet' ('longs and yearns').

Listen out, shortly after this, for a *crescendo* on the words 'mein Leib und Seele freuen sich ...' ('my body and soul rejoice ...') leading into a *forte* (= loud) on 'in dem lebendigen Gott' ('in the living God'). This happens twice. Even though, as noted above, the cry in the psalm at this point is one of distress rather than joy, we can still savour the musical expression of intense feeling.

In section C, listen out for the fugal passage on the words 'die loben dich immerdar' ('they praise you for ever'). This creates a climax for the piece as it approaches its close, before the final restatement of the first words of verse 1. This short fugue is also an appropriate musical expression of the praise it is describing at this point.

Movement 5: Sadness and Comfort

So also you have sorrow now, but I will see you again, and your hearts will rejoice, and no one will take your joy from you. (John 16:22)

See with your eyes that I have laboured little and found myself much rest. (Ecclesiasticus 51:27)

As one whom his mother comforts, so I will comfort you.
(Isaiah 66:13a)

The nature of the contrast in Movement 5 of the oratorio is not so different from the one we found in Movement 1. The two Bible verses (or, in the case of the first, its immediate context) make use of the picture of a mother with a child. We can only speculate whether the selection of verses was made with that in mind or whether the choice has been fortuitous. In between them we have another verse from the Apocrypha.

John 16:22: sorrow now, but joy to come

The context of **John 16:22** is Jesus' Final Discourse to his disciples in the Upper Room on the evening of Maundy Thursday. This Discourse occupies chapters 13 to 16 of John's Gospel. In John 16:6 Jesus has announced to his disciples, 'A little while, and you will see me no longer, and again a little while, and you will see me.' Some commentators take the promise that the disciples will see Jesus again to refer to his Second Coming, but it makes better sense to understand Jesus to be speaking here (and in the following verses) of his impending death on the cross, followed by the resurrection. The first 'a little while' means the few hours left before his crucifixion, and the second 'a little while' means the time between Jesus' death on Good Friday and his resurrection appearances on Easter Sunday.

Jesus' announcement provokes confusion and concern among his disciples – they have no clear understanding of what Jesus is speaking about. They realise that Jesus is talking about his going away from them, and it should be plain to them that he is talking about his imminent death. In their minds, they are beginning to understand this – but in their hearts, they cannot assimilate this truth. In verse 20, Jesus seeks to clarify what he is saying: 'Truly, truly, I say to you, you will weep and lament, but the world will rejoice. You will be sorrowful, but your sorrow will turn into joy.' Jesus elsewhere refers to the cross as his enemies' 'hour': at his arrest, he said, 'But this is your hour, and the power of darkness.' (Luke 22:53) It is true that Jesus has repeatedly spoken of the cross as *his* 'hour'.[119] But, undeniably, Jesus' crucifixion seemed to mark his enemies' victory, and no doubt the 'world', as represented by the secular and religious authorities of Jerusalem, did 'rejoice', while Jesus' friends did 'weep and lament'. But, Jesus was saying here, their sorrow would turn into joy.

It is in John 16:21 that Jesus uses the picture of a mother with a child, or more precisely a mother in childbirth. He says, 'When a woman is giving birth, she has sorrow because her hour has come, but when she has delivered the baby, she no longer remembers the anguish, for joy that a human being has been born into the world.' There is sorrow, anguish and pain in the process of giving birth, but the end-result is joy. Jesus then applies this truth to the disciples in the words of the verse which we find at this point in the oratorio – verse 22. There is sorrow for the disciples in all that the cross will mean in terms of separation and suffering, but that sorrow will be replaced by joy because of all that Jesus will have achieved by his atoning death.

There are two things to notice from John 16:21, quoted in the previous paragraph. The first is Jesus' deliberate use of the word 'hour', which – as was mentioned above – is the way Jesus repeatedly describes his death on the cross. In other words, Jesus is not using the picture of childbirth arbitrarily: it is a deliberately chosen metaphor to explain the

---

[119] It is in John's Gospel that we find most of Jesus' references to the cross as his 'hour'. The first instance is John 2:4. That reference and the subsequent ones all point to Jesus' death as a future event, until Jesus' final week of ministry in Jerusalem, when some Greeks wish to see Jesus and he announces, 'The hour *has come* for the Son of Man to be glorified.' (John 12:23, my italics)

significance of his death. The second thing to notice here is that the result of Jesus' saving death is the bringing to birth of a new order: it is the dawning of a new age. Earlier in John's Gospel Jesus had been acclaimed, by the inhabitants of a Samaritan town, as 'the Saviour of the world.' (John 4:42) Now that Jesus has died as 'the Lamb of God, who takes away the sin of the world,' in John the Baptist's words (John 1:29), the gospel will be preached to people of all nations.[120]

The wording of John 16:22, the verse used in the oratorio, is interesting. We might have expected Jesus to say, 'So also you have sorrow now, but *you will see me* again' (my italics). After all, it is the turning of the disciples' sorrow into joy that is being spoken of. But, in fact, the verse reads, '... but *I will see you* again' (my italics). The point being made here is that it is what Jesus does – not what they do – that is foundational to their relationship with him. The apostle Paul makes a similar point in writing to the Galatians: 'But now that you have come to know God, or rather to be known by God ...' (Galatians 4:9). Of course, it is the privilege of every Christian believer to know God, but the fact that he knows us gives solid ground for assurance of our security in him.

Finally, in John 16:22, we notice that the joy that Jesus promises his sorrowing friends will never be lost: '... no one will take your joy from you.' One commentator quotes the testimony of a Korean martyr before his execution by the Communists: 'You may take away from me my life, but you can never take Christ from my heart.'[121]

Ecclesiasticus 51:27: toil now, but rest to come

Ecclesiasticus 51:27 appears very near the end of this long apocryphal book as part of the writer's summing up of his message.[122] He

[120] This explains the significance of what was mentioned in the previous note. The Greeks who wished to see Jesus represented the first fruits of the worldwide harvest of the gospel. Their coming to Jesus triggered his announcement that his death on the cross would happen very soon.

[121] B. Milne, *The Message of John* (Leicester: Inter-Varsity Press, 1993), 233-234.

[122] The apocryphal Book of Ecclesiasticus is not to be confused with the biblical Book of Ecclesiastes.

recommends the reliability of his teaching on the grounds of his own personal experience. He has worked hard, he says, to find his rest; but his toil has been small (either in degree or in duration – depending on the translation) in contrast with the greatness of the rest he has found.

As was commented in connection with the earlier verse selected from the Apocrypha, we may well wish that Brahms had chosen a verse from the canon of Scripture. The word 'rest' in that verse is, of course, highly appropriate to the theme of Everlasting Rest. If Brahms was looking for a verse that mentions the promise of 'rest', an obvious choice would be Matthew 11:28, which was referred to in the Introduction to this part of the study. Jesus says in that verse, 'Come to me, all who labour and are heavy laden, and I will give you rest.' One highly speculative reason for Brahms to decide to look in other directions may be the fact that Handel's setting of this verse in Matthew chapter 11, and the two subsequent verses, in his *Messiah,* would have been very well known. Possibly, he may have wished to avoid appearing to want to improve on the work of an accomplished composer of an earlier generation. But Matthew 11:28 would have pointed clearly to Jesus as the only one who can provide 'rest' in the deepest sense of the word, both in this life and the life to come.[123]

Isaiah 66:13: comfort from the Lord

The choice of **Isaiah 66:13** (the first and second parts of the verse, not the third), by contrast, is extremely felicitous. In the earlier discussion of Matthew 5:4, the very first Bible verse included in this oratorio, we saw that Jesus' promise that those who mourn will be comforted is an echo of Isaiah 40:1: 'Comfort, comfort my people, says your God.' Just as that verse in Isaiah came at the very beginning of a new section of the Book, which consisted of words of encouragement to a disobedient people who would suffer exile in a foreign land, this verse (Isaiah 66:13) comes very near the end of that section (and of the Book as a whole),

---

[123] However, see footnote 128 below, and the comment in the text to which it belongs, for an instance of the use in the *Requiem* of Bible verses which are common to both Handel and Brahms.

and again announces '"comfort' to God's people. These two references to 'comfort' may be seen as two bookends for the whole of that major section of Isaiah.[124] In Isaiah 40:1, God announces in effect what *his people will* experience: 'You will be comforted.' In Isaiah 66:13, he promises what *he, their God,* will do: 'I will comfort you'.

Two further things stand out about this promised 'comfort'. First, it is a maternal comfort. As mentioned above, the choice of this verse connects with the inclusion of John 16:22 by virtue of the picture of mother and child in each. Interestingly, Isaiah has used the picture of childbirth just a little earlier in this same chapter. Jerusalem is said to give birth – painlessly! – to 'a son', to 'children' and indeed to 'a nation' (Isaiah 66:7-8). This is a powerful picture, in terms of abundant fruitfulness, of the restoration of God's people after exile. In addition, we are meant to see an echo of the Garden of Eden of Genesis 2, because the birth will be pain-free.[125] People are called upon to 'rejoice with Jerusalem' and even to regard her as their mother (Isaiah 66:10-11), because the people being called upon are in fact her children. The picture of fruitfulness switches for a moment from that of motherhood to that of a splendid river:

> For thus says the LORD:
> "Behold, I will extend peace to her like a river,
> And the glory of the nations like an overflowing
> stream." (Isaiah 66:12a)

But then, in verse 13 (the verse used in the oratorio), we return to the picture of a mother. However, now the 'mother' is no longer Jerusalem, or Zion, but God himself: 'As one whom his mother comforts, so I will comfort you; you shall be comforted in Jerusalem.' (Isaiah 66:13) Earlier in Isaiah, God had compared his love for his people with a mother's love: 'Can a woman forget her nursing child, that she should

---

[124] Another reference to God's comfort within this section is Isaiah 51:12: 'I, I am he who comforts you'.

[125] Pain in childbearing is one of the results of the Fall (Genesis 3:16).

have no compassion on the son of her womb? Even these may forget, yet I will not forget you.' (Isaiah 49:15)

The other thing to notice about God's 'comfort' in Isaiah 66:13 is its location. Brahms does not include the whole of the verse in his *Requiem.* But the verse properly concludes with the words, 'you shall be comforted in Jerusalem.' This is important because it is spelt out here that God's people will no longer be in exile in Babylon – they will have returned to their home.

What to Listen out for in the Music of Movement 5

Movement 5, it will be recalled from the Introduction, is the item that Brahms added after the Bremen première.

Listen out for the way the soprano soloist takes a dominant role in this movement, with the orchestra acting as an accompaniment. This is the first – and only – time that the soprano soloist takes part in the *Requiem*. Her entry is all the more strikingly fresh for its deliberate delay.

Listen out for the quiet, reflective tone of this movement. We are given much to enjoy from the lovely, flowing and expressive phrases of the melody. Prominent parts for each of the higher-pitched woodwind instruments enhance the beauty of the music.

Listen out for the interesting and unexpected shape of the movement. The general shape is A – B – A, which by now comes as no surprise. A is John 16:22 and B is the apocryphal verse, Ecclesiasticus 51:27. But what is very different is that the chorus do not sing any of those two verses at all, but instead they (and they alone) sing the words of Isaiah 66:13 – and they do so as an accompaniment to the soloist's verses in each of the three parts of the movement. In each section, the soloist sings her verse, and then at the end of her first statement of the verse (or a bit before the end, in the case of John 16:22 each time), the chorus enter with their harmonized singing of Isaiah 66:13. So, whenever the chorus are singing, the soloist is singing as well – but singing different words. Another way of looking at it is as three verses of a hymn (the soloist's A – B – A), each verse with a refrain – but the chorus are singing that refrain while the verse is still being sung!

Listen out for an interesting feature near the end, where the soloist and chorus do almost come together. While the soloist sings, 'ich will euch wieder sehen' ('I will see you again' – from John 16:22), the chorus sing, 'ich will euch trösten' ('I will comfort you' – from Isaiah 66:13).

The 'ich will euch' ('I – will – you') from both soloist and chorus echo each other.[126] This is very skilful craftsmanship.

Listen out for an occurrence of the U.M. – perhaps not so obvious this time. But in section B the first part of the entries for the soprano, contralto and tenor voices of the chorus appears to be an inverted form of that motif.

[126] In case some readers are not familiar with German, the word order in that language follows a different pattern from English, which is why the sequence of the three words translating 'I will you' is not odd.

Movement 6: Time and Eternity

For here we have no lasting city, but we seek the city that is to come. (Hebrews 13:14)

Behold! I tell you a mystery. We shall not all sleep, but we shall all be changed, in a moment, in the twinkling of an eye, at the last trumpet. For the trumpet will sound, and the dead will be raised imperishable, and we shall be changed.
... then shall come to pass the saying that is written:
"Death is swallowed up in victory."
"O death, where is your victory? O death, where is your sting?"
(1 Corinthians 15:51-52, 54b-55)

"Worthy are you, our Lord and God, to receive glory and honour and power, for you created all things, and by your will they existed and were created." (Revelation 4:11)

The first verse chosen for Movement 6, from the last chapter of the Letter to the Hebrews, contrasts the temporary nature of life on earth with the permanence of the life to come in heaven: here and now we experience the limits imposed by time, but in the age to come Christian believers will know the solid joys of eternity. This antithesis has been evident earlier in the oratorio, of course. The verses selected from 1 Corinthians 15, the great resurrection chapter of the Bible, focus on the change that will be ushered in at Christ's return, when believers receive their resurrection bodies to equip them for living in eternity. Such breath-taking glimpses of the heavenly home rightly evoke a response of praise to God in the words of the verse chosen from Revelation 4.

Hebrews 13:14: seeking the city that is to come

The word 'city', which comes twice in **Hebrews 13:14**, is used only three other times in this Bible book. Each time, the word points to the permanent heavenly home, which is to be the goal of every Christian believer; and keeping our sights fixed on that destination is the essence of living by faith, a major theme of the Letter to the Hebrews. We look forward with the eye of faith, of course, because that future home is unseen. As Hebrews 11:1 puts it, 'Now faith is the assurance of things hoped for, the conviction of things not seen.'

Two of those three other occurrences of the word 'city' in Hebrews come in chapter 11, where we are given a tour through the Old Testament. We are shown many examples of men and women of old, living before the time of Christ, who were looking forward by faith to the fulfilment of God's promises. These promises centre on Jesus and all that he would usher in by both his First and Second Comings. Those instances of the word 'city' in Hebrews 11 appear in the part of the chapter that focuses on Abraham. In verse 10, we are told that Abraham '... was looking forward to *the city* that has foundations, whose designer and builder is God.' (my italics). He was looking forward to a permanent home, which was a far cry from the nomadic existence in tents which he had adopted from the time he obeyed God's call. The following verse speaks of Abraham and his descendants, and they all (as a group) continue to be the people being spoken of in the following verses up to verse 16, which is where we find the second mention of 'city' in this chapter: '"But as it is, they desire a better country, that is a heavenly one. Therefore, God is not ashamed to be called their God, for he has prepared for them *a city.'* (my italics). Without these verses, we might summarise the Old Testament from Abraham to Joshua by saying, 'Abraham showed his faith in God by obediently setting out on a journey, which brought him to the Promised Land of Canaan. Later, after the people of Israel lived for a period in Egypt (first as guests, then as slaves), Moses led them out of that country and Joshua led the people back to the Promised Land. In this way God's promise to Abraham was fulfilled.' But that understanding of Abraham and his descendants is challenged by what the writer of the Letter to the Hebrews is telling us. These verses in Hebrews 11 tell us that Abraham and his descendants were looking forward not simply to the land of Canaan (Israel) but – beyond it – to heaven, which is spoken of here as 'the city that has foundations', the city 'prepared for them' by God.

It is true, of course, that God's promise to Abraham included 'the land' (Genesis 12:1). It is true also that we should notice the sense of fulfilment in Joshua's statement to the people in Joshua 23: '... you know in your hearts and souls, all of you, that not one word has failed of all the good things that the LORD your God promised concerning you. All have come to pass for you; not one of them has failed.' (Joshua 23:14) But these truths must be placed within the larger context. Arriving in the land was not the end of the story for God's people: conquering the land had to be followed by the hard work of occupying it, and that task was never fully accomplished. Abraham arriving in Canaan in Genesis 12, and Joshua leading the people across the river Jordan into the land in Joshua 3 – 4, were important staging-posts in the history of God's people. In the Bible's Big Picture, however, the real goal of the pilgrimage is heaven. The writer to the Hebrews wants us to know that this has always been the case for the people of God, both those who lived in Old Testament times and those who have lived (or are still living) under the New Testament.

The other mention of 'city' in Hebrews, prior to Hebrews 13:14, is in Hebrews 12:2. At this point in the Letter, the writer wants to persuade his readers not to revert to an Old-Testament-only form of Judaism. So, he spells out how everything that is on offer to them through Christ is far superior to the old covenant. He says: 'But you have come to Mount Zion and to the *city* of the living God, the heavenly Jerusalem ... and to Jesus, the mediator of a new covenant, and to the sprinkled blood that speaks a better word than the blood of Abel.' (Hebrews 12:22-24, my italics)

The final mention of 'city' in Hebrews, which comes in the verse used here in the oratorio (Hebrews 13:14), applies this seeking of the heavenly city to all Christian believers. In the discussion of Movement 4, we saw Paul's words to the Philippian Christians: 'But our citizenship is in heaven...' (Philippians 3:20). Philippi was a Roman colony in northern Greece and its people were proud of their Roman citizenship; being a citizen of heaven, however, is a higher honour. John Bunyan rightly understood the Christian life as a pilgrimage in his classic book 'Pilgrim's Progress', recounting the journey of Christian from the City of Destruction to the Celestial City. In the very first sentence of the book, even before the story has properly begun,

Bunyan describes this life as 'the wilderness of this world.'[127] In this way, John Bunyan establishes a connection between the pilgrim of his book and God's pilgrim people in their wilderness wanderings.

Another important Bible section which focuses on heaven as a city is the final two chapters of Revelation. The apostle John sees 'a new heaven and a new earth.' This vision is immediately described as 'the holy city, new Jerusalem, coming down out of heaven from God ...' (Revelation 21:1-2). The description of the city, in all its splendour and beauty, continues throughout this chapter and into the next.

The goal of the Christian life is future and it is, as yet, unseen. But it is an exciting future to look forward to.

1 Corinthians 15: the future resurrection

1 Corinthians 15:51-52 and 54b-55 come in the closing section of an important Bible chapter concerning resurrection. In the opening verses, Paul affirms the fact of Christ's resurrection. He reminds his readers of the basic truths of the Christian gospel, which he has both 'received' and 'delivered' (vv 1-4). He lists some of the appearances of the risen Jesus to groups of people and to individuals, including himself (vv 5-11). He wants to draw out some of the momentous consequences of Jesus' rising again – that we can have a solid *faith*, assured *forgiveness* and a secure *future* – by showing how they would not exist if Christ had not been raised from the dead (vv 12-19). At this point in his argument, he states again the glorious truth, 'But in fact Christ has been raised from the dead' (v 20a). He goes on to explain how Christ's resurrection is the guarantee of future blessings for those who belong to him (vv 20b-28). He spells out the enormity of what must follow from denying the resurrection (vv 29-34).

Then, from verse 35, Paul tackles the subject of the Christian believer's future resurrection body. We focus here on the verses from this section that are selected in the *Requiem*. Interestingly, at this point Brahms

[127] J. Bunyan, *The Pilgrim's Progress* (Harmondsworth: Penguin Books Ltd, 1965), 39 (first published 1678 – 85).

makes use of verses that also appear in Handel's *Messiah* – this is the only time that occurs.[128]

In verse 51, Paul's attention is focused on what will happen at Christ's return, when the history of the world will come to a sudden end. He calls on his readers for their undivided attention: 'Behold!' Ironically, he wants them to 'see' something that is now invisible. The word 'mystery' means something that once was a secret but is now revealed: what we might call an open secret. One of the wonders of the Christian gospel is that truths once hidden are now made known through the coming of Christ. So, Paul announces the revealed truth: 'We shall not all sleep, but we shall all be changed.' The 'we ... all' both times refers to Christian believers. Paul is not concerned here with what will happen at the end of time to the whole of humanity. Christians who are living on earth at that time will not die, in contrast to all previous generations of believers. The word 'sleep' here is chosen as the way to refer to death, because Christians no longer have anything to fear in dying: death for a Christian believer means falling asleep and then waking up in the presence of Jesus, just as happened with Jairus' daughter (Mark 5:22-24, 35-43). Jesus described this little girl's death as 'sleeping' because her death was not final – she was raised to life. The Christian who 'falls asleep' in death wakes up *immediately* in the presence of Jesus. We can be sure of this from the promise of Jesus to the penitent criminal crucified with him: 'Truly, I say to you, *today* you will be with me in Paradise.' (Luke 23:43, my italics)[129] But having said all that, the Bible's promise of the resurrection body, as here in 1 Corinthians 15, is associated with what will happen at Christ's Second Coming. At that time, according to Paul here in verse 51 of the chapter, a great change will occur for all Christians, both those who have died

[128] The verses in 1 Corinthians 15 that appear in Handel's *Messiah* (Part III) are vv 51-53 and vv 54b-57. So, both oratorios make use of vv 51-52 and 54b-55, and both omit verse 54a.

[129] Another instance of 'falling sleep' to mean the physical death of a believer occurs in Matthew 27:52, as was noted in the earlier discussion of Bach's *St Matthew Passion.*

in all the preceding years, generations and centuries, and also those alive in that final generation.

Verse 52 tells us more about that great change. It will be instantaneous. It will be 'in a moment', which translates a word from which we derive our English word 'atom', meaning 'that which cannot be divided', the smallest amount of time possible. The phrase 'in the twinkling of an eye', meaning the time it takes to cast a glance, has been in use since 1302 and is to be found in all major Bible translations including William Tyndale's New Testament and the Authorised Version of 1611. 'The last trumpet' is linked in Jesus' teaching with the events of the end of time (Matthew 24:31), and Paul refers to it in 1 Thessalonians 4:16 in connection with Christ's return: it is the signal for the dead to rise. When they do so, their new resurrection bodies will be 'imperishable'.

In the one-and-a-half verses that Brahms omits (vv 53-54a), Paul fills out the content of this momentous transformation:

> For this perishable body must put on the imperishable, and this mortal body must put on immortality. When the perishable puts on the imperishable, and the mortal puts on immortality...

It is a pity that the oratorio does not include these great statements, although we have a glorious affirmation to come in verses 54b-55 about the death of death. But in verses 53-54a, Paul gives more information about the nature of the resurrection body. Decay and death will be no more. How different the new will be from the old! Yet, alongside the discontinuity between the old and the new, there is also real continuity, as shown by the fourfold use of the word 'this' in the Greek text, twice in verse 53 and twice in verse 54. Modern translations make this difficult to spot: the NIV omits all four instances of the word 'this', and the ESV retains only the first two. So, the 'corrected' version of verses 53-54a, with the four occurrences of 'this' in italics, should read:

> For *this* perishable body must put on the imperishable, and *this* mortal body must put on immortality. When *this* perishable puts on the imperishable, and *this* mortal puts on immortality...

The point being emphasised here is that it is the same body that dies that is also raised to life. The resurrection body is gloriously different, but at the same time it is the same person.

The twice-repeated phrase 'put on' in verse 53 (putting on the imperishable and immortality), as if these things were items of clothing, indicates that the body is not the real person but an outer layer. It is as if, in the life to come, the real person will put on another suit of clothes. CS Lewis had all this in mind when he wrote to a Christian friend who was terminally ill with cancer, to encourage her to view the prospect of death positively: '"Can you not see death as the friend and deliverer? It means stripping off that body which is tormenting you; like taking off a hairshirt or getting out of a dungeon."'[130]

Having looked at the one-and-a-half verses that Brahms does not use, we return now to those which he does include. In verse 54b, Paul announces the fulfilment of Old Testament prophecy concerning the complete victory over death when Christ comes again. The Old Testament verse quoted is from Isaiah 25:8, which reads in full as follows:

> He will swallow up death for ever;
> and the Lord GOD will wipe away tears from all faces,
> and the reproach of his people he will take away from all the earth,
> for the LORD has spoken.

[130] C.S. Lewis, *Letters to an American Lady*, ed. C. Kilby (London: Hodder and Stoughton, 1969), 114.

'Swallowed up in victory' (1 Corinthians 15:54b) is a powerful metaphor for the complete destruction of death. The reference to God wiping away tears from all faces is echoed in Revelation 21:4 as part of the picture of the new heaven and the new earth, where there will be unbroken fellowship between God and his people. 'Reproach' (in the verse in Isaiah) is a reminder of the curse that death, as the consequence of sin, represents for the human race, but one day it will be completely removed.

Verse 55 is another Old Testament quotation, which Paul says will also be fulfilled at Christ's return. The words Paul uses are his rendering of Hosea 13:14:

> O death, where is your victory?
> O death, where is your sting?

The tone of this verse is one of exultation. This is a victory-cry over a defeated enemy. The fact that we still have to face death (unless we belong to that generation who are still alive at Christ's Second Coming) does not lessen the certainty of that joy. The picture in the second half of the verse is of a bee or a scorpion, whose harmful sting Christ has drawn by taking it upon himself, and therefore death is now harmless to all who are in him.

The following verse of 1 Corinthians 15 – verse 56 (not included in the oratorio) – goes on to explain that it is not death itself that is harmful, but the fact that death is 'the wages of sin' (Romans 6:23). The 'sting' of death is 'sin'. But now that sin is pardoned, as far as the Christian believer is concerned, death has no sting – Christ has paid the price for sin once and for all. This is the glorious truth for Christian believers, but the assurances of these verses do not apply to those whose sin remains unforgiven. Sin has an unexpected ally, from which it derives its power, namely 'the law'. The law is of divine origin and is therefore 'holy and righteous and good' (Romans 7:12), but the law is totally incapable of offering salvation.[131] The law sets the standard we ought to reach but never do. The law takes us prisoner and condemns us.

However, we round off this discussion on a positive note – as Paul does in verse 57: 'But thanks be to God, who gives us the victory through our Lord Jesus Christ.' The Christian believer can rejoice in Christ's complete victory over death and sin and law. Victory over *death* is assured by Christ's resurrection. Victory over *sin* is assured by Christ's death for us as our substitute. Victory over *law* is assured, because Christ has replaced the 'reign' of sin with that of grace (Romans 5:20-21).

Revelation 4:11: God is worthy to be praised

Such great and glorious truths as have been declared in the verses that Brahms has included from 1 Corinthians 15, let alone the verses which he has omitted but are implied all the same, demand a further response of praise. This is provided by **Revelation 4:11**, which is the final verse of a chapter that records the apostle John's vision of God the Creator. Here is not the place to unpack the content of that vision in full. Instead, the following comments give a brief explanation of the setting of that verse.

In his vision of Revelation chapter 4, John attempts to put into words something that almost defies the capability of human language. He tells us something of what he *saw*: the display of colour and the stream of movement. It may come as a surprise that John never really describes God. He cannot, because of God's awesome majesty. He also tells us something of what he *heard*, as the royal court declare God's eternal splendour and his utter purity. There is a particular focus on God's holiness: he is 'holy, holy, holy' (Revelation 4:8), which is an echo of the seraphim's praise of God in Isaiah's vision of God in chapter 6 of his book (Isaiah 6:3). In the Hebrew language, 'holy, holy' would be the way to express the term 'very holy' So, a three-times repeated 'holy' indicates what can only be described as a super-superlative, 'holy to the ultimate degree'.

---

[131] See Romans 5:12ff, 7:7ff, 10:4.

Our verse from this chapter, selected for the conclusion of Movement 6 of the oratorio, consists of the words of the twenty-four elders, seated on thrones around God's throne. To call God 'worthy' means to 'worship' him, i.e., to ascribe 'worthship' to him. He alone is 'worthy' to receive glory, honour and power. They praise God for his creation of 'all things'. It is due to his will that they were created and have their being.

The pastoral purpose of the recording of this vision, as indeed of the whole of the Book of Revelation, is to give encouragement to Christian believers who are living in danger of persecution and adversity. In the first chapter of the Book, John has described himself as his readers' 'brother and partner in the tribulation and the kingdom and the patient endurance that are in Jesus' (Revelation 1:9). Christians are to fix their eyes of faith on 'the kingdom', of which they are citizens (and about which this Bible Book will tell them more), at the same time as they face the harsh reality in this life of 'tribulation'. As they do so, they will be enabled to stand firm with 'patient endurance'. In the light of this vision of God's majesty and glory, they can be assured that God has not turned his back on the world that he created. He made all things, including them, for his own purpose. Evil will not have the last word, because the Sovereign God is in control.

Powerful as this message is, we might wonder if Brahms has selected the most appropriate Bible verse at this point. The passages from Hebrews and 1 Corinthians have pointed us to the Christian believer's home in heaven: the 'city' that is to come (Hebrews) and the future resurrection life (1 Corinthians). The theme is God's grace in redemption. Revelation 4, on the other hand, has as its major theme God's majesty in creation. A better choice for a final verse might have been one or other of two hymns of praise, also beginning with the word 'worthy', taken from the following chapter:

> Worthy are you to take the scroll and to open its seals,
> for you were slain, and by your blood you ransomed people for God

> from every tribe and language and people and nation,
> and you have made them a kingdom and priests to our God,
> and they shall reign on the earth. (Revelation 5:9-10)

and:

> Worthy is the Lamb who was slain,
> to receive power and wealth and wisdom and might
> and honour and glory and blessing!
> (Revelation 5:12)

The vision of Revelation 5 is the companion to that of chapter 4. Chapter 4 records a vision of God the Creator. Now comes a vision of God the Redeemer, the Lamb who has conquered through his death. One or other of these two songs of praise might have been more appropriate here, because they would explain how it is that sinners can be qualified for the life to come. It is only through the shed blood of Jesus, who died on the cross, in order to purchase 'a ransomed people for God'. It might be pointed out that the second of these alternative Bible extracts forms part of the exciting and well-known conclusion of Handel's *Messiah*. It is possible that Brahms decided for this reason to select a different Bible verse. The exclusion, or the inclusion, of Bible verses that are used in that other great oratorio has been discussed already in this study, and there are arguments on both sides of the issue. We shall never know whether such thoughts went through Brahms' mind.

What to Listen out for in the Music of Movement 6

Like Movement 2, this movement is most dramatic. As was explained in the Introduction, Movements 2 and 6 (the second and the second to last) mirror each other in that respect. But while much of Movement 2 was taken up with a funeral march, by contrast we now hear the triumphant celebration of resurrection-victory.

The shape of Movement 6 is quite without complications. Brahms straightforwardly takes us in order through the verses that we have been discussing, without going back to an earlier verse.

Listen out for the prominent role of the baritone soloist again in this movement.

Listen out for the subdued setting of the chorus's singing of Hebrews 13:14 and for the way they are interrupted by the baritone soloist. He announces the words of 1 Corinthians 15:51 concerns the change that awaits Christian believers on the Last Day. The chorus respond in hushed chords.

Listen out for the way the soloist's entry echoes that striking phrase, which was heard in Movement 2, with the octave leap upwards. This time, however, the leap is just less than an octave – though it is still a recognisable echo. In view of the intended connection between Movements 2 and 6 (referred to in the Introduction and above), we can be fairly sure that this musical echo is deliberate.

Listen out for the momentary halt in the music, as the soloist moves into verse 52 and sings the words 'in einem Augenblick' ('in a moment'). Then we move into the section about 'the last trumpet' (although in the German text the word used is 'Posaune', which is really 'trombone'). The music becomes exciting at this point, with full – and loud – chorus and orchestra (not least the brass section and timpani), as is fitting for the message of resurrection to an imperishable body.

Listen out for the soloist's announcement that the word of Scripture will be fulfilled, and the chorus's response, which is extensive and triumphant. They revel in the content of that Scripture, namely the assurance of victory over death and hell.

Listen out for what appears, shortly after that, to be the music coming to a conclusion on the final repeat of the words 'Wo ist dein Sieg?' ('"here is your victory?"). However, immediately the contraltos begin a new theme, 'Herr, du bist würdig ...' ('Lord, you are worthy ...').

Listen out for the first three notes of the contraltos' line, because they are another appearance of the U.M., albeit in an inverted form. And we hear that same inverted form of our unifying motif from the sopranos, basses and tenors in turn in their opening music in this part of the movement.

Listen out for, and enjoy, the extraordinary and masterful fugue, which runs from this point onwards until the end of the movement. While it is interspersed in places by the four voices of the chorus singing more chordal sections, the fugue keeps breaking out again.

Listen out, twice during this latter part of the movement, for unmistakable, and thrilling, strides upward through five octaves from the low strings and tuba to the high trumpet and violins. And so, the movement reaches its glorious conclusion.

Movement 7: Toil and Rest

'... Blessed are the dead who die in the Lord from now on.' 'Blessed indeed,' says the Spirit, 'that they may rest from their labours, for their deeds follow them!' (Revelation 14:13b)

Revelation 14:13: Future rest from present labours

Just as the *Requiem* began with a Bible verse describing those who mourn as 'blessed', so it ends with another verse describing a group who merit the same description, namely 'the dead who die in the Lord'. This phrase clearly means those who die as Christian believers, because 'In the Lord' or 'in Christ' is the most frequently used term in the New Testament for those who have put their trust in the Lord Jesus. In a very real sense, they are incorporated 'in him' and they are identified 'with' him. They have died with him, are buried with him, are raised with him, and are exalted with him.[132] The very first part of this verse, **Revelation 14:13**, which refers to the 'voice from heaven', is omitted by Brahms. But we are given the words spoken by that individual (whom, very probably, we are meant to identify as God the Father), and we hear the words of agreement of the Spirit (i.e., God the Holy Spirit). Bearing in mind that 'the Lord' is Jesus, God the Son, this may well be considered as one of the instances in the Bible of all three Persons of the Trinity being identified in the same verse.[133]

The occurrences of the word 'blessed', both at the start of the oratorio and here at its conclusion, act as 'bookends' (to repeat the word used in the discussion of Movement 5 in connection with the word 'comfort',

---

[132] See, for example, Ephesians 1:1-14, where the preposition 'in' is used several times in connection with 'Christ' or other words referring to him: nine of them are clear examples of the inclusion of believers 'in Christ'. See also, among many other possible examples, 2 Corinthians 5:17 and Colossians 3:1-4.

[133] In the carefully ordered structure of the Book of Revelation, the word 'blessed' is used 7 times. The number 7 is used in various ways in the vocabulary and the structure of this Bible book and indicates completeness. The 7 instances of 'blessed' in Revelation (sometimes known as 'macarisms', from the Greek word for 'blessed') are 1:3, 14:13 (here), 16:15, 19:19, 20:6, 22:7 and 22:14.

both at the beginning and also towards the end of a major section of the Book of Isaiah). The technical term for this is an 'inclusio'. The effect of this repetition of 'blessed', at the beginning and the end of the *Requiem*, is to provide a sense of coherence and completeness to the work, quite apart from the emphasis given to this particular word.

At the beginning of this chapter of Revelation, the apostle John sees Jesus as 'the Lamb', accompanied by 144,000 individuals, each with the name of Jesus and of the Father written on their foreheads, all of them standing on Mount Zion (Revelation 14:1). There are several important truths from this first verse of the chapter, all of which have a bearing on the description of Christians which we are given in verse 13, the verse chosen for Movement 7 of the work:

- They stand on 'Mount Zion'. As was noted in the discussion of verses from Psalm 84 in Movement 4, Mount Zion (the hill in Jerusalem where the temple stood) becomes a symbol in the Bible for heaven. In case the phrase 'the dead who die in the Lord' suggests the image of row upon row of coffins or a vast cemetery, we are being told clearly that Christians who have died are already alive and triumphant in their heavenly home.
- Jesus is described as 'the Lamb'. We have met that description of Jesus in a number of Bible verses earlier in this study.[134] Each time, that phrase speaks of Jesus' sacrificial death on the cross. The Christian believers of verse 13 are 'in the Lord', and therefore in heaven, solely on the basis of Christ's substitutionary death for them.
- The number '144,000', describing God's people, is not meant to be understood literally. It is a symbolic number of completeness (12 x 12 x 1000 – the number 12 is suggestive of the 12 Old Testament tribes and the 12 New Testament apostles). Revelation 7 also speaks of the '144,000' (Revelation 7:4), but this number of God's people is to be equated with the description of God's people a few verses later in the same chapter, as 'a great multitude that no one could number'

[134] 1 Peter 1:18-19 (in the discussion of Movement 2); John 1:29 (in the discussion of Movement 5); and Revelation 5:12 (in the discussion of Movement 6).

(Revelation 7:9). The assurance of Revelation 14:13 applies to every Christian believer, whether they have lived their lives on earth in the past, or live them now in the present, or will live them in the future.

- The name of Jesus and of his Father written on the foreheads of Christian believers is to be understood as a symbol of their security in heaven. They belong to Jesus and to the Father: they are his eternal possession.

As was mentioned in the discussion on Movement 6, the purpose of the Book of Revelation is to give pastoral encouragement to Christians living under pressure (the 'tribulation' of Revelation 1:9). What tremendous motivation for steadfast Christian living *here and now* is provided by the certainty of the security and 'blessedness' of believers in the *there and then* of heaven to come! They are weary from their toil, which is what the word used here for 'labours' suggests – but they are assured of 'rest', not in the sense of passivity or idleness, rather in the sense of knowing the joy of the end of all pain. This is an important aspect of the Christian believer's assured Everlasting Rest.

The words 'from now on' are best understood as referring to 'blessed', not to 'the dead who die in the Lord'. In other words, it is not that those who have died from that point of time onwards are more blessed than those who had died previously. Rather, all those who have died as Christians are assured of a blessedness which is for ever. The Spirit's answer is literally 'Yes!' (rather than 'Blessed indeed').

One further point should be included. Shakespeare's Mark Antony declares:

> The evil that men do lives after them;
> The good is oft interred with their bones.[135]

However, faithful Christians can be assured that their deeds follow them into the life beyond the grave. This gives dignity to all the work

---

[135] W. Shakespeare, *Julius Caesar,* Act III, Scene 2, ll.81-82.

in which Christians engage. Christians can know that we are 'created in Christ Jesus for good works, which God prepared beforehand, that we should walk in them.' (Ephesians 2:10) Whatever Christians achieve by God's grace will cause ripples that travel into eternity.

What to Listen out for in the Music of Movement 7

Movement 7 is sung by the chorus without soloists.

As mentioned in the discussion in the Introduction about the symmetrical structure of the *Requiem,* Movements 1 and 7 mirror each other. Both begin with the word 'Selig' ('Blessed'). And both have the same shape: A – B – A. A represents the first half of the Bible verse and B the second half.

Listen out for the first entry of the sopranos at the beginning of the movement as they sing without the other voices, and for the entry of the basses who follow them immediately, singing the same opening phrase, similarly without the other voices. The first word for both voices is 'Selig' ('Blessed'), and the first three notes for both voices provide another occurrence of the U.M. in its inverted form.

Listen out for the solemn tone of the voices in this first part of the movement, both in those opening phrases for the sopranos, and then the basses, on their own – and then for all four voices as they come together.

Listen out for the change of tone as we come into section B of the movement, and hear the words 'Ja, der Geist spricht' ('Yes, says the Spirit'). This change of tone is produced first by these words being sung without the sopranos (just by the contraltos, tenors and basses), and then by the words 'daß sie ruhen von ihrer Arbeit' ('that they may rest from their labours') being sung without the sopranos and contraltos (just by the tenors and basses). In other words, there is a two-step reduction of the higher-pitched voices, so that we hear only the lower-pitched voices. Also, at this point, the added accompaniment from the trombone further increases the mood of solemnity.

Listen out, at this point of entering properly into section B, for a change of key (from F to A).

Listen out for further prominent entries by brass instruments in this part of movement.

Listen out for the transition from section B back to the second section A, which is marked by a return to the original key, and by the tenors (on their own) singing 'Selig sind die Toten' ('Blessed are the dead'). Their first three notes (on the word 'Selig') are a restatement of the U.M. in its inverted form, and their singing of the words 'sind die Toten' provide the U.M. in its original form.

Listen out for further instances of the U.M. from the sopranos, after all four voices have joined together again, and also from the orchestra.

Listen out for the harps towards the close of the movement, as at the close of Movement 1. This is even more striking, since they have not played since the middle of Movement 2.

Listen out for the final word sung by the chorus. This has been mentioned already in the Introduction. It is that significant word 'selig' ('blessed'), which was also the very first word of Movement 1. The symmetry of the work is complete.

Conclusion

What impact have these great oratorios made on you? Everything we experience through any of our senses leaves its impression on us. Whether consciously and deliberately, or subconsciously and automatically, we evaluate all that we see or hear or taste or touch or smell. May I invite us, therefore, consciously to evaluate our response to the musical masterpieces of Haydn, Bach and Brahms?

Assuming that your response to these oratorios is a positive one, which I hope is the case, I would venture to suggest that we will place ourselves in one of the following categories. The first two are very common. They are also very appealing. It may seem very bad manners for someone to say that they are wrong or inadequate, but that is, in fact, the case, as will be explained. However, there is a third response, which I want to commend – and we will come to that very soon.

The first inadequate response might be labelled ENJOYMENT ONLY. There is, of course, nothing wrong with enjoyment. God 'richly provides us with everything to enjoy.' (1 Timothy 6:17) To enjoy a good piece of music is right and proper. If this book has helped to increase anyone's enjoyment of these three oratorios, it will have been worthwhile. But the quibble is with the word 'only'. When a musical work is being used to convey the message of the Bible, our response must go further. Handel's words, quoted in my earlier book on his *Messiah,* are worth repeating. Once, when *Messiah* was being performed, Lord Kinnoul congratulated Handel on a splendid entertainment. Handel replied, 'My Lord, I should be sorry if I only entertained them; I wished to make them better.'[136] We may wonder how Haydn, Bach or Brahms may have responded if someone had complimented them in the same way.

The second response which does not go far enough might be given the label IMPROVEMENT BY SELF-EFFORT. This could, of course, be the

[136] James Beattie, 'Letter of May 25 1780', published in W. Forbes, *An Account of the Life and Writings of James Beattie, LL.D.* (1806), 331.

way Handel's words, quoted above, are understood. But such a response falls short of the ideal. Individuals may be moved deeply by what they hear or read or see performed, and as a result they may resolve to be 'better'. But that it in itself will not make them good enough for God. An emotional, or even a religious, experience may make an impact at the time, without producing lasting effects. The Book of Daniel tells us about Nebuchadnezzar, king of Babylon. He was impressed by the clear explanation that God gave Daniel concerning the king's mystifying dream (Daniel 2). And he was deeply moved when he witnessed the miraculous preservation of three young Jewish men whom he had consigned to the fiery furnace (Daniel 3). But neither of those experiences brought about Nebuchadnezzar's conversion – that happened through a more direct and personal experience of God's grace when he found himself under God's judgement (Daniel 4).

We cannot truly become *better* people without at the same time becoming *new* people. No amount of self-effort will make us good enough for God. Genuine Christianity is not the result of trying hard to improve one's thoughts and words and deeds. Attempts to make oneself 'better' by self-effort are characteristic of moralism, legalism or religion without Christ. Genuine Christianity is the outflow of a life that has begun 'to put on the new self, created after the likeness of God in true righteousness and holiness.' (Ephesians 4:24) Being a Christian is not turning a new leaf but beginning a new life. It is to 'be born of the Spirit', 'born again' (John 3:6 and 7). Anyone who is in Christ is a 'new creation' (2 Corinthians 5:17). John Stott memorably described the difference between moralism and true Christianity in terms of the difference between two trees. In a comment on Jesus' words, 'Whoever abides in me and I in him, he it is that bears much fruit' (John 15:5), he wrote: 'Thus the Christian is likened to a fruit tree, not a Christmas tree. For the fruit *grows* on a fruit tree, whereas the decorations are only *tied* on to a Christmas tree.'[137]

---

[137] J. Stott, *Christ the Liberator* (Downers Grove: InterVarsity Press, 1971), 55.

Religion is an inadequate word to use of true Christianity, because it suggests that I have to do things to make myself acceptable to God. *Relationship*. by contrast, is what lies at the heart of genuine Christianity, and it comes about as a result of God's grace in Jesus, and through his saving death on the cross. Paul draws out the contrast between Religion and Relationship in Philippians 3. He describes his earlier life as a Pharisee when, in terms of 'righteousness under the law' he might have been regarded as 'blameless' (Philippians 3:6). But he writes off all his 'religious' credit on account of his life-changing encounter with the Lord Jesus. He says, 'I count everything as loss because of the surpassing worth of *knowing* Christ Jesus my Lord.' (Philippians 3:8, my italics) Nothing, not even a familiarity with the truths of the Bible, must be allowed to become a substitute for coming to Jesus personally in order to receive life. A genuine Christian must be able to say, like Paul, 'I *know* whom I have believed' (2 Timothy 1:12, my italics).

This leads us to the third response – the right one – to the three oratorios of this study. It can be labelled as KNOWING GOD MORE AND MORE. These three musical masterpieces are certainly to be 'enjoyed'. They should also lead us to want to become 'better' (as Handel said of his great oratorio, *Messiah*), but this will not come about by self-effort. Rather, it will happen as the result of being made new in Christ, knowing him as Lord and Saviour. That will lead to a life-long process of knowing God – Father, Son and Holy Spirit – more and more.

Haydn's *The Creation* helps us not simply to know more about creation. It encourages us to want to **know God as the Creator**. As we take in the truths of Genesis 1 in particular, and also Psalms 19 and 104, we are given understanding of these truths about God:

- His *awesomeness*. The majesty, beauty, vastness, intricacy and variety of 'the heavens and the earth' are truly breath-taking. The creation of mankind should lead us to ponder on the amazing truth that each of us is God's handiwork. As David wrote, '"I praise you, for I am fearfully and wonderfully made."' (Psalm 139:14)

- His *grace.* Genesis 1 tells us that:

  'God created man in his own image,
  in the image of God he created him;
  male and female he created them.' (Genesis 1:27)

  Genesis 3 reveals to us that, before the Fall, the first human pair walked and talked with God in the garden. We should marvel that God should have such purposes of grace for men and women.
- His *care.* We have been reminded, for example in Psalm 104, that God sustains his creation. 'These all look to you, to give them their food in due season,' (Psalm 104:27) Even after the Fall, God cares for all he has made.
- His *sovereignty.* He is the Lord over all his creation, and nothing happens beyond his control and authority. Therefore, we recognise our personal accountability to him.
- His *holiness.* 'Good' is a recurring word in describing God's creation – culminating in the statement, 'And God saw everything that he had made, and behold, it was very good.' (Genesis 1:31) Although Haydn's oratorio is mainly concerned with Genesis 1 and 2, we have noticed its strong hint of the Fall to come in chapter 3. We recognise that it was human sin – our sin – that led to God's creation being spoilt. Our relationship with God, our relationship with one another and our relationship with our environment have all been marred by our sin. So, knowing God's holiness and our own sin must lead to penitence.

Bach's *St Matthew Passion* enables us to take in the wonder of God's work of salvation in the death of his Son on the cross – and as a result to **know God as our Redeemer.** In the words of Isaac Watts,

When I survey the wondrous cross
on which the prince of glory died,
my richest gain I count but loss
and pour contempt on all my pride.[138]

[138] I. Watts, 'When I survey the wondrous cross', in *Hymns and Spiritual Songs,* 1707.

We learn these great truths about God:

- His *righteousness.* Because he is the God of holiness, he must punish sin. When Jesus hung on the cross, God laid on him the sin of the world and poured out his judgement on him. In this way, Isaiah's prophecy about the Suffering Servant was fulfilled:

  > All we like sheep have gone astray;
  > we have turned – every one – to his own way;
  > and the LORD has laid on him
  > the iniquity of us all. (Isaiah 53:6)

  John the Baptist's identification of Jesus was also proved correct, when he pointed to Jesus and said, '"Behold, the Lamb of God, who takes away the sin of the world."' (John 1:29)
- His *love.* The cross of Jesus displays God's judgement but, at the same time, it supremely displays God's love. 'But God shows his love for us in that while we were still sinners, Christ died for us.' (Romans 5:8)
- His *forgiveness.* So many Bible verses spell out the wonderful truth that God cleanses his people from their sin, for example Jeremiah 31:34: '"For I will forgive their iniquity, and I will remember their sin no more."' We have seen how, on the evening before his crucifixion, Jesus spoke of the fulfilment of that verse, when he said, '"... for this is my blood of the covenant [i.e. the new covenant of Jeremiah 31], which is poured out for many for the forgiveness of sins."' (Matthew 26:28)

Brahms' *Requiem* points us unmistakably to the future prospect of heaven, which Richard Baxter described as 'The Saints' Everlasting Rest'. We are reminded that we can **know God as the Rest-giver.** Through a variety of Bible verses, we have been directed away from the frustrations and sorrows of this 'vale of tears' to the 'solid joys and lasting treasure' of heaven to come.[139] In particular we have seen how sorrow is replaced by joy; transience by permanence; mortality by

---

[139] The phrase 'vale of tears' derives from Psalm 84:6 in Wycliffe's translation of 1395 ('valei of teeris') and the *Bishops' Bible* of 1568 ('vale of teares'). 'Solid joys and lasting treasure' – see Footnote 114.

security; longing by fulfilment; sadness by comfort; time by eternity, and toil by rest.

It was noted in the earlier discussion that Brahms might have made use of Matthew 11:28 but sadly did not. That verse promises 'rest' to come, and it also makes plain our need to come to Jesus as the one who gives that rest: '"Come to me, all who labour and are heavy laden, and I will give you rest."'

As a closing paragraph to this study, let me suggest a prayer of response. The prayer uses the plural pronouns 'we' and 'us', but I hope that we may want to make it our own personal prayer.

Lord God,
You have revealed yourself as Father, Son and Holy Spirit.
From everlasting to everlasting you are God.
We praise you as the CREATOR:
You are the maker of all things visible and invisible.
Heaven and earth are full of your majesty and glory.
You uphold the universe with the word of your power.
We praise you as the REDEEMER:
At the time of your sovereign choosing,
the Word became flesh and dwelt among us.
He humbled himself by becoming obedient to death,
even death on a cross,
the Righteous for the unrighteous,
that he might bring us to God.
We praise you as the REST-GIVER:
You invite us to come to you,
to lose our burdens of sin and toil,
to find in you our dwelling place.
We pray that we may know you more and more
in your life-giving word,
as your Spirit shines his light on the pages of Scripture and into our hearts.
We pray that, knowing you, we may love you more and more
and may serve you all our days. Amen.

Appendix 1: Index of Biblical and Apocryphal References

This list includes verses and passages that are discussed in the study but does not include those that are referred to in passing.

A. SCRIPTURE

B. APOCRYPHA

Appendix 2: Index of Major Topics and Bible Characters

PART 1 – CREATION

PART 2 – CROSS

PART 3 – EVERLASTING REST

(N.B. Some of the themes overlap, e.g., 'sadness' and 'sorrow', 'death' and 'mortality'.)

Appendix 3: Musical Glossary

alto: see 'contralto'.

anthem: an independent piece of choral music which may be sung as a non-essential part of a church service.

antiphon: two different sections of a choir singing alternately, as if responding to each other.

aria (or *air*)*:* a solo vocal piece of melodious character.

arioso: a short but aria-like, sustained, developed vocal piece.

arpeggio: a chord which is spread, as would be played on a harp (with which the word is connected) – i.e., the notes are heard one after another.

bar: a segment of time corresponding to a specific number of beats in which each beat is represented by a particular note value and the boundaries of the bar are indicated by vertical bar lines.

baritone: the male voice which has a pitch between bass and tenor.

bass: the lowest of the male voices.

Baroque: when applied to music, this term refers to the distinctive musical style of the 17th and early 18th centuries.

block chord: the style of harmonic progression, in which the four vocal lines sing the same words in the same metre and rhythm as each other, as when a church-choir sings a hymn or as in a Bach chorale. This style of music is known as 'homophony'.

cantata: in Baroque music, the term is applied to a work for several solo voices and chorus, etc., much like a short oratorio.

cantus firmus: a fixed melody to which other voices are added.

chamber music: instrumental music played by a small ensemble, with one player to a part, the most important form being the string quartet.

chorale: see 'block chord' above.

chorus: (1) a piece within the oratorio for the four-part choir to sing, rather than a soloist. (2) another word for choir.

chromatic: introducing notes not forming a part of the prevailing key. A chromatic scale, or sequence, progresses by semitones.

Classical: music written in the European tradition during a period lasting approximately from 1750 to 1830 (i.e., following the Baroque period), when forms such as the symphony, concerto, and sonata were standardised.

clavichord: in appearance this instrument, when opened, resembles a small rectangular piano. It was often in the form of a box to be placed on a table but sometimes had its own legs. It was in use from the 14th century to the end of the 18th century.

coda: a passage added to any composition, or section of music, to give a stronger sense of finality.

compound time: this contrasts with 'simple time'. Whereas the beats in simple time divide into twos, the beats in compound time divide into threes. The difference can be illustrated by saying aloud the following two phrases, where the stressed syllables are in italics. As an example of simple time, we can say, '*Don't* for*get* to *catch* your *train*.' As an example of compound time, we can say, '*Phone* me as *soon* as you're *there*.'

continuo: an independent bass line, usually realised on a keyboard instrument, in which numerals written underneath the notes indicate the kinds of harmony to be played.

contrabassoon: also known as a double bassoon. It resembles a bassoon (a low-pitched wind instrument) but is longer, curves around on itself twice and is pitched an octave lower.

contralto: the lowest of the female voices. The shortened form 'alto' is normally used for males with this pitch of voice.

cor anglais: an instrument belonging to the oboe family. It can be described as an alto oboe with a pitch a fifth (approximately half an octave) below that of the oboe.

counter-tenor: male alto.

crescendo: gradually getting louder in volume.

crotchet: a musical note which represents the normal 'pulse' of a piece, its time-value being half that of a minim.

da capo: literally means 'from the head'. It is found at the end of some items of music and indicates going back to the beginning again and continuing until the word *Fine* (= 'end').

diminished seventh: the interval which is one semitone less than a minor seventh. A minor seventh upward from C would be B flat – i.e., in the minor key beginning on C, the seventh note would be B flat. The diminished seventh above C is therefore B double flat, which is the same as the note A.

diminished seventh chord: a diminished seventh chord is formed by a note together with three notes above it, each at an interval of a minor third. It inevitably includes the note which is a diminished seventh above it. So, the diminished chord beginning on C will consist of C, E flat, G flat and B double flat (which is the same as the note A).

diminuendo: gradually getting softer in volume.

dotted crotchet: any note which is 'dotted' (i.e., has a dot printed immediately after it) is lengthened in its duration by half.

dotted rhythm: repeated sequence of a dotted note (i.e., lengthened by half) followed by a note which has half the normal value.

duet: a piece of music for two vocalists or instrumentalists, with or without accompaniment.

dynamics: the variation in loudness between notes or phrases.

forte / fortissimo: forte means loud; *fortissimo* means very loud.

fugue: a piece, or section, with sustained use of counterpoint, which means that one part enters with a phrase, which is then more or less exactly copied by other parts in succession, while the earlier part(s) is/are still playing (or singing). This style of music is known as 'polyphony'.

harmony: the combination of different notes, or lines of notes, by vocalists or instrumentalists. Depending on the context, it can be the opposite of 'unison' (see below) or 'discord'.

harpsichord: this type of domestic keyboard instrument was popular from the beginning of the 16th century to the end of the 18th century and is associated with Baroque music.

home key: the tonality of the piece of music, as indicated by its key-signature. It is the key in which the piece would normally be expected to begin and finish.

homophony: see 'block chord'.

key: refers to the adherence in a piece of music to the note-material of one of the major or minor scales – see 'minor' below. The key is known by whichever note the scale (major or minor) begins and ends on.

key-signature: the marking at the beginning of the piece (and of each line of the music) of its home key. The marking takes the form of one or more 'sharps' (moving the relevant note up a semitone) or 'flats' (moving the relevant note down a semitone).

libretto: the Italian word for 'little book', meaning the literary text of an opera or oratorio.

major: see 'minor'.

minor: best explained by contrast to its opposite, which is 'major'. The scale of C major consists of the white notes on a piano keyboard: C-D-E-F-G-A-B-C. The scale of C minor in its so-called 'harmonic' form consists of the notes: C-D-Eb-F-G-Ab-B-C. A minor key sounds more mournful than a major key.

movement: a distinct major section within a larger piece of music, such as a symphony or concerto. In this study the term is applied to the separate items within an oratorio.

obbligato: when attached to the 'part' of any instrument in a score, the implication is that the part in question is essential to the effect.

oboe d'amore: this was a member of the oboe family and is now obsolete. It was intermediate in size between the oboe and the cor anglais.

oboe da caccia: this was a member of the oboe family and is now obsolete. It was a predecessor of the cor anglais, which nowadays takes its place when older music, scored for an oboe da caccia, is played.

octave: the interval between one note and another which is eight steps above it or below it, counting inclusively – i.e., when ascending, or descending, the scale from that first note by eight steps (counting inclusively). Two notes an octave apart, played or sung together, have a hollow-sounding quality.

oratorio: an extended setting of a religious libretto for solo vocalists, chorus and orchestra, and designed for either a concert or a church performance, i.e., without scenery, costume or action.

overture: in Baroque (and early Classical) music, the word meant a piece of instrumental music intended as the introduction to an oratorio or an opera.

pause: the note, chord or rest, over which a 'pause' sign is indicated, is to be prolonged at the performer's will. It does not mean a silence (unless it is a rest – i.e., a mark indicating the absence of music – over which the pause sign is written).

piano / pianissimo: piano means soft, quiet; *pianissimo* means very soft.

pizzicato: the word means 'plucked' and generally refers to string instruments (violins, etc.) being plucked with the fingers instead of being bowed.

quartet: a piece of music for four vocalists or instrumentalists, with or without accompaniment.

quaver: a musical note with the time-value of one-half of a crotchet.

recitative: a style of solo vocal composition in which ordered melody, rhythm and metre are largely disregarded in favour of some imitation of the natural inflections of speech and accompanied by only the continuo or by additional string instruments; *secco* (= 'dry') recitative is accompanied only by the continuo, while *accompagnato* (= 'accompanied') recitative is accompanied not only by continuo but also by the string section of the orchestra.

requiem: the word generally means the Mass for the Dead, as found in the Roman Catholic liturgy. The text has been repeatedly set by composers. But some requiems show notable differences, particularly the one by Brahms.

ripieno: literally 'filling out'. The word, as used by Bach, refers to supplementary performers.

rolled chord: the notes of the chord are played quickly in order, from the lowest to the highest, instead of simultaneously.

Romantic: when applied to music, it refers to music of the 19th century, which was marked by an emphasis on originality and individuality, personal emotional expression, and freedom and experimentation of form.

semitone: the smallest interval used in normal music, as for example between the notes B and C.

*siciliana (*or *siciliano):* a musical piece with the time signature 6/8 or 12/8 (which means, respectively, two or four beats in the bar, each consisting of a dotted crotchet). The piece has a slow lilting rhythm. The Christmas carol 'Silent Night' is a well-known example of a piece making use of the 'siciliana' rhythm.

sonata: type of musical composition, usually for a solo instrument or a small instrumental ensemble, that typically consists of two to four movements, or sections, each in a related key but with a unique musical character.

sonata form: a type of composition in three sections (exposition, development, and recapitulation) in which two themes or subjects are explored according to set key relationships. It forms the basis for much Classical music, including the sonata, symphony, and concerto.

soprano: the highest of the female voices, above mezzo-soprano and contralto.

staccato: the word means 'detached'. The note is played in an abrupt, detached way.

suite: a set of short instrumental compositions, often with the pieces being in the same key or a related one.

symphony: when referring to works from the Classical or Romantic periods, it means a large-scale orchestral work intended to be played in the concert hall. It is usually in four movements.

syncopation: accenting a note which would normally be unaccented. Syncopated rhythms, therefore, are felt to go against a regular pattern of strong and weak beats which would be expected from the time signature of the piece.

tempo: speed.

tenor: the male voice that is next in height above a bass and a baritone, but lower than counter-tenor.

ternary form: the shape of a piece of music that falls into three parts, with the third part being essentially a repeat of the first – i.e., the shape is A-B-A.

tierce de picardie: the phrase means 'a Picardy third'. It is a major chord at the end of a piece of music in a minor key. The middle note of that chord, which is at the interval of a third above the bottom note, is therefore one semitone higher than it would be if the chord were still in the minor.

time signature: the composer's indication in the score of the metre of the piece of music.

timpani: the Italian word for kettledrums.

tone painting: musical description, by harmonic, melodic, or rhythmic means, of the words of a text.

trio: a piece of music for three vocalists or instrumentalists, with or without accompaniment.

triplet: a group of three notes in the space of two, i.e., three evenly spaced notes in the space of two notes but of the same rhythmic value.

unison: a line of music provided by more than one vocalist or instrumentalist, all singing or playing exactly the same notes.

viola: a string instrument, shaped like a violin, but a bit larger, and therefore it plays notes of a lower pitch than a violin.

viola da gamba: a member of the viol family of string instruments, now obsolete and superseded by the violin family. The viola da gamba was the last survivor of the viol family and was still in use until the end of the 18th century. It resembled the cello, which has replaced it.

Appendix 4: A comparison of the Gottfried van Swieten and Vincent Novello versions of the libretto of *The Creation*

The following consists of extracts from the Vincent Novello version of the libretto of *The Creation* (1860), which has been used in the first section of this study, and it is shown here in ordinary italics.

The majority of the Novello version is the same as the version produced by Gottfried van Swieten (1800), but the original wording of lines in the van Swieten version which have been altered by Novello is shown by the parts printed in bold italics, to the right of the Novello text.

Not all of the libretto of *The Creation* is included in this appendix – only those movements where there have been changes from the original van Swieten version. A series of asterisks indicates each time that movements from the libretto have been omitted.

The source of the van Swieten text is: *The Creation – eClassical* (http://eclassical.com>art71).

PART ONE
SCENE 1 (The First Day)
****
3. Aria and chorus
URIEL

Now vanish before the holy beams	
the gloomy shade of ancient night.	***the gloomy dismal shades of dark***
The first of days appears!	
Now chaos ends and order fair prevails.	***Disorder yields to order the fair place***
Affrighted fly hell's spirits, black in throngs;	***Affrighted fled hell's spirits black in throngs***
down they sink in the deepest abyss	***Down they sink in the deep of abyss***
to endless night	

CHORUS
Despairing, cursing rage attends their rapid fall
A new-created world springs up at God's command

SCENE 2 (The Second Day)
4. Recitative

RAPHAEL

And God made the firmament, and divided the waters which were under the firmament from the waters, which were above the firmament, and it was so. (Gen.1.7)

Now furious storms tempestuous rage;
Outrageous storms now dreadfu arose;
like chaff by the winds impell'd are the clouds,
as chaff by the winds are impelled b the clouds.
by heaven's fire the sky is inflam'd,
By heaven's fire the sky is enflamed,
and awful thunders are rolling on high.
and awful rolled the thunders on high
now from the floods in steam ascend
reviving showers of rain,
the dreary wasteful hail, the light and flaky snow.

****

SCENE 3 (The Third Day)

****

7. Aria

RAPHAEL

Rolling in foaming billows,
uplifted, roars the boist'rous sea.
Mountains and rocks now emerge,
their tops among the clouds ascend.
their tops into the clouds ascend.
Through th' open plains, outstretching wide,
in serpent error rivers flow.
Softly purling, glides on
through silent vales the limpid brook.

****

9. Aria

GABRIEL

With verdure clad the fields appear,
delightful to the ravish'd sense;
by flowers sweet and gay
enhanced is the charming sight.
Here fragrant herbs their odours shed;
Here vent their fumes the fragran herbs,
here shoots the healing plant.
With copious fruits th' expanded boughs are hung;
By loads of fruit th' expanded bough are press'd

in leafy arches twine the shady groves;

to shady vaults are bent the tufty groves;

o'er lofty hills majestic forests wave.

the mountain's brow is crown'd with closed wood.

****

11. Chorus

CHORUS

Awake the harp, the lyre awake,
and let your joyful song resound!
Rejoice in the Lord, the mighty God!
For he both heaven and earth
has clothed in stately dress

In shout and joy your voices raise!
In triumph sing the mighty Lord!
For he the heaven and earth
Has clothed in stately dress.

SCENE 4 (The Fourth Day)

****

13. Recitative

URIEL

In splendour bright is rising now the sun,
and darts his rays; a joyful happy spouse,

and darts his rays, an am'rous joyful happy spouse,

a giant proud and glad
to run his measur'd course.
With softer beams, and milder light,
steps on the filver moon through silent night.
The space immense of th' azure sky,
a countless host of radiant orbs adorns.

Innum'rous host of radiant orbs adorns

And the sons of God announced the fourth day,
in song divine, proclaiming thus his power.

****

PART TWO

SCENE 1 (The Fifth Day)

****

19. Trio

GABRIEL

Most beautiful appear, with verdure young adorn'd,
the gently sloping hills; their narrow sinuous veins,
distil, in crystal drops, the fountain fresh and bright

URIEL

In lofty circles play, and hover in the air,

in lofty circles play, and hover thro' the sky

the cheerful host of birds; and as they flying whirl	***the cheerful host of birds. And in th flying whirl***
their glitt'ring plumes are dyed as rainbows	***the glittering plumes are died, a rainbows***
by the sun.	***by the sun.***
RAPHAEL	
See flashing thro' the deep in thronging swarms	***See flashing thro' the wet in thronge swarms***
the fish a thousand ways around.	***the fry on thousand ways around.***
Upheaved from the deep, th' immense Leviathan	
sports on the foaming wave	

GABRIEL, URIEL and RAPHAEL
How many are thy works, O God!
Who may their number tell?

****
SCENE 2 (The Sixth Day)
****
22. Recitative
RAPHAEL

Straight opening her fertile womb,	
the earth obey'd the word,	
and teem'd creatures numberless,	
in perfect forms and fully grown.	
Cheerful, roaring, stands the tawny lion	
With sudden leap the flexible tiger appears.	***In sudden leaps the flexible tige appears.***
The nimble stag bears up his branching head.	
With flying mane, and fiery look,	
impatient neighs the noble steed.	***Impatient neighs the sprightly steed.***
The cattle, in herds, already seek their food	***The cattle in herds already seeks h food***
on fields and meadows green.	
And o'er the ground, as plants, are spread	
the fleecy, meek and bleating flocks.	***The fleecy, meek and bleating flock.***
Unnumber'd as the sands, in swarms	***Unnumber'd as the sands, in whirl***
arose the hosts of insects.	
In long dimension creeps,	
with sinuous trace, the worm.	

23. Aria
RAPHAEL
No heav'n in fullest glory shone;
earth smile'd in all her rich attire;
earth smiles in all her rich attire;
the room of air with fowl is fill'd;
the water swell'd by shoals of fish;
by heavy beasts the ground is trod.
But all the work was not complete;
there wanted yet that wondrous being,
that, grateful, should God's pow'r admire,
with heart and voice his goodness praise.

****

25. Aria
URIEL
In native worth and honour clad,
with beauty, courage, strength, adorn'd
Erect, with front serene, he stands
to heav'n erect and tall, he stands
a man, the lord and king of nature all.
His large and arched brow sublime
The large and arched front sublime
of wisdom deep declares the seat!
And in his eyes with brightness shines
the soul, the breath and image of his God.
With fondness leans upon his breast
the partner for him form'd
a woman, fair and graceful spouse.
her softly-smiling virgin looks,
of flow'ry spring the mirror,
bespeak him love, and joy, and bliss.

****

27A. Trio
GABRIEL, URIEL
On thee each living soul awaits;
from thee, O Lord, all seek their food;
from thee, O Lord, they beg their meat;
thou openest thy hand,
and fillest all with good. (Psalm 104:27-28)
and sated all they are.

RAPHAEL
But when thy face, O Lord, is hid,
But as to them thy face is hid,
with sudden terror they are struck;
thou tak'st their breath away,
they vanish into dust (Psalm 104:29)

GABRIEL, URIEL and RAPHAEL
Thou sendest forth thy breath again,
and life with vigour fresh returns;
revived earth unfolds new strength
and new delights (Psalm 104:30)

Thou lett'st thy breath go forth again,
revived earth unfolds new force

PART THREE

SCENE 1

28. Orchestral introduction (morning) and recitative

URIEL
In rosy mantle appears,
by music sweet awak'd,
the morning, young and fair.
From heav'n's angelic choir
pure harmony descends
on ravish'd earth.
Behold the blissful pair,
where hand in hand they go;
their glowing looks express
the thanks that swell their grateful hearts.
A louder praise of God
their lips shall utter soon;
then let our voices ring,
united with their song.

by tunes sweet awak'd
From the celestial vaults
their flaming looks express
what feels the grateful heart.

SCENE 2

29. Duet and chorus

ADAM, EVE
By thee, with bliss, O bounteous Lord,
both heav'n and earth are stor'd.
This world so great, so wonderful,
thy mighty hand has fram'd.

the heav'n and earth are stor'd

CHORUS
For ever blessed be his pow'r,
his name be ever magnified.

ADAM
Of stars, the fairest, pledge of day,
that crown'st the smiling morn;
and thou, bright sun, that cheer'st the world,
thou eye and soul of all!

Of stars the fairest, O how sweet
thy smile at dawning morn
How brighten'st thou, O sun, the da

CHORUS	
Proclaim in your extended course	
th' almighty pow'r and praise of God.	
EVE	
And thou that rul'st the silent night	
and all ye starry hosts,	***and all ye starry host,***
spread wide and ev'rywhere	
spread wide his praise	
in choral songs about	
ADAM	
Ye mighty elements, by his pow'r	***Ye strong and comb'rous elements***
your ceaseless changes make;	***who ceaseless changes make,***
ye dusky mists, and dewy streams,	
that rise and fall thro' th' air.	
ADAM, EVE, CHORUS	
Resound the praise of God our Lord.	
Great his name, and great his might.	***Great is his name, and great his might.***
EVE	
Ye purling fountains, tune his praise;	
and wave your tops, ye pines.	
ye plants, exhale, ye flowers, breathe	
to him your balmy scent.	***at him your balmy scent.***
ADAM	
Ye that on mountains stately treat,	
and ye that lowly creep;	
ye birds that sing at heaven's gate,	
and ye that swim the stream;	
ADAM, EVE, CHORUS	
Ye creatures all, extol the Lord;	***Ye living souls, extol the Lord;***
him celebrate, him magnify.	
ADAM, EVE	
Ye valleys, hills, and shady woods,	***Ye vallies, hills, and shady woods,***
made vocal by our song,	***our raptur'd notes ye heard,***
from morn till eve you shall repeat	***from morn till ev'n you shall repeat***
Our grateful hymns of praise.	

CHORUS

Hail, bounteous Lord! Almighty, hail!
Thy word call'd forth this wond'rous frame,
the heav'ns and earth thy pow'r adore;
thy pow'r adore the heav'n and earth
we praise thee now and everymore.

SCENE 3

30. Recitative

ADAM

Our duty we have now perform'd,
Our duty we performed now
in off'ring up to God our thanks.
Now follow me, dear partner of my life,
thy guide I'll be; and ev'ry step
pours new delights into our breasts,
pours new delight into our breast,
shows wonders ev'rywhere.
Then may'st thou feel and know
the high degree of bliss
the Lord allotted us,
and with devoted heart
his bounties celebrate.
Come, follow me, thy guide I'll be.

EVE

O thou for whom I am,
my help, my shield, my all,
thy will is law to me;
so God our Lord ordains;
and from obedience grows
my pride and happiness.

31. Duet

ADAM

Graceful consort, at thy side
softly fly the golden hours;
ev'ry moment brings new rapture,
ev'ry care is lull'd to rest

EVE

Spouse adored, at thy side
purest joys o'erflow the heart;
life and all I have is thine;
life and all I am is thine
my reward thy love shall be

ADAM, EVE

The dew-dropping morn, O how she quickens all!	
The coolness of ev'n, O how she all restores!	
How grateful is of fruits the savour sweet!	
How pleasing is of fragrant bloom the smell!	
But, without thee, what is to me	
the morning dew, the breath of even,	
the sav'ry fruit, the fragrant bloom?	
With thee is ev'ry joy enhanced,	
with thee delight is ever new,	
with thee is life incessant bliss;	
thine it all shall be.	***thine it whole shall be.***

SCENE 4

32. Recitative

URIEL

O happy pair! And happy still might be	***O happy pair! And always happy yet***
if not misled by false conceit.	
ye strive at more than granted is;	***ye strive at more as granted is;***
and more desire to know, than know ye should.	***and more to know, as know ye should.***

33. Quartet and chorus

Sing the Lord, ye voices all,	
magnify his name thro' all creation,	***Utter thanks, ye all his works***
celebrate his pow'r and glory,	
let his name resound on high.	
Jehovah's praise for ever shall endure.	***The Lord is great. His praise shall last for aye.***
Amen. Praise the Lord. Utter thanks.	***Amen. Sing the Lord. Utter thanks.***

Appendix 5: German Text of Brahms' *Requiem*, with English Translation

The German text was selected by Brahms from the Lutheran Bible. The English is the author's translation.

MOVEMENT 1

Selig sind, die da Leid tragen, denn sie sollen getröstet werden.

Blessed are they who bear sorrow, for they shall be comforted. *(Matthew 5:4)*

Die mit Tränen säen, werden mit Freuden ernten. Sie gehen hin und weinen und tragen edlen Samen, und kommen mit Freuden und bringen ihre Garben.

Those who sow with tears shall reap with joy. They go forth and weep and bear precious seed, and come with joy and bring their sheaves. *(Psalm 126:5-6)*

MOVEMENT 2

Denn alles Fleisch, es ist wie Gras und alle Herrlichkeit des Menschen wie des Grases Blumen. Das Gras ist verdorret und die Blume abgefallen.

For all flesh, it is as grass, and all the glory of man as the flower of the grass. The grass has withered, and the flower has fallen away. *(1 Peter 1:24)*

So seid nun geduldig, lieben Brüder, bis auf die Zukunft des Herrn. Siehe, ein Ackermann wartet auf die köstliche Frucht der Erde und ist geduldig darüber, bis er empfahe den Morgenregen und Abendregen.

Be patient now therefore, dear brothers, until the coming of the Lord. Behold, the farmer waits for the precious fruit of the earth and is patient for it, until he may receive the early and latter rain. *(James 5:7)*

Aber des Herrn Wort bleibet in Ewigkeit.

But the word of the Lord endures forever. *(1 Peter 1:25a)*

Die Erlöseten des Herrn werden wieder kommen, und gen Zion kommen mit Jauchzen; ewige Freude wird über ihrem Haupte sein; Freude und Wonne werden sie ergreifen und Schmerz und Seufzen wird weg müssen.

The ransomed of the Lord shall return, and come to Zion with songs; everlasting joy shall be upon their heads: they shall obtain joy and gladness, and sorrow and sighing shall have to flee away. *(Isaiah 35:10)*

MOVEMENT 3

Herr, lehre doch mich, daß ein Ende mit mir haben muß, und mein Leben ein Ziel hat, und ich davon muß.
Siehe, meine Tage sind einer Hand breit vor dir, und mein Leben ist wie nichts vor dir. Ach, wie gar nichts sind alle Menschen, die doch so sicher leben. Sie gehen daher wie ein Schemen, und machen ihnen viel vergebliche Unruhe; sie sammeln und wissen nicht, wer es kriegen wird. Nun Herr, wess soll ich mich trösten? Ich hoffe auf dich.

Lord, do please teach me that I must come to an end, and that my life has a limit, and that I must pass away. Behold, my days are a handbreadth before you, and my life is as nothing before you. Alas, all mankind is as nothing at all, though they live as if they are secure. So they walk like a shadow and give themselves much useless unrest; they gather riches and do not know who shall possess them. Now, Lord, in whom shall I take comfort? I hope in you. *(Psalm 39:4-7)*

Der Gerechten Seelen sind in Gottes Hand und keine Qual rühret sie an.

The souls of the righteous are in the hand of God, and no torment touches them. *(The Wisdom of Solomon 3:1)*

MOVEMENT 4

Wie lieblich sind deine Wohnungen, Herr Zebaoth! Meine Seele verlanget und sehnet sich nach den Vorhöfen des Herrn; mein Leib und Seele freuen sich in dem lebendigen Gott.

How lovely are your dwellings, Lord of hosts! My soul longs and yearns for the courts of the Lord: my body and soul rejoice in the living God.

Wohl denen, die in deinem Hause wohnen, die loben dich immerdar.

Blessed are they who dwell in your house: they praise you for ever. *(Psalm 84:1, 2, 4)*

MOVEMENT 5

Ihr habt nun Traurigkeit; aber ich will euch wieder sehen und euer Herz soll sich freuen und eure Freude soll niemand von euch nehmen.

You now have sorrow; but I will see you again, and your heart shall rejoice, and no one shall take your joy from you. *(John 16:22)*

Sehet mich an: Ich habe eine kleine Zeit Mühe und Arbeit gehabt und habe großen Trost funden.

Look at me: I have had toil and labour for a short while, and I have found much comfort. *(Ecclesiasticus 51:27)*

Ich will euch trösten, wie Einen seine Mutter tröstet.

I will comfort you, as one whom his mother comforts. *(Isaiah 66:13)*

MOVEMENT 6

Denn wir haben hie keine bleibende Statt[140], sondern die zukünftige suchen wir.

For here we have no lasting city, but we seek the one to come. *(Hebrews 13:14)*

Siehe, ich sage euch ein Geheimnis: Wir werden nicht alle entschlafen, wir werden aber alle verwandelt werden;

Behold, I tell you a mystery; We shall not all sleep, but we shall all be changed;

---

140 "Statt" is the spelling in older German of the word for "city." In modern German, the spelling is "Stadt."

und dasselbige plötzlich, in einem Augenblick, zu der Zeit der letzten Posaune. Denn es wird die Posaune schallen, und die Toten werden auferstehen unverweslich, und wir werden verwandelt werden.

and that will happen suddenly, in a moment, at the time of the last trumpet[141]. For the trumpet shall sound, and the dead shall rise imperishable, and we shall be changed.

Dann wird erfüllet werden das Wort, das geschrieben steht: Der Tod ist verschlungen in den Sieg. Tod, wo ist dein Stachel? Höll, wo ist dein Sieg?

Then shall be fulfilled the word that is written: Death is swallowed up in victory. O death, where is your sting? O hell, where is your victory? *(1 Corinthians 15:51-52, 54b-55)*

Herr, du bist würdig zu nehmen Preis und Ehre und Kraft, denn du hast alle Dinge geschaffen, und durch deinen Willen haben sie das Wesen und sind geschaffen.

Lord, you are worthy to receive praise and honour and power, for you have created all things, and through your will they have their existence and are created. *(Revelation 4:11)*

MOVEMENT 7

Selig sind die Toten, die in dem Herren sterben, von nun an. Ja, der Geist spricht, daß sie ruhen von ihrer Arbeit; denn ihre Werke folgen ihnen nach.

Blessed are the dead who die in the Lord from now on. Yes, says the Spirit, that they may rest from their labours; for their deeds follow them. *(Revelation 14:13)*

[141] Literally, the word "Posaune" means "trombone," but "trumpet" is the word used in most English versions.

Also by Robert Bashford

This book provides a commentary on the message of Messiah. Handel's great oratorio gives a marvellous portrayal of the Person and Work of Jesus Christ: the anticipation of his coming, his birth, his ministry, his sufferings and death, his resurrection, and his ascension – plus also the proclamation of the Gospel to the world, and Christian assurance of resurrection life beyond death.

The main focus of this study is the selection of Bible verses that make up the work, compiled by the librettist Charles Jennens. At the same time there is also a certain amount of comment on the music, showing how Handel's distinctive skill contributes towards clearly expressing the message.

The aim of the book is that readers may deepen their understanding of the Bible passages included in the work and enjoy Handel's Messiah all the more – and as a result know Christ better.

From our new Christian Leadership Series

Bishops – A Concise Study summarises the key points of the argument of Martin's major study *'Bishops Past, Present and Future'* (Gilead Books 2022). It is designed to meet the needs of those who would like to know the answers to the three questions about bishops noted above, but who would balk at tackling the 800+ pages of the original book.

This concise study is published in the hope that will help many in the Church of England, both ordained and lay to think in a more informed fashion about how bishops should respond to the challenges facing the Church of England at this critical point in its history as it considers how to move forward following the publication of the Living in Love and Faith material.

Other Books Published by the Latimer Trust

Reformation Anglicanism: Essays on Edwardian Evangelicalism is a superb set of essays arising from the Moore Theological College symposium on Reformation Anglicanism held in 2019.

Featuring essays from various reformation scholars, this collection of articles focuses on some foundational documents (e.g. *Book of Homilies, Articles of Religion*) and foundational reformers (e.g. Thomas Cranmer, Martin Bucer, Heinrich Bullinger) involved with the English Reformation, and its Edwardian phase in particular. This edited volume not only offers a sustained focus on the often-neglected mid-Tudor phase of the Reformation but explores new avenues of research on overlooked subjects such as the *45 Articles of Religion,* John Ponet's *Short Catechism,* the *Reformatio Legum Ecclesiasticarum,* the ministry of John Hooper, and the memory of Martin Bucer. Students and scholars alike will benefit from this fresh examination of these anchors of Anglicanism which were hotly contested both then, and now.

Come, Let Us Sing seeks to help us reform the musical dimension of church life by bringing biblical clarity to two key questions: Why do we come together? and why do we sing together?

In answer to the first, Robert Smith navigates a path through the contemporary 'worship word wars', concluding that we gather both to worship God and to encourage others. Two questions must, therefore, be asked of everything we do: Does it glorify God? and does it edify others?

As to why we sing, Smith unpacks three principal functions of congregational singing in Scripture – as a way of praising, a way of praying and a way of preaching. In so doing, he explores the necessity of singing scriptural truth, the value of psalmody, the place of emotions, the role of our bodies, and how singing expresses and enriches our unity.

Come, Let Us Sing is a timely call for the church to reclaim its biblical musical heritage and reform its musical practice

www.ingramcontent.com/pod-product-compliance
Lightning Source LLC
LaVergne TN
LVHW041114080826
845145LV00007B/1812